Minestrone for the Mobster's Soul:

Minestrone for the Mobster's Soul:

Life Lessons from the Movie Mafia

Bobby Madura and Joey DiBruno

Aventine Press

Published by Aventine Press
1023 4th Ave #204
San Diego CA, 92101

ISBN: 1-59330-540-0

Library of Congress Control Number: 2008928711
Library of Congress Cataloging-in-Publication Data
Minestrone for the Mobster's Soul:

Printed in the United States of America

ACKNOWLEDGMENTS

You don't get nowhere alone.
Max, *Once Upon Time in America*

By the time *Minestrone* was ready to be served up, we found it hard to believe looking back, how many cooks had added to the pot. We thank them all for the necessary ingredients and/or the special flavors they added. If we've missed anyone, hey, meet us for some lemon chicken at Tufano's—on us.

Detailed critique and/or editing of the book was done by Anne Ociepka, agent Michael Murphy, Jeff Vance, and Kevin Mulvaney and Adam Witty of Advantage Media Group.

Three critiques and numerous phone consultations were given by Renaissance man, Rus Bradburd, English professor at the University of New Mexico and former assistant basketball coach at University of Texas at El Paso and New Mexico State for 14 years. Rus is the author of numerous published short stories and the memoir, *Paddy on the Hardwood,* which describes his two years coaching professional basketball in Ireland while working on his fiddle-playing and fiction-writing.

Besides Rus, Doug Gorman's and John Kuri's critiques helped set us on the path to personalize *Minestrone* developing it from a bunch of movie quotes and lessons to a memoir of events on the West Side in Chicago in the 1950s and 1960s.

Guys who lived it with us or told us their stories (and the particular lessons they imparted) were Carlo Pedone (Family), Sam Pedone (Trust, Betrayal, and Business), Simone Pedone (Family), Wally Wydra (Politics), Cliff Courier (Friendship and Religion), Tom Gayne (Ambition and Family), Randy Kalemba (Betrayal), and George Demos (Politics).

Important lessons or details were provided by Joe Czupek (Trust), Lester Connor (Business), Will Rey (Respect), Andrea Lukens (Love), Laura Mulligan (Family), and Jerry Sichting (Trust).

Our moms, Jean Madura and Wanda Sakwa, gave us details long before they or we knew how we'd use them, while on their jobs they met Sinatra, Al Martino, and other Italian crooners.

People who offered suggestions, acted as sounding boards, stimulated our thought processes, obtained movie quotes, found neighborhood details, or just plain put up with our obsession were Katie Ociepka, Donna Chainas, Brent Haskins, Dennis McCann, Bob Monahan, J.B. Bickerstaff, Jim Boylen, Jim Brewer, Rex Kalamian, and Stan Kellers.

Agent and publishing assistance were offered and suggested by Andrew Blauner, Mark Boyle, Steve Bulpett, Pat Croce, Jerome Kersey, Gary Sacks, Curt Sampson, Dick Versace, and Pat Williams.

Photos and media by Andrea Lukens, Carlo Pedone, Katie Ociepka, Brian Babbitt, Aleksandar Dzikic, Tom Gayne, Shane Doyle, Ryan Semanko, and Chad Folkestad.

PREFACE

The choices that you make will shape your life forever.
Calogero (voiceover), *A Bronx Tale*

We make our own choices, we pay our own prices.
Violet, *Bound*

On December 14, 1999, a customs agent in Port Angeles, Washington, became mildly suspicious of the answers given by a man entering the U.S. by ferry from Canada with his car. She could have shrugged it off and not taken the extra time and effort to search the car. Instead, she made a decision, a choice. She had her fellow agents search it. The agents discovered the explosives this would-be terrorist was planning to use to blow up L.A. airport. The "Millennium Plot" was foiled. Some time in her Life she learned the Lesson to trust her instinct and intuition—to trust the fact that the brain, her brain, could pick out and process thousands of facts in a second and reach a possible conclusion.

On July 10, 2001, FBI agent Ken Williams in Phoenix sent a memo to FBI headquarters warning that there was an "effort by Osama bin Laden to send students to the U.S. to attend civil aviation" schools. No one at headquarters *decided* to follow up and investigate this "effort" in any serious way. Lessons had not been learned

On August 16, 2001, the Immigration and Naturalization Service arrested a Middle Eastern flight school student who had little interest in take offs and landings but who just wanted to know how to steer a 747. A Minneapolis FBI agent told his Washington office that this sounded suspicious and that a 747 loaded with fuel could be used as a weapon. Nothing was done because internal bureaucratic rules did not allow sharing of information between agencies. Agents in both Washington and Minneapolis did nothing. By not observing the Life Lesson of Carefulness nothing was done. They *decided* to let the matter drop and the 9/11 plot continued. The agents in both these cases had learned the Life Lesson of bureaucracy rather than that of taking proactive responsibility for their jobs.

Closer to home, my home, a young man woke in the morning of October 14, 2003, in the northern suburbs of Chicago. No doubt he felt a thrill of expectation knowing he had in his wallet a ticket that would gain him entrance to Wrigley Field and most likely (he felt,) give him the opportunity to see his team, the Chicago Cubs, clinch their first pennant in 58 years and go on the World Series. No one could have predicted what would happen to him, and there is no way he could have consciously decided ahead of time what action he would take when a foul ball began dropping out of the sky in his direction. However, the instinctive "me-first" Life Lesson of his generation *decided* for him. Though his actions did not begin to approach the magnitude of those who are charged with protecting our country, his particular life was changed forever.

Each day that we walk out our door we don't know whether we will be confronted with a decision that might be life-altering. The only way we can be prepared is to have learned our *Life Lessons* throughout our lives so we're ready when a situation presents itself. *Minestrone for the Mobster's Soul* presents some of these lessons. It's often too late to start learning them on the spot.

Introduction

"Hey, I'm trying to catch the Cub score from yesterday," my cousin Joey "DB" DiBruno said loudly as I tried to change the channel on the car radio. It was late Spring of 2007 and we were driving south on Lake Shore Drive on a Saturday morning toward Oak Street Beach. It was the first day warm enough to get some sun.

To us, though, it could have been the late 60's or early 70's again. On that curve of sand under the high rises across the drive, we'd seldom fail to happen upon some sweet secretary, nurse, or stew we'd met on Rush Street the night before. Or the night before that. My thinning hair and DB's whitening hair seemed to be the only discernible difference between those days and now.

"I'll save you the suspense. They lost," I answered as he punched the button returning the voice of Mike North to the speakers.

"This *jamoke* talks about everything but sports—give the fucking score, will you," Joey kept up, knowing that I had no idea what the

Cubbies had done. After another ten minutes of no sports talk, the WSCR talk radio head started into a discussion of mob movies. Our attention picked up. Within minutes guys were calling in to give their opinions and host North was putting together a top ten list.

Before we got to Addison, we each had our own list. Our trip to Oak Street Beach and our hopes of running into somebody we knew was becoming secondary.

Numbers one and two were a given, we both agreed. "In what order?" Joey asked, which pissed me off.

"Brando set the table for everything," I said, not doubting for a second that I was right.

"Owh! I think we can debate that point. Think about how DeNiro played the young Corleone—there hasn't been a better acting job since." And it was on.

Some caller on the radio suggested *Miller's Crossing* for the top ten, and we switched to WBJZ, smooth jazz, as we passed Fullerton. We both put *Goodfellas* in the number three slot with little debate, but I had a beef at Joey's sticking *A Bronx Tale* in at four.

"I'm going with *Donnie Brasco*," I demurred, and so it went. We agreed to disagree on the 4 and 5 slots, but settled on *Casino* at six with little discussion.

Then it was my turn, "I'm going off the board here—*Scarface* with Pacino is my number seven."

Joey disagreed. "Is that even a mob movie? It's about the Cuban drug trade and Pacino uses that fucked-up accent." I knew how he felt about *Scarface* and was ready with my history about how it was a re-make of the original in 1932, which starred Paul Muni, which was itself based loosely on Chicago's real Scarface, Al Capone. Besides, I just liked it, and so did everybody else.

We both agreed that Scorsese's latest, *The Departed,* had to be up there, even though the Italians got their asses kicked in it. From that point on the arguments never ended. And probably never will.

*****

It had been over thirty years since we jacked that Biarritz for our boss, Vito, that helped us get started. Though we were no longer in that kind of business, "Bingo Biancuso" at Patrick Cadillac still made sure DB got a deal on his new Escalade that was available to few others. For better or worse, reputation stays with you forever—that's one lesson.

And it had been over ten years since I had done my ninety days in Cook County Jail after St. Francis social club got raided and closed down. It took almost a year to find out how and why the cops cracked us. I took my medicine rather than fight it. I happened to be in the club when the cops came in, so I took all the responsibility. DB skated free though I'm sure the fuzz would have tried to get me to rat if they had thought he was a bigger fish than I was. When I got out, I thought it was time for a change. We'd been trying to be legit since.

Look, before you think this is written by a couple of wiseguys trying to win some sympathy they don't deserve, hang on a minute. We never had to kill anybody. And we didn't rob or steal. Well, not any more than your usual politician or salesman, or the average Joe like you might do if you thought you would get away with it, and—if you had the balls.

No, we were just two kids who grew up on the West Side of Chicago in the 50's and 60's. We learned the rules of the neighborhood and thought they were the rules of the world. We acted accordingly. Did your old lady ever warn you about hanging out with the wrong crowd? Well, it's not our fault she would have eliminated just about everybody that we grew up with.

Instead of worrying about graduating from school, we graduated from pilfering old man Stefano's grocery store and hitting the Jewel's supermarket. Stefanz ran a book out of the back of his store, but we never let the thought of his mob connections stop us. Just the opposite— he'd be distracted in the back (or we'd distract him), while we'd make off with Playboys or a handful of Topps baseball cards from behind the counter. By the time he got pinched for gambling, we were arranging our own five-finger discounts at the supermarket, pocketing our parents' grocery money in the bargain. This was long before they put in those video cameras to watch you. A long trench coat with deep pockets sewn on the inside held a lot of spaghetti, though we'd have to take the tomatoes out as soon as we got outside so they wouldn't get squished.

Setting a garage on fire to help a friend's old man collect insurance? No problem. Breaking into Ryerson grammar school on the weekend? Hey, there was no after school program in our neighborhood back then, so you had to create your own. The kids in the suburbs had swimming pools and tennis teams and all kinds of duper shit. We had to establish a no-child-left-behind policy ourselves.

Joey and I never got caught for anything, except for the social club, or the "gambling den," as the *Sun Times* called it. I don't recommend walking as fine a tightrope line as we did, but looking back at it I realize we balanced on the edge between the law and the Outfit, or the Mob as you might call it, that controlled our turf. Neither one destroyed us. We think we learned a few lessons along the way and one of the reasons we wrote this was to pass these lessons on to you. That probably sounds like we think we're smart, like we outwitted the system or something. For a while, we thought so too, Now we know we were just lucky. When your ma told you there are some dumb, crazy fucks out there, and they'll wreck your life, she was right (though she may not have put it just that way). Something we did kept us out of the line of fire of these wackos, but you'll get to meet a few of them in these lessons.

You've heard the story that when you're growing up, you have a turning point where you either turn bad or you turn good? That's a lot of bullshit. If there's a turning point, it's one where you either get smart or you stay stupid. Look at the classic movie script cliche, where two brothers or friends grow up in a bad environment like Hell's Kitchen or the Bowery (it's always New York City). They have the same upbringing, but one becomes a criminal and the other becomes a cop or a priest. It does happen, but it isn't a matter of who's good and who's evil. It's a matter of smart and stupid. You can be a stupid criminal and get caught by the law and you can be a stupid "straight" and put time in at a boring job, while your life ebbs away. Either one puts you into a kind of prison.

But you can be smart either way too. Smart doesn't mean following some made-up laws that let the government control the loot. In the past hundred years, the U.S. government has outlawed alcohol, gambling, sex for money, high interest rates, various drugs, you name it. The same government has come right back and made these things legal in certain places and taxed the hell out of them. Do those taxes go toward good things for people? Sure, some of it does. But most of the money from those sources goes to keep the same political mob in power.

Some of you might say you're with me so far, but you don't like the violence that is associated with illegal behavior. You want to see violence? Get caught by the government and see what happens to you in custody or in prison. Others of you might say that alcohol, drugs, and sex are okay, but something like extortion is bad? Go to Washington, D.C. and you'll see real extortion. Don't give me good and evil. Smart and stupid is what's it's about.

We decided to be smart. And we decided to be as successful as we could be without taking undo risks. We didn't want to murder, rob, or beat innocent people. We did want to supply the public's desires through an organization or a business—that was the first key to our success. Not letting anyone mess with that success was the second.

Our main line of work, although it took years to get there, became operating the St. Francis Social Club on the Avenue—that's west Chicago Avenue, my friend. You'll read some of the details in the Business chapter, but for now let's just say that St. Francis's provided guys like you a respectable and safe place to gamble and make contacts for loans, women, and other stuff you might want. We sent so many guys to Vegas and Atlantic City that we were practically running a travel agency. Later we had a couple of restaurants on the side too, and those grew into our main business.

Oh sure, we had to pick off a few Caddies and Lincolns in our day or had our crew do similar jobs, but when possible we made sure we took them from addresses on the North Shore where people wouldn't miss them. They'd be covered by insurance anyway. Yeah, I know, that raises insurance rates. But the rates go up on those kinds of cars owned by those kinds of people—kind of a tax on rich pricks for the benefit of the rest of us. You could call it a Robin Hood kind of thing. And if you read your history, you know that stuff about him always taking from the rich and giving to the poor was also a bunch of crap. He kept plenty. Just think about his name—"Robbin" and "Hood." Give me a break. This shit has been going on for centuries. I think in our little way we might have done more good and deserve a better rep than ol' Mr. R. Hood.

I'd like to think my life story and lessons would stand on their own and that you'd learn something from them alone. But then again, if it weren't for the movies, I probably never would have thought of writing them down. In 1972 a phenomenon happened that makes these lessons more real to the average Joe (or Giuseppe). *The Godfather* hit the big screen. Overnight, the mob movie replaced the cowboy movie in reflecting American values. I realized immediately that the lessons—honor, respect, family, and so on—taught in *The Godfather* and the films it spawned were the ones I grew up with. You and the rest of the general public realized the same thing. Cowboy values—always wear the white hat; win the right way or not at all; love your horse, not your woman, etc.—were a fantasy. The real world had been waiting for a new code, for new lessons.

Before Brando's Don Corleone, it was Gary Cooper in *High Noon*, Marshall Dillon (James Arness) in *Gunsmoke*, or Paladin (Richard Boone) in *Have Gun Will Travel* who reflected an America that still thought it lived in the wide open spaces of the Old West. Alan Ladd in *Shane*, Jimmy Stewart in *Liberty Valence,* or John Wayne in just about anything—they epitomized who Americans thought they were.

Within a few years in the late 1960's and early 1970's, everything changed. Three of our greatest Americans, with the whitest hats, were gunned down in front of us. Riots in our cities, a surge in crime rates, and a war in Asia in which we weren't always the good guys taught us we lived in a world with new rules. Instead of the wide open spaces, we noticed we lived in narrow, crowded cities. John Wayne wasn't considered for the role of *Dirty Harry*. Instead, we got our advanced degrees in life from Brando, Pacino, and DeNiro, and eventually, Gandolfini.

Whether America wants to admit it or not, its code and values are the same as those of the mob movie. The Mob itself doesn't necessarily live up to these values any more than anyone else does, but these codes for life do come from Old World roots. And today, the values have come full circle. That is, made guys and wannabes watch the movies, are affected by the themes, and start taking on the traits of these films. FBI surveillance tapes are full of mob suspects imitating the movies consciously and unconsciously.

Though mob movies illustrate the life lessons better than we ever could, we thought our experiences would make the lessons more practical. In each chapter I'm going to tell you a true story from the old neighborhood that points out what Joey and I learned. They're all in chronological order as we grew up, except the last one, the Religion chapter. It affected us the most, but it was also the scariest and we didn't want to fuck up your mind at the start.

After each tale of our lives that I tell, DB investigates what the movie mob—Scorsese, Coppola, Puzo, and their characters—have to say about that lesson.

Look, we're not telling the stories that follow to get off on our own egos or anything. A lot of things worked out great, but some things didn't. And I know a lot of you guys have stories to tell as well. We just wanted you to know where we've been and how we developed a so-called philosophy of life. People don't always listen and learn anyway. People are who they are, and they usually continue being who they are. But because we love the mob movies, we thought maybe, just maybe, you'd enjoy looking at what's behind them. And that, who knows, you just might find something to change your life. If not, fuck it. Enjoy the movies, the quotes, and the lessons anyway. After all, as a young Sammy "the Bull" Gravano is quoted as saying (in Selwyn Raab's 2005 book, *The Five Families)* after he first saw *The Godfather* in 1972:

> *I left the movie stunned. I floated out of the theater. .....*
> *that was our life. It was incredible. Not only the Mob*
> *end, not just the mobsters and the killing and all that*
> *bulllshit, but that wedding....the music, the dancing, it*
> *was us, the Italian people.*

Non-Chicagoans who read this aren't going to get all the street references. Really, no disrespect, but all I can say is, get a fuckin' map. I'm a little tired of hearing about the Lower East Side or Beverly Hills myself, like I'm supposed to take turns genuflecting toward one coast or the other.

The idea behind this collection of life lessons from the mob movies started when I had time to kill in the joint and is written for guys like you. The bright idea to list and rank every mob and Mafia film ever made might have come from a radio sports program, but I've got to believe one of us would have thought of it on our own anyway. Either way, I hope after reading this book you'll feel that my ninety day vacation (paid for by your taxes, by the way) that first spawned this idea was worth it.

Never rat on your friends and always keep your mouth shut.
Jimmy Conway (Robert DeNiro), *Goodfellas*

*Because as soon as these tough guys today get caught and they're
facing hard time, they sing better than Pavarotti.*
Paul Castellano (Chazz Palminteri), *Boss of Bosses*

1. Omerta: The Code of Silence

If "omerta" was in my old man's vocabulary, I never heard him use it.
Matter of fact, I must have been in my 20's before I even heard the
word in the neighborhood. Nevertheless, omerta is one of the most vital
rules in life and the only place to start our lessons. Although the actual
word didn't matter, then or now, I understood the concept since I was
about six years old. While we memorized our Ten Commandments from
Sister Annunciata in our first grade classroom at Our Lady of Angels,
we were learning other commandments on the street after school that
were just as important. Check that. They were more important. Sister
could have added two commandments right off the bat:

XI: Thou shalt not tattle on anybody.

XII: Thou shalt keep private anything that happens within thy
family.

These commandments seemed wired into our genes. Other messages
took a little longer to seep into our subconscious. Like the lessons we

got from our buddy Charlie Mazzuca's mother in the summer of 1960, when I was twelve and my cousin Joey "DB" DiBruno was thirteen.

Say what you want about that global warming shit today, summers seemed a lot hotter in the late 50's and early 60's in Chicago. Everybody was sweating his balls off except the lucky pricks who had window air conditioners so they could sleep at night. We had fans in our house, but all they did was blow the hot air back at you that was ricocheting off the concrete. We'd look for any way to keep cool.

Late morning or early afternoon we'd head over to the corner store and suck on a two cent ice cup until we saw Rocco Elia strutting down the street to the corner, carrying a huge wrench. "Get ready, boys, Niagara Falls is heading your way." Rocco was a weight lifter and his Dago T made his muscles look even more ripped. He still lived right in Little Italy, off Taylor Street, what's mostly the U of I-Circle Campus and hospitals now. Some of his buddies had moved west though, like our parents, and he hung out a lot up by us near Chicago Avenue and Pulaski because his girl friend lived there.

Rocco's straw was tilted on his head while he leaned over to roll up his Big Yank baggy blue pants to knee level. Seconds after his wrench went to work, the corner fire hydrant was open and every kid in the neighborhood was running into the spray generated by the board he attached to it. Old guys were driving their cars up for a free wash, and my girl friend Sharon and other budding twelve year olds were getting their short-shorts and blouses soaked. Kids today don't know what they're missing. The fun lasted just long enough until the coppers showed up and shut down the hydrant. They'd ask the little kids, "Who turned on the hydrant?" They never got an answer, and their smirks seemed to indicate they didn't expect one either. Sometimes their own kids were playing in the water. There'd be a lull for a while as kids went home to eat a bit of lunch or get some Kool Aid, but it didn't take long for Rocco to re-open the hydrant after the cops left. This game went on all summer long.

We loved that cool water, but we also loved to head over to Charlie Mazzuca's house which was not far from Ryerson grammar school. It's not that we were that crazy about hanging with Charlie. It's just that when we rang the doorbell, his old lady would usually be the one who opened the door. She had her own way of keeping cool that consisted of wearing little more than a bra and a half slip. And she was a good-looking broad for somebody's mother. DB and I pretended to fight to ring that bell, but neither one of us could stop staring at her after she'd answer, "Hello boys, come on in, Charlie's in the bedroom." It wasn't until years later that I realized she knew full well the effect she was having.

We'd walk past old man Ray Mazzuca sitting at the kitchen table already pounding down a Schlitz at 10 AM. If Charlie was half asleep or taking his time, we didn't mind because Mrs. M kept walking around toweling her sweat off. We did have to listen to Ray bitching about his financial woes though. There were the bills he couldn't pay, his car that needed work, and his "fuckin' garage" that was falling apart with a door he could barely close, which held a Nash Rambler nobody would steal anyway.

One day I was listening to this bullshit, doing my best to keep my hard-on in my pants as usual. I was sneaking another peek at Mrs. M who was adjusting the strap that had slipped onto her shoulder, when she added her two cents onto her old man's list of woe. "If your 'fuckin' garage' would only burn down, we could at least collect some insurance on it."

DB and I looked at each other at the same time. We had never heard anyone's mother use language like that, let alone been in the presence of a grown, busty woman half-undressed, but that wasn't what got our attention. We had simultaneous reactions: "We can help these people," I muttered. With one eye on Mrs. M I double checked with Ray about his insurance. "Sure, Crazy Louie's old man's got me locked up with premiums on everything, and that ain't doin' me any fuckin' good either," he bitched as he swigged his beer. I just kept looking at him, smiling. Finally I saw a little grin on his chubby kisser, as he started to say, "What're you guys..."

"Come on, Charlie," I yelled out, interrupting Mr. Mazzuca, this time while staring directly at his wife. "Let's hit the street." Even though we were young, Ray knew who we ran with and he knew we had an idea. We didn't have to say anything to him, nor him to us. The deal was set. I fantasized being rewarded by Charlie's "old lady" (I realized years later she was probably only about thirty-five), but I knew deep down that would never happen. Nevertheless, I don't think the plan would have hatched if she hadn't been around.

We planned the torch job on Mazzucas' garage (car included) down to which way we'd run once it got going. We wanted to do it as late as possible, but we didn't want to arouse our parents' suspicions, so 11 o'clock was as late as we dared. It was still light out till 8 o'clock and we said we were going to be at Charlie's till curfew.

Usually not many people were out at that time on a week night in our neighborhood. There was one kid, though, who routinely parked himself in the doorway in front of the six-flat apartment building he lived in, and sure enough, that night Little Petey was there, sneaking a smoke and just generally hanging out. His doorway was across the street from the alley and the garage was the second one in, giving him just enough of a vantage point to see it.

We couldn't just ignore him, so we walked up. "What's happening?" was his hello. Either we'd have to tell him or be dicks and scare him away, in which case he'd be more curious about what was going down. At the last moment, I thought of a third alternative. We liked Petey. He used to pull off small-time pranks himself. Although he "wasn't no Einstein," as Fr. Baldini used to say, he never got into any big trouble, and when he got older he was pretty straight. I don't think he was Italian either, from what I remember. But that didn't matter, growing up in our back yard. We figured we could trust him not to say anything. But if he got involved with us, that would guarantee his silence. Plus we could get him to do some of the dirty work, so we let him in on the action.

The only problem was that Petey had on this St. Mel high school track t-shirt.

"You've gotta take that stupid shirt off though," I told Little Petey.

"It's my brother's shirt. I can't go inside to get another shirt, they'll hassle me about going back out. Besides, Bobby, I'll run faster with this track shirt on if I need to."

"He can be recognized in that," DB chimed in.

Petey had never gotten caught for any trouble, so if anything bad happened, the cops would go easy on him. We were all young—they'd go easy on all of us. Still, when you've got a plan, you should stick to it. I should have put off the torch job for another night, or just made him take off that shirt, but I didn't always have all the common sense I should have even at what I thought was the ripe old age of twelve.

"Let's just go for it, ain't nobody around anyway," I told DB.

We took some greasy rags and paper and stuffed them in a couple of garbage cans. Petey dragged the cans across the alley next to the garage. He probably did it quietly, but it seemed like you could have heard the metal grinding against the pavement all the way to Humboldt Park.

"Fucking cut that noise, Petey," I spit out at the guy who was doing all the work for us.

Petey stopped in the middle of the alley, "Can't we just torch the damn garage the way it is?"

"Then it won't look like no accident," I answered, getting irritated. I punched Joey in the arm and gave him a look and we ran out and each grabbed a handle on the can and tiptoed it over to the garage.

We threw a match and a cigarette into the can and waited for something to happen. We had already learned that any fast-burning stuff would have the arson cops sniffing around for sure. We wanted it to look like it was possible some dumb drunk was walking through the alley and threw a cigarette or a match in the can. We encouraged the fire with another match and when the shit finally ignited, it went up so fast we were lucky we didn't catch fire ourselves. An unexpected shudder hit me at the same moment as the heat. The rush of flame flashed me back two years, when we were caught in a much more horrific blaze. My eyes caught DB's and I knew he was feeling the same thing. And was probably thinking the same thing too—"what the hell were we doing!"

This was a couple of years before the first Mayor Daley put in bright streetlights every twenty yards in the city. We went from dark shadows to spotlight instantly. And there was Petey in his goddamn purple shirt for any neighbor peering out a window to see.

"Run, Petey!" I tried to whisper a yell. "This ain't 4th of July fireworks at the lake."

I jammed my Cubs hat over my eyes and started sprinting—you would have thought I had won that track letter—but when I cranked my head back about fifty yards down the alley, I saw Petey still staring at the fire, like he was in wonder or something, and the purple t-shirt was like bright neon, with a "Catch me" sign on it. Finally he started running.

Sure enough, an old lady fingered him the next day, with her whole family nodding in agreement behind her, non-Italians who hadn't learned what omerta meant. Petey took his stupid shirt to St. Charles (the juvey home) for the next 30 days after taking a beating from his old man. But he kept his mouth shut and left us out of it.

Franky Catalano Jr., the son of the precinct captain in our neighborhood, went to court with Petey and Petey's old man. He told us that when the judge asked Petey if he had a friend that helped him start the fire, Petey froze for a minute. The whole caper had been my idea, and it was probably the worst thing Petey had ever done up to that point. No doubt he could have copped a plea and gone home. Well, he could have gone to his house. But his home was much more than just his house. His home was the neighborhood, and the neighborhood had rules.

"I like to do things alone," he finally told the judge. "I don't have no friends. I only wanted to set the garbage can on fire 'cuz I like to see things burn."

Of course, he did have friends, and he always would. Just like the kids at the fire hydrant, nobody ever "said nuthin' 'bout nuthin.'" Charlie Mazzuca said that his father Ray told him that the arson squad told Ray some dumb kid was playing with matches. Ray never said anything directly to us about the fire. All he said was that he'd take care of us. On the day he collected the fire insurance he handed us an envelope. Petey never said anything, of course, but when he came home, we took care of him. We felt like pros, like big shots now. Petey never wore that t-shirt again, though. And Mrs. Mazzuca? Well, she never took care of us, but she was a comfort all the same, late at night, when we were alone.

Lessons from the Movie Mob on Omerta

Nobody likes a "rat." A stool pigeon, a stoolie, a fink, a snitch, a pig that squeals, a canary who sings, a rooster who crows. Names for the rat are legion, because contempt for him is universal and knows no bounds. The term "rat" came about naturally, describing what most people consider the lowest, filthiest form of life. In *The Departed*, Jack Nicholson's character ups the ante by calling them "cheese-eatin' rats." There are two kinds of prisoners in our jails who get the roughest treatment by inmates (and often by guards too). Tops is the guy who you are unfortunately going to meet in the next lesson, one who harms young children. Close behind is the rat.

*All right, so there's a snitch. We find 'em, we cut his prick
off, leave it in his mouth, leave 'em on the street.*
Sonny Black (Michael Madsen), *Donnie Brasco*

Omerta is the art of keeping silent rather than saying anything that
would get a friend in trouble. Loyalty to the law of omerta is as deeply
branded in Americans' skulls as loyalty to the home team. Students learn
not to "tattle" on each other. Cops don't turn each other in. Businessmen
usually won't spill the beans on other businessmen. Whether you're
criminal or straight, if you've got any code of conduct at all, you don't
rat.

Though Americans have strong feelings about not being a snitch,
they're nothing compared to omerta's importance to Italians and Italian-
Americans. Omerta is in our DNA. We were immigrants, Catholics,
strangers in this new land for decades. What most Americans don't know
is that for a hundred years before we arrived here, most of our ancestors
felt like strangers in Italy as well. Sicilians and southern Italians were
treated like foreigners by early Italian governments and later were
despised by Mussolini. Learning to cover for each other became second
nature (Some of this still hasn't changed in Italy). Omerta helped us
survive.

> *We have in our tradition something called omerta, what
> some people might think of as a code of silence. In my
> world, omerta is a noble principle. It praises silence and
> scorns the enformer. Omerta is an injunction against
> allowing yourself to be the instrument of another man's
> downfall. Omerta, however, does not mean that a man
> cannot say what he feels.*
>
> Joe Bonanno, original capo of one of the "Five (crime)
> Families," who died   of old age in 2002, defining omerta
> in the movie, *Bonanno: A Godfather's Story,* taken from
> his book of the same name.

Minestrone for the Mobster's Soul starts with omerta because our
lives started with it. All the rest of the lessons, virtues, and rules that we
live by are nothing without it. Omerta is the strongest value in Mafia

and mob movies, just as it is in real life. Ratting? You don't have to fuhgeddaboudit, because you doneventinkaboudit.

Early mob movies echoed the same theme. In the 1930s it was Rico (Edward G. Robinson):

> *We got to stick together. There's a rope around my neck*
> *right now and they only hang you once. If anybody turns*
> *yellow and squeals, my gun is going to speak its piece.*
> *Little Caesar*

But if you think omerta is something that only applies to criminals or Mafia types, think again. Omerta may come into play any day you step out of your house or go to work. When to apply the "art of omerta," or when not to, can make the difference between your obtaining a job or a promotion or not.

In circumstances when you may least expect it, omerta can be a matter of life and death, not just for a wiseguy, but even for you, Joe Citizen. You might be an office worker or a dockworker like the one who witnessed a "canary" being tossed from a roof in the 1950's movie classic, *On the Waterfront*:

> *I've been on the docks all my life and there's one thing I*
> *learned. You don't ask no questions and you don't answer*
> *no questions, unless you want to wind up like that.*

After watching the "rat" being thrown from the roof, another worker evokes laughter from the others when he remarks,

> *...he could sing, but he couldn't fly.*

To Italians, "a rat is a rat." That's because we know what "our thing" is and we are loyal to it. Though omerta is powerful in American culture, there is some debate about when to rat and when not to rat. We'll let you be the judge. When a student sees another student bring guns or bombs to school is he ratting on that student if he goes to authorities? Is a cop ratting on another cop when he tells his chain of command the second cop is a criminal himself? Is a military prison guard ratting when he sees another guard torturing a prisoner against military law?

You civilians face the law of omerta every time you see a fellow employee signing a false time card or false expense report. You face it when you see your company make thousands, eventually adding up to millions, by defrauding the public. In each case, you've got to decide what is "this thing of yours" that you are loyal to. You've got to decide if you are a bigger rat by saying nothing. Protecting some false idea of omerta can be just as bad as giving someone up. It can mean protecting some horrific evil. Knowing the difference can be a matter of life and death for you or your friends.

In *On the Waterfront,* Charlie (Rod Steiger) talks to Terry (Marlon Brando) to get him to "investigate a meeting being held by Father Barry (Karl Malden):

Get the names and numbers of all the players.

At first Terry doesn't understand his role:

Why me, Charlie? I feel funny going down there. Besides, I'd just be stoolin' for you.

Charlie sets him straight:

Let me tell you what stoolin' is. Stoolin' is rattin' on your friends, the guys you're with.

Americans have a word for those who talk at the right time. We call them "whistle-blowers" instead of rats or stool pigeons. "Whistle-blower" gives you a nice image of a policeman directing traffic or running after a thief, not an image of a traitor. But one man's whistle-blower is another man's rat.

The FBI are a good example of fucked-up omerta. Problems with communications were rampant in their offices prior to, and even after, September 11, 2001. Did anyone speak up? Who knows how many agents knew the extent of these problems and were silent so that they wouldn't be ratting out their fellow agents or putting their own careers in jeopardy. Instead, the country got attacked and 3,000 were murdered. Finally a Minneapolis FBI agent became a "whistle-blower." An employee with real *stugots* (in this case, it was a woman) was the one who confronted the problem.

Then again, it was a woman who was one of the worst publicly known rats of the last decade. Remember Linda Tripp? She pretended to be a friend to Monica Lewinsky and then ratted her out, taping their phone calls that discussed "private matters." She even wore a wire when she met with Monica. She later went to prosecutors with intimate details of her "friend's" conversations. Without stool pigeon Linda Tripp there would have been no Clinton scandal. Without squealer Tripp, Clinton and the U.S. Congress would not have been distracted by whether what his dick did or did not do should be called sexual relations. This went on for over a year, while at the same time terrorists were plotting to attack our country. Without that *strunz* Tripp, Lewinsky's dress would have gotten dry-cleaned and saved us all a lot of fucking trouble.

Another side of omerta, though, involves more than simply not ratting on your friends. Sometimes it means just keeping your mouth shut. You don't have to consciously rat on a colleague to be guilty of breaking the code of silence. You don't even have to have bad intentions. *The Godfather and The Godfather, Part II* have scenes that are two of the best examples of this.

In *The Godfather*, Santino makes a remark during a meeting that his father and the family are having with Sollozzo. After the meeting, the Don tells him,

> *Santino, come here. What's the matter with you? I think your brain is going soft....Never let anyone outside the family know what you're thinking again.*

This scene is a subtle take on omerta's "code of silence." By opening his mouth, Sonny gets his father pumped full of bullets a short time later because he let "outsiders know what (he) is thinking." The Turk sees that if he wants to open up the drug business, it will be easier dealing with Sonny than with the old man, Don Vito. Getting rid of the Godfather therefore will smooth his path. Sonny, of course, never wishes to put his father in danger, but he shows a lack of judgment in not following his father's advice, nor Jimmy Conway(DeNiro)'s in *Goodfellas,* "...always keep your mouth shut."

Breaking the code of silence gets Fredo killed in *Godfather II*. He tries to enhance his tiny ego by showing that he knows important players. He unconsciously mentions that he has met Johnny Ola before, thus sealing his own doom when Michael overhears. He never learned the lessons his father learned decades before, when the young Clemenza asks the young Vito if he looked inside the package he entrusted him with:

> *I'm not interested in things that don't concern me.*

Every unnecessary bit of gossip you repeat around the office; every condescending remark you make about a relative; every little snip of information given oh-so subtly can be enough to break the code and get you into trouble. It's done every day, sometimes with just a look or a "tell." It can be done out of immaturity, stupidity or downright malice. It gives Mr. or Ms. Big Mouth some short term sense of importance, but it only comes back to haunt him or her. People who develop a rep for having a big mouth miss out on job advancement, financial opportunities, and friends and contacts, and never even realize it.

In contrast, Michael keeps omerta's code of silence perfectly when his wife Kay asks him if he had Carlo killed. She puts him under extreme pressure asking him three times. Each time he deflects the question or tells her not to ask him about his business. When she begins to ask a fourth time (and he realizes that she will take further silence as an admission of guilt), he interrupts:

> Michael: *Enough! All right, this one time. This one time
> I'll let you ask me about my affairs.*
> Kay: *Is it true? Is it?*
> Michael lies: *No.*

Think back to the first time you saw *The Godfather*. How would you have answered the same question in a similar situation? Would you be like Michael? Lie to the very end. Don't give in. Keep your mouth shut. Or would you cop a plea faster than you could say bada bing, badda boop: "This one time I'll let you ask me about my business. Yes, I did it. But, I had to do it. I'll stop it. It won't happen again. I promise."

Michael's sense of omerta's code of silence is complete. If he has to lie, he does. This lie to his wife is as excruciating as any violent act that takes place in the film.

And don't pretend you can avoid a lie just by keeping silent. The code of silence in the end always implies a lie. This is demonstrated perfectly in *A Bronx Tale*. The key character in the movie, a child, witnesses a mob killing. He keeps silent. In a scene as agonizing as the one between Kay and Michael, the police ask the kid about each of the suspects, one by one, as they are lined up against a wall. Both the little boy and the audience know that it is the last suspect Sonny (Chazz Palminteri) who did the killing. When the boy is asked about Sonny, he will either have to break the code of silence or lie. He lies. In this situation, most of us would have lied too. Maybe out of pure fear. The child's father (Robert DeNiro) deepens the moral ambiguity of the situation by telling the child that he did...

> *...a good thing for a bad man. Sometimes in life you gotta do certain things that you gotta do even though they're not right.*

How strong are omerta and the code of silence? You've heard that myth about "death-bed confessions"? Movies love to play those up. But those who are loyal to the code may not always confess. The ultimate homage to the virtue of omerta comes in *Hoffa* when Bobby Ciaro (Danny Devito) tells the story about one of their guys, Billy Flynn, who gets burned when they fire bomb a building. This guy has about two seconds left to live and has a chance to confess to a priest (who isn't supposed to tell anyone anyway). He can save his soul from hell by confessing the truth. Instead, he keeps the vow of omerta eternally:

> *Billy Flynn–third degree burns, 90% all over his body. The motherfucker can't stop smoking his cigarette–the fumes–some fucking thing–Vaboom! There he goes. Priest, who is Father Doyle, down at St. Margaret's, which you wouldn't know, asked him to confess. As he's dyin,' Bill Flynn looks the priest in the eye... 'Fuck you.'"*

I went to the police like a good American...I stood in the courtroom like a fool and those two bastards, they smiled at me. Then I said to my wife, for justice we must go to Don Corleone.
Bonasera, *The Godfather*

2. Justice

The blinding light of realization that this is an unjust world came to Joey and me when Buddy C, one of the main guys we ran with, came to us with a story about a young kid in the hood named Jasper. Today I know why Buddy's story disturbed me. Back then all I knew was I was pissed off and confused. In my gut I felt we had to do something—we had to enforce justice. Instinctively I knew no one else was going to do it.

Our families had moved west into K-Town when we were young kids. It wasn't really a town, but a bunch of streets that somebody got the bright idea to name starting with the same letter. There was Kedvale, Kildare, Keeler, and so forth. Further west you had "L" names like Laramie and Long, and then came the "M's" and the "N's." So I guess somebody could get a good idea of where you lived just by hearing your street. But the "K's" are the only one I ever heard anyone call a town. DB's old man bought a two-flat on Karlov, just off Chicago, and my family moved into the second floor flat. But the smarter families were going farther down the alphabet.

The situation involved Jasper, who lived on Kildare, and one of the priests in the parish. Yeah, you can see what's coming. Now we didn't have anything against religion, and we had had life and death issues thrust on us two years earlier. But back in '61, when I was only 14 and Joey was 15, what this collar did shocked us. Everybody was a lot more stupid about these things back then, or they pretended to be.

We had always joked that this particular priest was a little different. He seemed not real masculine-like, but we didn't really think a lot about it. We goofed on the guy, laughing behind his back, but at the time I'm sure we thought he was harmless. After all, he was a priest.

What Buddy told us was that the priest had been "laying hands" on Jasper. That's what they called it back then in the neighborhood. Joey was a soph at St. Mel's at the time, and I was a freshman at Austin High after the good Christian Brothers decided their paddles and other Catholic discipline weren't going to work for me. There were older and tougher guys on our streets, but for some reason Buddy chose us to tell about Jasper, and he seemed to be looking to us for an answer. Either the local connected guys wouldn't bother or Buddy and Jasper didn't know how to talk to these older guys about the situation. I don't know.

We went to see the kid to get the story straight from him. Jasper wasn't one of our gang or anything, he didn't even hang with us. He was just a quiet kid, you know, the kind that other kids picked on sometimes. He was what you'd call "meek," the ones that are supposed to inherit the earth, right? Well, he inherited something different from Father Fannuch.

I don't know much about psychology, even now, let alone in my early teens, but it seemed like I knew by instinct that I had to talk to Jasper gently and in a quiet place. So we got Buddy to stand watch at the end of this alley behind the school while we talked.

I opened with, "Okay, Jasp, I want you to know that we're on your side no matter what, just tell us exactly what you told Buddy about what's been happening with you and the Father."

DB was like taking mental notes or something. He looked to be in a trance.

At first, Jasper was tongue-tied and wasn't saying much. "Uh, uh, Father has me stay after Mass every day to help him."

Knowing what I do now, I'm surprised Jasper said anything, but I guess we were already establishing a reputation on our streets as guys you could trust.

Finally, he started coming out with it. "Father takes me to his room, and we try on all these cassocks and surplices and other church clothes. I have to take off my regular clothes and Father does too. He says it's just like in a locker room."

"Jasper, you should tell your parents," DB finally blurted out. He had been muttering stuff under his breath most of the time that Jasper was telling the story. Sounded like, "jeez….sheeeit…..fckkk," not even whole words that you could hear clearly. I don't think he really wanted to hear any more. Frankly neither did I.

"I've tried. I've tried," choked Jasper. Now this was the first time the kid started crying. Before that he was just telling the story to us like a robot or like he was telling us about somebody else.

"As soon as I start telling them that Father keeps me after, they start talking real fast about how good it is that I'm an altar boy and stuff, and then they change the subject. I stopped trying to say anything to them. I know they'll just think I'm bad."

I'm not going to relate every detail Jasper told us because I get too damned mad even now. But it doesn't seem like Father physically hurt him. He just used to touch him and then get off on it, sometimes in front of the kid.

People trusted the priests in those days and believed in the whole representative of Christ thing. I can see now that Jasper's folks just didn't want to face any damn part of what was happening. We didn't have any experience in this kind of shit ourselves, so we didn't know what to think or do at first. We were not ready to rebel against all our religious upbringing at this point in our lives, but the thought of this particular priest listening to Confessions and handing out Communion made our skin crawl. Any confusion we had soon turned to anger and we knew that justice had to be served. We were going on pure instinct, and didn't know until decades later how right we were to be enraged.

We knew that every Friday night after Bingo, Father F would bring the evening's take back to the rectory to keep in the safe. The arrogant prick usually walked over unprotected, figuring that nobody would ever bother him or rob him because he was a priest. We decided that I'd hide behind some big bushes on the little walkway to the priests' house and DB would be in a dark doorway across from where I was. I could see DB, but the priest couldn't. We were ready on the next Friday night, and sure enough, right on time came Father F.

Just as he turned into the walkway and out of the street lights, Joey, with his fedora pulled down as far as it would go, called out to him from the doorway, "Howyadoin', padre?" As the priest turned to face the voice greeting him and started to utter some kind of greeting, I stepped out of the bushes behind him and got him at the base of the skull with my Louisville Slugger, and he went to the ground. We both took part in the rest of the damage, with shots to the head, ribs, and an extra hard kick in the balls. He was clutching the bag with the bingo money tightly by this time though, and we hadn't thought to use the element of surprise to grab it immediately. But as DB whispered in the rev's ear like we had planned, "This was for Jasper," so that this robe-wearing cocksucker would know this wasn't just a robbery, he loosened his grip on the bag.

The frock landed in the hospital for a couple of weeks with a concussion, broken nose and about four broken ribs. We didn't plan to kill him, but we later realized we easily could have without wanting to. Maybe something was holding back the force of my swing.

It was the perfect crime, if you want to call it that. The priest probably didn't recognize us. Yet if he did, he couldn't say anything lest the real reason for the beating come out. He let the police assume it was a mugging.

Joey wanted to divide our share of the bingo money by three and give a third to Jasp, but I nixed that idea. I probably just wanted to keep the money for myself or didn't want to take the chance of letting somebody know what we did, but now I know it was the right decision anyway. Getting money for what happened or feeling responsible for the priest's beating was the last thing the poor kid needed to deal with.

"Okay, so let's put a third of ours in an envelope in the collection basket on Sunday with a message to the pastor that this is for Father F's hospital bills and that he'd better leave little kids alone and better be gone from our parish," was Joey's next suggestion. I said, "Screw that, I'm not giving them anything." I don't know if he ever put any of his half in the basket, but these days I'm even more glad I didn't go along with it. You read where priests are getting away with everything short of murder.

Our man of the cloth immediately requested a transfer to another parish when he was released from the hospital, so we never saw him again. The people in the parish felt bad for him, thinking he was traumatized by our changing neighborhood and wanted to get away. No one learned the truth till years later, though there were few parishioners left by that time. Did he get the real message? Did it do him any good? I don't know for sure. We used to wonder how many kids he was playing with in his new "flock," and from the stories that have come out nowadays across the country, maybe it was a lot. But we got him out of our parish and he would never bother our people again.

Considering the times, I think we did the right thing. Today maybe it would be different. Justice is a little swifter for priests who abuse little kids now. They've been winding up in the slammer. At the same time, Holy Mother Church has been bankrupting itself paying out tens of millions to victims. I hope Jasper got some of that.

In prison, abusers often get a more permanent form of justice as well. There was this Father Geoghan guy on the East Coast, whose jail time was cut short when he accidentally wound up in a cell with some maniac who decided to save the taxpayers the cost of years of incarceration. The padre got a slow strangulation instead. Funny, but the guards had a hard time finding the keys to the cell fast enough to rescue him. Geoghan got his, but are you going to tell me we should have waited 30 years for those other black robes to catch up to guys like Father F? I don't think so.

Another collar, Father Shanley up in Boston, was getting ready to do an eight year term when I was first writing this. His lawyer said that putting him in prison was like giving him a death sentence. I'm sure the kid who got raped by him many years ago is hoping it is. The early line on Shanley was nine months, and I was taking the under. Guess he's still hanging in there, but if I was there, I'd make sure I won that bet.

Lessons on Justice from the Movie Mob

Justice is one of the most important ideas in any society. If you don't have justice, it's every man for himself. And if that's the case, there's no honor, respect, loyalty, or you name it. On the other hand, we live in a pretty unjust world anyway. That's why you always hear people hoping for justice at some vague future time:

"May God punish him for that!"
"May you rot in hell."

Whoever's saying those things doesn't sound like he's expecting justice real soon.

Or sometimes you'll hear:

"What goes around comes around"

Yeah, like because the Earth is round you think it's going to spin enough so that some wrong-doing cocksucker is finally going to get what's coming to him from the other direction. I guess it sounds good, but you know what—it doesn't usually happen. People point to the one time when the asshole gets what he deserves, but they forget about the other ten times when he doesn't. And yet we are told we should look to the law and the government for justice.

Justice is an ideal that we all agree is something good. We all think that society should be the one to enforce justice. Okay then, what is society? It is all of us. We aren't always going to wait around for some angel or some doofus in a black robe to come down from on high to bring it. If our laws and courts can't make justice happen, some other part of society is going to have to step up to do the job. I happen to think that is the right thing to do. Maybe that comes from my ancestry. We hardly ever saw any legal justice in southern Italy. The police and courts were controlled by someone else, someone unjust, and they were only out to screw us.

Now you can agree or disagree with whether another part of society should mete out justice. But don't give me any crap about it being legal or not. Something being legal doesn't make it right. What that old black lady down in Alabama did when she took a seat in the front of the bus in the 1950's was illegal. But she was right. And you can't disagree that when a Mafia or mob movie portrays justice being done it is reflecting what our values are and what the average Joe and Jane want to happen.

Remember when Bonasera comes to Don Corleone looking for justice at the beginning of *The Godfather?* His daughter had been beaten by two men, yet the scum that committed the offense were allowed by a judge in our wonderful court system to walk free. What happened? Why did this judge, supposedly dispensing "justice," let them walk? I don't know. Maybe the bastards had a good lawyer. Maybe this was their first offense. Maybe the judge got paid off. Maybe... maybe.... who cares? The fact is that justice was not visited on those who deserved it.

Bonasera may have wanted revenge, but the Don agrees to dispense justice. He also makes sure he teaches other lessons to Bonasera about respect and friendship before he agrees to dispense the justice. What happens next is one of a hundred things that makes *The Godfather* superior to all other movies. A lot of movie directors would have relished throwing in an extra scene of violence, showing these guys getting their nuts fed to them as kind of a last supper. What do we see in *The Godfather*? Nothing. Why? Because we don't need to. When the Don has given his word, we have no doubt about what will happen. That's justice. Compare that to what our courts dispense.

Some of the virtues of the mob movie code depend on whether you are part of "our thing" or not. For instance, the mob may consider a certain person a man of honor if he follows its codes of conduct (such as omerta), even though he murders for the mob. The outside world judges him as a murderer, and the mob accepts that he has no honor in this outside society. But when it comes to justice, I say to you that the mob is often more just than "society" is—in any comparison.

Consider the kind of justice you get from the FBI, for instance. I hate to get started on the FBI because the list of shit they have bungled is so long it would bore you.

> Gotti: *Russo, you know what FBI means, right?*
> Russo: *Why don't you tell me!*
> Gotti: *Forever Bother the Italians*
> *Gotti*

Funny? Maybe. What they really are is Forever Bungling Investigators. They knowingly let innocent men rot in jail to protect their sources; they protect killers; they frame innocent people; they've killed more innocent people than the Mafia has (read about Waco or Ruby Ridge); they let terrorists attack the U.S. when they had information in their computers about them. (he's not learning how to land the plane, so what?)You want more? I could give you plenty more if I had the space.

I've got to admit, the FBI has had men who worked hard to protect this country and who have treated us with honor and justice, but for the most part they've become their own thing, their own mob. People call it bureaucracy. Exactly. Bureaucracy is just a mob protecting its turf and protecting themselves. They keep their own vow of silence rather than expose injustice. The FBI's lack of justice goes back to the very beginning. In the 1960s they bugged civil rights leaders, presidents, and anyone who might be a threat to "their thing."

I had no beef with that panty-waist J. Edgar Hoover; after all, he left the mob alone for 30 years. He had his turf, the mob had its turf. But don't kid yourself. Hoover was *capo de tutti capi* on his turf—not even presidents would mess with his organization, because he had the goods on all of them. But he sure didn't bring justice to "his thing," if you consider his thing America and freedom. In the 30's he'd go after Dillinger, Baby Face Nelson, and individual criminals to make a big name for himself. Meanwhile, these were the Mafia's golden days. These were the days in which they prospered and made the millions that smart wiseguys used as the cornerstone of their fortunes when they went legit or semi-legit.

Our system dispenses better justice than the FBI or other parts of civilian society. Yes, we use deceit (like advertisers); we extort (like lobbyists and politicians). And we punish those who cross us (like the courts and jails). But we give citizens what they want and therefore we profit from it. In the 20's and 30's we gave them booze. Today we give them gambling (like every fucking state lottery, riverboat casino and Indian reservation). We give them prostitution (this is illegal?). And we give advanced education to suckers who are looking to score. When punishment needs to be delivered, we do so. Our perps don't wait 20 years on death row to be fried. We do it quickly and cleanly (unless there is a further lesson to teach). But we do not punish those who do not deserve it. Occasionally, there is a little "collateral damage" shall we say. It happens. The FBI can tell you plenty more about that too.

> *The people in Chicago love us. Why? Because we give*
> *them what they want.*
> Ralphie Capone *(Titus Welliver), The Lost Capone*

And we give them justice. If Bonasera comes to us, he gets justice. If he cries to the cops, odds are he'll get a stick in the eye. Justice—like respect—if it is not given to us, we must take it.

You need to make sure you don't confuse justice with pure revenge though. Revenge is another matter. A couple years after we dispensed justice to the padre an event occurred that was seared into our memory, as well as all other Americans. President Kennedy wasn't Italian, but he was our first Catholic president and a leader we respected. He sounded and looked like the kind of guy who lived by the right code. The fact that JFK's death was immediately revenged by Ruby, a mob-connected guy from Chicago, has got to be more than just a coincidence on some level. I wish Oswald had lived a while longer to see him squirm and to find out more about who set him up. We'll never know if killing him was just pure revenge or a way of covering up a mob hit.

In Italy, our ancestors engaged in revenge feuds for decades, even centuries. Hundreds have been buried through the years in the same city or province. It was part of the code.

> *Vendetta—traditional Sicilian justice. Every killing*
> *demanded another.*
> Bonanno (Martin Landau), *Bonanno, A Godfather's Story*

But revenge is not necessarily justice. It is counterproductive. It's not businesslike, you could say.

> *Whenever you go for revenge, you better dig two graves*
> *– one for your enemy and one for yourself.*
> Lucky Luciano (Gian Maria Volonte) to Joe "The Boss"
> Masseria, *Lucky Luciano*

Human beings have always found revenge a compelling theme, from ancient literature to current films. Revenge means seeing the evildoer get his just deserts. It means having justice done. It means making sure that what comes around goes back around. An orgasm of emotion is unleashed in the act of getting even.

The life lesson you must gain from watching these films, however, is that you must control this demand on your manhood—this revenge—rather than let it control you. As Bonanno said, every killing demands another and once the blood starts flowing it becomes impossible to turn it off.

> *You're like me. We forgive nothing.*
> Don Corrado (William Hickey), *Prizzi's Honor*

Revenge often consumes and kills the one who gains it, whether or not the vengeance is successful. Revenge is often fueled by a hatred that clouds your mind. It lets your emotion rule you; it leads to errors in judgment; it destroys reason. These emotional reactions might also give the enemy a chance to turn the tables on you or give the law a reason to punish you, the avenger.

Remember Don Vito Corleone returning to Sicily to exact revenge on the aged Don Ciccio in *Godfather II*? He does it coolly and methodically, many years later. This coolness results in justice, not revenge.

"Revenge is a dish best served cold," a great thinker said once. (Or as Tony Soprano provided his view on it, which came out something like, "Revenge is best served with cold cuts.")

Another example is when Sonny Corleone goes wild with revenge upon hearing his sister is being physically abused in *The Godfather*. This allows his enemies to lie in wait at the toll booth to kill him. Contrast that with Michael, who is expressionless as he kills Sollozzo and Capt. McCluskey in the restaurant. He is not enacting revenge for his father's near assassination. He is just coldly taking care of business, and taking care of justice too.

Hate produces a hot revenge, not justice. You must control your emotions so you do not destroy yourself.

> *To a dirty trick, show a smiling face.*
> Sammy the Bull, *Witness to the Mob*

Politics and crime, they're the same thing.
Michael to Tomasino. *Godfather III*

3. Politics

In our early teens, we spent most evenings hanging out in the schoolyard. We were either at Ryerson south of Chicago Ave. and east of Pulaski Road, or we'd go up to Nobel, where a small time gang, the Kedvale Gents, hung out. Nobel was across from Franky Catalano, Jr.'s house. Franky was six years older than I was and his dad was the precinct captain. And although we knocked out at least one window on his old man's house, he was the guy who initiated us into a lot of the sports we played. Believe it or not, there were times that we played baseball or shot hoops like normal American youths (or *utes* as Joe Pesci would say).

We were lucky back in the day. We didn't have to get dressed up in some fancy uniforms and wait to get carted off by our old ladies to a ball field where the parents watch you, the coaches tell you who's playing where, and the umpires boss you around. We weren't indoctrinated into some hierarchy for the benefit of adult egos. Our parents were dead tired by the time they came home, and just sent us out "to play," so our games were democratic. We played what we wanted, when we wanted, and with who we wanted. The games included softball with a 16" Clincher, pinner or "hit em out, touch football, field goals, and of course every variation of basketball from Horse to full court.

My favorite was "fast pitching." Polacks north of us called it "strike-em-out." Essentially a baseball game, the genius of "fast-pitching" was that you only needed two guys to play, a pitcher and a batter (though your could have fielders too). For a strike zone, you either drew one with chalk on the side of the school building or used the partitioned brick blocks just below the school windows that were universal on all Chicago public school construction. That made the strike zone a little big, and it didn't matter how tall you were, everybody had the same zone.

You used a dime rubber ball and kind of gauged how far 60 feet-six inches was away from the plate and drew a line on the concrete for the mound. Sometimes there'd just be a natural line or crack that you'd use. You could make that dime ball curve, drop and do all kinds of stuff you couldn't do with a real baseball. The batter wouldn't run anywhere after swinging. Whether he got a single, double, triple, or home run depended on how far the ball went. A homerun was a crack off old man Catalano's house or into his yard. We didn't try to hit his windows or anything, but if there was collateral damage we'd all run.

The pitcher would try to strike you out or get you to hit a ground ball that he could field, which would also be an out. There were foul lines, of course, and other rules were as close to baseball's as possible. You'd always be either pitching or batting–none of that standing in right field for half an hour with your glove up your Little League ass. Sometimes you'd pretend one major league team was playing another and announce the batters as they came up. One guy would be the Cubs and he'd enjoy stepping in there with the best Ernie Banks batting stance he could muster, bat sticking straight up like it was the extension of a bone coming out of the right side of his body. In '61, toward the end of our schoolyard careers, it would have been Billy Williams, Ron Santo, Kenny Hubbs, and a host of other greats joining Ernie at the plate (and still the Cubs finished in seventh). The opposing guy would have to choose another NL team (interleague play was unthinkable then, even in the schoolyard).

Eventually basketball dominated Chicago playgrounds as it still does today. You can still find a few fast-pitching games here and there though. On the other hand, if you go to the suburbs, you'll usually find rows of beautiful basketball courts with nice new nets and no one playing. Guess the kids are at home on their computers.

The "City that Works" worked for us, and if I could go back to any time in my life, I'd be playing fast pitching out against the school wall in a Chicago minute. I never once saw any rules about fast pitching or any of the other sports we played written down, but every kid in the neighborhood knew them. As we got older we learned the rules about how the city worked as well. These weren't written down either—that made them even more important. Couple that with what our friends and the older guys in the Outfit taught us and we had a first class education.

The overriding theme we grasped was that Mayor Daley's city had its own Outfit. Its own Organization. Its own Syndicate. Its own political Mafia, if you want to use that term. Back then it was known as the Machine. It couldn't have had any other name. It was efficient, well oiled, and produced results. It kept the neighborhood running by ensuring services, providing jobs, and helping residents with problems. It did most of this with a velvet glove, though it could use an iron fist when necessary. It expected loyalty, just as the Outfit did. The Machine and the Outfit shared many common goals that made it natural for them to work together. Their primary priorities were to stay in power and reap the benefits of that power. The erstwhile career of our neighbor and big brother, Franky Catalano, Jr. was a prime example of just how the city, and the Machine, worked. The Outfit had its *capos* (captains); the Machine had its precinct captains.

Franky Jr. was as stand-up a guy as you could imagine. Never in any real trouble, he didn't hang unduly with guys connected to the mob. He knew everyone in the neighborhood, though, because of his father's position as precinct captain. He also knew the code of the street, or the Avenue in this case, and never violated it. After all, the code of the city his father worked for and the code of the Avenue were close to the same. One of the few from the Avenue who graduated college, Franky's ambition was to be a teacher in the Chicago Public School system. When he got his first assignment, it was at Sullivan, a cushy high school on Chicago's far North Side that some teachers with decades of seniority couldn't get assigned to.

Whatever ball game we were playing, it ended like clockwork each evening at seven o'clock when Franky's old man came home from work at his phony city job downtown. He'd always be toting a paper bag with a six pack of Old Style and a half pint of Jim Beam from Armanetti's Liquors under his arm. Mr. Catalano was a World War II veteran and had won a purple heart fighting somewhere in Europe. He still had some shrapnel in his back and the booze helped ease his discomfort. That made the drinking more acceptable. It was the way old-timers took care of pain back then. Franky Sr. had never finished high school, let alone taught in it, but he had more power than a lot of people in the city, power that somehow resulted in his son being "lucky" enough to be placed in a top school in his first position.

If you had somewhere to go at 7 PM, you didn't need a watch, you just looked for Franky's old man. This human clock also kept the neighborhood humming as the local political power. If your garbage wasn't picked up, if your street needed plowing in winter or needed cleaning in summer, if some neighborhood punks (like us) were harassing you, or if you had any other beefs with city services, you didn't call some anonymous voice downtown. You'd ask Catalano–your precinct captain—to take care of it for you. If your cousin just moved in and needed a job, Franky would find one for him. After all, a garbage truck could always use a third man, so that everybody had more time for a smoke or a nap during the day.

Before civil service, to become a fireman or policeman or to obtain almost any public job, you had to have somebody sponsor you. That was usually your alderman or ward boss, who in turn got candidates from their precinct captains. If the job applicant was particularly connected or helpful in the precinct, he might get a construction job like our friend, Donnie "The Wrench," nicknamed because he never carried one, or any other tool for that matter. Call that corruption? I'd call some lawyer sitting on his fat ass making $300 an hour corruption. The little guy had a right to a little of the cush.

Of course, once a year or so was when you took care of old man Catalano for all those favors. That was usually in early November, but there were local elections in the spring as well. Catalano would go door to door encouraging everyone in the house to vote and to vote Democratic. His son helped him make the rounds. Franky Jr. didn't much like this political work but he had to help his father. Most of the people signed whatever he presented and nodded in agreement that they would vote the right way. Did citizens worry that anybody would know which way they voted? I'm sure many did. And maybe the Machine could find out,

I don't know. But it didn't really matter. As long as you paid lip service and as long as Alderman Keane and Mayor Daley were re-elected, the Machine ran smoothly. And they always won, with huge margins.

One thing they would know, though, was if you had voted at all. If you had not done your civic duty by late in the afternoon of voting day, Franky or one of his helpers would "come looking for you"–that's the only way I can put it. They'd offer to drive you to the polling station (it was usually practically next door anyway) or watch your kids while you voted. They were very polite and so helpful that you really had no excuse for not doing your patriotic American duty.

Very few people refused to vote, were dumb enough to put up a Republican sign, or antagonized Franky in any way. Why would they have wanted to displease him anyway? Catalano was their friend and always helped them any way he could. As for those few who did stand out in opposition–you know what? Their garbage got picked up too. But if they had any special problem, they couldn't go to Franky for a solution. And if you know life in the city, lots of special problems can come up.

We never failed to get a Christmas card from the Alderman. Of course it was Franky and his old man who had to write out all the cards and send them with the Alderman's return address. If any came back to the Alderman, he'd have a word with the old man. A precinct captain was supposed to know all who lived in his precinct. If a voter had moved out, it meant that a new voter probably moved in. The captain should have visited and welcomed the new family to the neighborhood, taken note of all eligible voters in the family, and checked to see if they registered to vote in the future.

He was also supposed to note which voters moved out because those people would need to be stricken from the voting rolls. Or maybe not. If a loyal Dem moved back to the old country, to another state, or even to the suburbs, the county election board didn't automatically take him off the rolls unless someone bothered to tell them. And likewise, if that loyal citizen moved on to that ultimate precinct in the sky, election officials might not be notified in a timely manner. Was it possible that this past citizen of the precinct might be so loyal that he'd travel hundreds or thousands of miles or do a Lazarus and in some magical way appear and cast his ballot in the next election? That's what made Chicago such a fantastical place. Everything was possible. Anything could happen. And often did.

Say you, a loyal member of the precinct, got a traffic ticket. You had a lot of options. Of course, if you were smart, you wouldn't even have received the ticket. You would have dealt directly with the cop, making some excuse about not being able to get out of work to go to court, and then adding the old reliable: "Can't we take care of this right here?" Most of the time he'd be glad to let you "take care of it right here," and he'd collect the "fine" right on the spot.

If you didn't know how the system worked, Chicago's finest was ready to school you on the spot. Their motto then and now is "To serve and protect." To grease the wheels the officer would initiate the dialogue himself with another famed catchphrase: "Whaddaya wanna do about this?" making no move toward getting his pencil and ticket pad out. He'd say that a couple of times until you got the picture and replied, "Can't we take care of this right here?" Most people already knew the system, though, and had a $20 bill ready next to their license all the time and accidentally gave them both to the officer. They'd be on their way in seconds with a stern warning to be more careful.

For many years it was kind of hard to get a traffic ticket in the city of Chicago, unless the officer didn't like you or "your kind" for some reason. He'd have to issue some tickets, after all, to show he was working in between donut stops. So if you had bad luck to actually get a ticket, your next option (besides just paying it) would be to note the police badge number (found on the ticket) and give it to your precinct captain. He would find out if that officer usually appeared in court on the days he was assigned. If he wasn't in court as a witness against you, the case was thrown out. Officers who showed up in court were in the minority. Many citizens would rather pay the ticket than take time off from work to show up in court. But those who showed up knew they'd be judged innocent if the cop wasn't there.

If you got a ticket from a cop who usually *did* show up, your precinct captain could put you in touch with a lawyer who hung out in the halls of the courthouse. You'd meet him outside a specific traffic courtroom. He would walk up to the double doors, look through the crack in between them, and see who the judge was. If the judge was "the wrong one," he'd tell you to go in, get a continuance, let him know the date and time, and he'd meet you again. This scenario would be repeated if he didn't get the right judge. Finally, on the right day, he would look in and say, "Let's go." You'd walk in and check in with the bailiff. When court started, your case was first up. Charges were read, the judge dismissed them, and you were out the door. You paid the lawyer a fee perhaps larger than your fine, but a small price to keep from staining your perfect driving record, losing your license, or increasing your insurance rates.

Now, if none of this worked you could simply ask your precinct captain or someone else who was politically connected to "fix" the ticket. You'd pay for the privilege, in loyalty and greenbacks.

Other public functions were handled in similar fashion. Each had its own quirks and different people might be involved. But almost all of them could be handled. Want to get out of jury duty? Done. Want to get a construction permit? You could fill out the correct forms and follow the rules and do it yourself. It was a lot faster, though, if you did it through your connections. Plus, if some problem cropped up, you'd have no choice but to ask for unofficial help. You'd pay a service charge and you'd have to be loyal to those who helped you. It was a lot more benign than the mob, but just like the mob, you knew you'd be asked to repay the favor sometime down the line.

You'd vote Democratic in every election. If petitions had to be signed for candidates to run for office, you might be asked to help get them. You might be assigned to get fifty signatures and be given a hundred names and addresses. How you got them was up to you. If you felt you wanted to be on the up and up, you'd go out and actually get most of them. But if you got together with a bunch of other guys doing the same thing and sat around a large table passing pens and petitions around and got proficient in signing with your left hand, that made the job easier. Your ward boss wasn't going to ask questions.

Your clout could even get you into the National Guard when all the slots were taken. In those days that meant you might be fighting a flood on the Mississippi River, instead finding yourself ass deep in a swampy rice paddy in Nam with gooks sniping at you.

Most of this was seldom talked about and not very controversial. The Machine just worked, as naturally as breathing. The last thing that would have come out of Franky Catalano Sr.'s mouth would have been "You'd better vote Democratic, or else such and such might happen." He didn't have to.

That's why it wasn't surprising that Franky Jr. got his first job at Sullivan after he graduated. His father had a cushy city job most of his life. His son hadn't asked for any favors, but he got them anyway. He had always helped out his dad.

One day I was in the schoolyard firing that rubber ball against the wall, doing my best Bob Rush, actually believing my arm was getting strong enough to make the majors. I realized that I had to get the side out fast (the "side" was Nicky Macaluso) because I was ahead and it was about 7 o'clock. It didn't matter that Franky Jr. was too busy to hang out with us younger kids any more—our games still ended when his old man came home. Nicky kept fouling and fouling off everything I threw up there though. I finally asked some lady who was passing by for the time and she said it was a quarter after. Funny, I said to myself, that son-of-a-bitch Catalano is never late. Well, who knows? I thought. I wound up as if I was going to give Nicky my best fast ball and then pulled the string on it and he whiffed before the ball ever got there. I think he wanted to go home too.

I got home, had supper, and was watching TV a couple of hours later, when Greg Macaluso, Nicky's older brother who worked a graffiti blaster job that Catalano had gotten him, rang our door bell. My father came into the living room and told me, "Old man Catalano had a heart attack this afternoon. He died on the Pulaski bus, just before he got off at Chicago Ave." Strange, I had never heard my father call him "old man" before. We learned that Mr. Catalano was really only 51 years old.

Naturally Franky was as broke up as anyone would be losing his dad. A couple of days later at the wake he kind of spit out, part angrily, part sadly, through tears, "At least I won't have to ring those damn doorbells any more to get the vote out." I never had known how much Franky hated doing that stuff, or I just hadn't paid attention. But he was done with it.

Unfortunately the Machine wasn't done with him. You've heard about it being hard to get out of the mob once you're in? I learned that this was another similarity between the two. Although the punishment was less severe, it still sent the message. Franky's father's body was barely cold before the phone rang and Franky Jr. got word from the ward committeeman that they'd like him to be the new precinct captain and carry on his father's legacy.

Franky knew how things worked, but I don't think he really understood that there'd be repercussions if he refused. He was thinking about what might happen in the neighborhood, rather than his job. He thought of other people to recommend. He suggested they look for someone older. It didn't matter. The ward boss insisted he was the best one for the job. "Franky, you really know the ropes. We need you. Don't you like being needed? You do great at your school job, and we know you'd do great as precinct captain," the committeeman kept saying.

Franky kept refusing for the rest of the school year and into the summer. In early August, a startled Franky opened up his mail and found he had been transferred to Wendell Phillips High School on the South Side. Phillips was in one of the poorest, most crime-ridden areas of the city, an area where the students who did show up for class were not nearly as excited about education as the Jews and WASPs on the North Side.

"The City that Works" only works for you if you work for it. "The Boss," Richard, J. Daley, symbolized that motto. He embodied every quality a good don should have —and he never got his hands dirty. Even today, I see his face and Capone's together when I think of those who ruled the city in the last century. In true mob fashion, his son carries on the legacy to this day. Although the Machine is weaker, elections for mayor are still a foregone conclusion. Richy Jr. has beautified and modernized the city, cleaned up the way it does business, and gained respect from all sides. I'm sure he too has got to scratch somebody's back and grease some wheels when nobody's looking, but isn't that a small price to pay for a pol who can make things work.

Once when Richard "The Boss" Daley was questioned regarding nepotism or giving his sons unfair political breaks, his answer was clear: "If you can't help your kids, who are you going to help."

He succeeded in helping his kid in a way Don Vito Corleone could only dream of for his son, Michael:

> *I thought that when it was your turn, you would be the one to hold the strings –Senator Corleone, Governor Corleone, something.*

Richy Jr. holds those strings, but today he realizes that to get results he has to pull them in a different direction than his father did. Most mob bosses wouldn't ask for a better result for their sons.

Lessons on Politics from the Movie Mob

"The Machine is dead." "The Mafia is broken." You'll hear these pronouncements in Chicago about the Machine and nationally about the Mafia. These political and criminal organizations may be weaker. Depending how you define them, they might barely be on life support. Either way, that doesn't mean that politics in general is dead. That's impossible. As long as human beings interact, politics—the art of dealing with people to get what you want done—will always be alive, whether you're dealing with friends, relatives, or co-workers.

I hope you've never said the following: "I don't want that job because I don't like to play politics." If you have, I hope this lesson teaches you that that sentence is nonsense. You will play politics whether you dig ditches or become the mayor's right hand man. You'll need to deal with the foreman of the ditch-diggers, the guy slacking off his digging next to you in the ditch, and the guy hauling the muck away. They can make your life harder if you don't deal with them and easier if you do. Another definition of politics is the art of the deal. So deal, and get over it.

> *Let me be your friend. Even the strongest man needs friends.*
> Don Lucchesi
> *I'm flattered...You're a man of politics and finance, Don Lucchesi.*
> Vince Mancini
> *Godfather III*

One way of dealing is to find a mentor, or as Mike Royko used to say, "you need a Chinaman." (Why an inside guy with clout was called a "Chinaman" I couldn't track down, but it seems to go back a hundred years.) Find the guy who knows how to dig ditches the best, the fastest, the easiest, and follow his example. Find the guy who is most likely to become foreman next, and make sure he knows your skills and ambitions. Find out what he's into and you be into it. That doesn't mean you have to compromise your principles (assuming you have some). Ninety-nine times out of a hundred you can find a way to appreciate and share his interests. Just don't tell me you don't like to play politics

Soon, you too can become the mentor. Help others and they should be loyal to you. You are building a group, an organization, your own outfit, your own Mafia, if you will.

> Max: *You don't get nowhere alone.*
> Noodles: *I thought you were the guy that said he didn't like bosses. It sounded like a good idea then. It still does.*
> Max: *Let's just think about it, Noodles. They're gonna ask us to come in with them. There's a lot in it for us.*
> *Once Upon a Time in America*

> *A wise man once told me, Mr. Luciano, that if a man wants to succeed at this business, he has to make alliances.*
> Bumpy. *Hoodlum*

> *If Don Corleone has all the judges and politicians in New York, then he must share them or let others use them. He must let us draw the water from the well.*
> Don Barzini. *The Godfather*

Not only is it necessary to play politics, whether you're a janitor or the vice-president of the janitors' local, but the more you seek advancement in an organization, the more you are going to have to rely on your political instincts—in other words, your instincts in dealing with people.

But, the higher I go; the "crookeder" it becomes. Oh, where the hell does it end?
Michael, *The Godfather*

The politics doesn't end. But crooked is as crooked does. You'll have to the judge where to draw the line. Just don't tell me you don't like to play politics
It might have helped if the 43rd capo-in-chief of the U.S. had learned this life lesson in politics from the movie Mafia before he took over:

Michael (in Cuba) I saw an interesting thing happen today. A rebel was being arrested by the military police and rather than be taken alive, he exploded a grenade he had hidden in his jacket. He killed himself and he took a captain of the command with him. Right, Johnny?
Johnny Ola: *Those rebels, you know they're lunatics.*
Michael: *Maybe so, but it occurred to me, the soldiers are paid to fight, the rebels aren't.*
Hyman: *What does that tell you?*
Michael: *They could win.*
The Godfather, Part II

*You know, you live this goddamn life long enough and you know
you can't take anything with you except your honor.*

Neil Dellacroce (Anthony Quinn) on his death-bed,
to John Gotti. *Gotti*

4. Honor

"Jimmy, how's it going on the inside?" was always our greeting on the occasions we visited Jimmy D'Annunzio at Joliet.

"Joey and Bobby, Fuckin-ay," was always Jimmy's hello.

Matter of fact it was his favorite expression for just about everything. The first time we visited him, "fuckin-ay" meant something like "surprised to see you." On later trips it meant "glad to see you." "Fuckin-ay" had a lot of meanings. When Sandy Tortoni used to walk by us after school with short shorts on and little heels, there was Jimmy's "Fuuuuckin-aaaay." I guess that also meant "glad to see you," but there was a bit more implied perhaps, especially when Jimmy grabbed his crotch after she went by. Then there was the serious, quiet "Fuckin-eh" when Jimmy knew he was in big trouble. He had a different "fuckin-ay" for any situation. But if you think we had any trouble figuring out what he meant, fuckinay, fuhgeddaboudit.

Although Jimmy was a good friend who we had grown up with, he had no honor. He knew the rules—no dealing drugs, no doing drugs, no hiding profits from the boss—he just didn't follow them. And he never could fuckin-ay his way out of trouble once he was in it. In high school he stole a car and was part of a robbery that went wrong and that got a guy shot and killed. Since Jimmy was only 16 at the time, he got sentenced as a juvenile and back then they couldn't keep him once he turned 21.

"Fuckin-ay, no problem, my men, these jagoffs in here know not to mess with me. They treat me with respect and honor," was one of his answers when we asked how he was doing.

Jimmy would go on talking about what a tough and honorable guy he was in the pen, but he knew, and we knew, that other guys didn't mess with him because they figured he had connections, not because he was tough or a "man of honor." Plus some of his jail pals probably figured that being on Jimmy's good side might be a good career move.

But we were also realizing that his time in the joint was fuckin-ay fucking him up. Though we liked him personally, we could see that in the long run he was going to be bad for business. He was growing harder in the can, but not in a good way. Aligning himself with more common thugs and badasses, Jimmy was learning the wrong lessons, the tricks of the wrong trades, where only a few got promoted and the rest wound up terminated.

Detention center officials tried to get him into a real business, or at least a trade. They taught him to be a barber. They told him he could be set up with a nice career once he got out—and someday it would be Jimmy's Barber Shop. Yeah, right!

Jimmy was released in 1967 when he turned 21 and got one more chance to make it in this world. He could have gone straight or at least could have kept his nose clean in some of the regular rackets. He got the customary party with plenty of drinks and some young ladies who usually worked LaSalle Street. I mean, high class. Jimmy was a lower level guy and very young when he went in, but while in the joint, he had played the game right.

We were happy for Jimmy personally. He had done his time, kept his mouth shut, and was out of prison with his life ahead of him. And we still had hopes that he could join us in whatever came our way. But we knew that here was a guy who had developed a mean streak that lay hidden and that could erupt like Mt. Etna without warning.

Dutifully, or so it might have seemed to an outsider, Jimmy started working at Tony Vittore's barbershop on Chicago Avenue, near Monticello. We went in there for our trims, but we remained suspicious that Jimmy was not going to be satisfied with the income a barber makes, and that cutting hair wasn't the kind of action he craved. Plus, he was a little scary wielding that razor when he shaved the "mustache Petes," those ancient *paesans* from the Old Country.

A couple of months went by, though, and Jimmy seemed to be doing fine. We heard he had what you might call a part time job from the Outfit, roughing people up. That was right in keeping with his reputation because Jimmy had that cold look he could give you when he was pissed and that people immediately feared. Since they sensed he was capable of anything, he often didn't have to do anything. Apparently he was doing his work without getting too carried away or killing people that didn't need killing. Coupled with his haircutting job as a front, he seemed like what you'd call a model of prison rehabilitation.

One day we went to see Jimmy at the barber shop. We didn't need a cut or anything—we just wanted to shoot the shit and see how he was doing. We knew it was a Tuesday and the owner, Tony, usually wasn't there. As we pulled up, we noticed, wow, business was brisk. We sat outside in the car for a few minutes and guys were going in left and right. It was so busy that when some lady went in with her kid, they came right back out again. Guess Jimmy told her they were too busy and to come back tomorrow.

As we slid in finally, Jimmy was all "Joey and Bobby, how the fuck are you?" At least that's how I remembered it a little while later. DB says, it was "...how the hell are you?" We were talking for a few minutes and Jimmy was bitching about that "dumb fuck" Dooley who's taken over coaching the Bears and other sports news. I didn't notice anything out of the ordinary, but DB said later he saw what looked like a few potential customers approach the door, look us over, and walk on by or go away. One guy came in, looked at us, and made an appointment for a cut (who the hell makes a haircut appointment on Chicago Avenue?).

Finally a guy came in and mumbled "Can't you just take a little more off here than you did yesterday," and they disappeared in the backroom for a few minutes. The guy left with the same 'do he had when he came in from what I could see. As soon as Jimmy disappeared in the back room for a second, Joey and I looked at each other. Okay, maybe the sports talk was a little unlike Jimmy, and he seemed nervous, but that didn't tip us off to anything. Then I realized it! When we walked in, there was no "Fuckin-ay!" Something was wrong. Jimmy was selling more than his haircutting expertise.

Shit, I thought. Not that I've got anything against drugs personally if that's what people want to do, but outright dealing was not what the higher-ups wanted. They were old-school and didn't want their associates selling junk. I don't know if the Boss wanted the no drug rule because he personally didn't like drugs, or if he felt, like Vito Corleone, that dealing drugs was bad for business.

Drug-dealing makes it harder to get cops to look the other way. Judges, too, are not as likely to play ball because they might have the public on their ass if they are lenient with big bad drug-dealers. Also, guys who get pinched on a drug beef are up for longer sentences and might be more tempted to violate the law of omerta—to turn into rats in other words. Let the lowlifes deal that shit and take the heat—that was the idea in our hood.

Naturally, we kept our mouths shut, but word got back to the higher-ups in short order anyway. The Boss and his top lieutenants had a sit down with Jimmy and gave him the order – no more drugs. But Jimmy couldn't just sit around in the barber chair. He just laid low, hid things better, and still dealt. You should know that you can't hide things from the bosses for long.

Jimmy changed his m.o. and started meeting his contacts outside of the neighborhood. He kept dealing, while popping pills and doing a little "H" himself. He was getting more fucked up by the day. Although he kept the barber shop clean, everybody knew that if you wanted to score, Jimmy could deliver, whether it was reefer, speed, heroin, or whatever. One day some kids got pinched with some "H" over by Austin High School. They gave Jimmy up as the dealer and he was arrested.

We learned some lessons right then, years before we heard them in the movies. "To your enemy, show a smiling face" was one of them. The Boss got Jimmy bailed out the very next day, not easy to do on such a charge. If Jimmy had half a brain, it would have tipped him off right there. Since the Boss was anti-drug dealing, it was strange he'd have him bailed out so quickly. Of course if Jimmy had any brains he might not have been in this mess in the first place.

The Boss later perfected his response, with another guy, initials of C.C., who also violated the drug rule. The Boss let the judge throw the book at C.C., who wallowed in jail for seven years. The Outfit protected him in the joint. They sent visitors to make sure he was all right and kept in touch with him. He served his time and kept his mouth shut about his mob ties. When he got out though, he must have wondered why he didn't get the traditional "coming-home" party, with the booze and broads, and all. Since he went in on a drug bust, though, he might have figured it was natural that the Outfit didn't go out of their way to welcome him, since the Boss frowned on drugs. So C.C. just went home. Or maybe he thought there would be a surprise party. There was. The surprise came at a beef stand in Elmwood Park, when C.C. went out a couple of weeks later for a *sangwich*. And the surprise came in front of his family for good measure, which shows just how dishonorable the bosses felt it was to deal drugs in those days. You usually don't whack a guy in front of his family.

Jimmy was facing more prison time than C.C. would do and would be worthless to the Outfit. Furthermore, who knew whether or not he'd crack this time. Inside of a week, we were watching John Drummond on the Channel Two news and he was talking about this gang-related shooting in Cicero. Jimmy D walked out of a bar to his car on Cermak Road and took five bullets in the back and one in the head. The cops never found the hitter, of course. You know there are occasions when it makes more business sense to refuse bail.

In the case of Jimmy, the guy standing over him on the street after he plugged him was probably saying, "It's not personal Jimmy, its only business." It's a concept that runs through almost every film concerning this thing of ours. But he also might have said something about Jimmy's lack of honor, lack of any code or willingness to fit into an organization, something that an old timer like Joe Bonanno would say years later.

Since when has the love for money become more important than honor? Narcotics is a dirty business.
Bonanno, A Godfather's Story

Lessons of Honor from the Movie Mob

Honor is believing in something and following through no matter the consequences. It is one of the highest values in American society, almost as high a value as it is in Italian life. A man must serve his country with honor. An athlete must honor his team and mates. Students strive for the honor roll. But we all know soldiers, athletes, students, and ordinary citizens who have dishonored their cause, their thing. Matter of fact dishonor seems more on the rise lately. All the more reason that people will look up to someone who displays it.

Even if Americans do not believe in a particular cause, they will usually respect those who act with honor in support of that cause or belief. John Gotti was one of the last of the classic Italian-American Mafia godfathers. Gotti may have been as ruthless as those who came before him. He had the previous head of the Gambino family—Paul Castellano—assassinated. Unfortunately, Gotti also had another quality that was different from those who originated this thing of ours. Instead of trying to stay in the shadows, he wanted to wear the crown in public. He had to be the big shot, a celebrity. His ego was one of the reasons given by those who engineered his downfall.

Maybe he didn't follow the image of what a don should be, yet in terms of "our thing" Gotti kept his honor to the very end. He went to the can, died in the can, and never copped a plea. He fought as hard as he could in every trial, and when he was convicted he shut his mouth and did his time until his last breath.

Will movies be made twenty years from now sentimentalizing this honorable man, this cruel Mafia boss, John Gotti? It's already started. A series, *Growing Up Gotti,* has already played on television, featuring the Dapper Don's daughter, Victoria. (You can bet I watched the first episode, and if Gotti were alive, he'd take out a contract on the producers of this pile of garbage.)

Look at Al Capone—he's almost a cartoon character today. He's a marketing tool for tourism. You can visit "The Hideout, Al Capone's Northwoods Retreat" in Wisconsin—it's recommended by AAA! Or visit a museum and take a tour dedicated to his deeds in Chicago. In the future, maybe you'll be able to go to Gottiland in Queens. I can see a tour right now. We'll visit his Ravenite Social Club and then end with dinner at

Sparks Steak House where Big Pauly got clipped. Maybe John Jr. will be out of prison long enough to be our tour guide. If not, there's always Victoria.

Gotti deserved his fate, yet he embodied at least one of the qualities that society reveres—honor.

Gotti's principles and beliefs may have been immoral, but being true to them, even in the face of a lifetime prison sentence, is no less a thing of honor. His "protégé" Gravano seems to think Gotti had no honor:

> *Where was the honor? Where was the loyalty there? Where was the brotherhood? DiBono was bringin' Paul envelopes every week, envelopes with my money. Loyalty, obedience, honor – these things don't mean anything anymore? ...*
> Gravano, *Witness to the Mob*

But it was Gravano who ratted out the entire mob to save his skin. Gotti kept the code of silence.

> *Here we are, you and me sitting, facing each other like enemies. Maybe you thought you would kill me. But you won't because besides all our differences, we are joined by blood and history and you, cousin, you still believe you are a man of honor.*
> Bonanno, *Bonanno, A Godfather's Story*

If there is anything Bobby and I have tried to follow to the hilt it is this code of honor. We made our decision about not dealing dope long ago. We had rules—parameters, as Gotti called them. And we stuck with them We made our promises, or choices, and we lived by them. In the case of drugs we thought these parameters were practical as well:

> *It's better to make two hundred million with no risk, than five hundred million with the Feds up my ass. Can't you see that? Doesn't anybody see that? Am I the only one?*
> Paul Castellano (Chazz Palminteri) *Boss of Bosses*

The other lessons in this book may help you to be successful in life, put money in your pocket, bring you friends and allies. Honor will often bring you those benefits too, but it will sometimes temporarily result in the opposite. Honor may mean you must act against your own interests—stick to the code you believe in even if it harms you.

You make a promise to a friend, you keep it—even if it costs you.

You accept a job from your boss, you complete it—even if it becomes harder than you figured.

You are born to a family, you defend them against all outsiders—even if it means your injury or your death.

> *Look, I'm from Brooklyn, I was born poor. I'm not saying that bein' poor means you don't have to live by the rules. I hate that crybaby stuff. I made my own choices. There are certain promises that a man makes that carry more weight than a hundred Bibles full of law. And you live by these promises. And if you don't, you should be dead anyway.*
> Paul Castellano (Chazz Palminteri), *Boss of Bosses*

Some straights laugh about "honor among thieves." Honor, like so many other values we hold sacred, is sometimes violated, just as ethics are in any group of men. That doesn't make honor less important to us. It's actually more important.

In our world we have to depend on a person's word, backed by his honor. We don't sign contracts for most of our business. We have to avoid transactions that most people take for granted. The honor of our word is important because it's all we have. Imagine one of us filling out an insurance form—what are we going to put as our occupation—wiseguy? Are we going to list all our income sources to apply for a mortgage? Are we going to make out a will and list all the assets? Are we going to pay income tax on all our income? (That's tripped up more than a few of us.) No, instead, we deal with each other as much as possible and give our word, our word of honor. If we can't pay cash, we borrow from friends. Income tax, we avoid whenever possible. We're already paying the street tax. When one of us is killed, his wife and children are taken care of by his "other family." That's our insurance.

Tom Hagen: *Francis, when a plot against the emperor failed, the plotters were always given a chance to let their families keep their fortunes.*

Frankie Pentangeli:*.....they went home and they killed themselves. Then nothing happened and their families were taken care of.*
The Godfather, Part II

Frankie knew what he must do for his family as a man of honor. Only you can decide how much honor you will live with. Rich man, poor man—honor is a trait that people emotionally respond to, whether it be found in a saint who gives his life for his beliefs or a sinner who lives by the code he professes.

You see, all our people are businessmen.
Their loyalty's based on that.
Michael Corleone (Al Pacino), *The Godfather*

5. Loyalty

For decades, Freddie "the Pol" Polito controlled much of Chicago's jukebox business from his operation, The Music Man, on west Grand Avenue. The Pol was technically a mob boss but he stuck strictly to the juke business. When we were in our early 20's, Joey and I wound up working for him.

"Did-did you guys deliver those new boxes on Fillmore Street yet?" Freddie would whine when he got a new order.

"No, Mr. Polito, the place isn't even open for three hours yet," I'd say.

"Okay, okay, tell me when they're in there." The Pol was a real nervous, paranoid kind of guy. Working there made you feel uneasy, like every move you made was being watched. It probably was. Whatever we had to do, he was all over our ass to get it done yesterday. I guess he didn't want to lose one second of those juke boxes earning their keep. Or us either for that matter.

But Freddie the Pol was our boss, and we were loyal to him. His right hand man Tony Frangione was also loyal to him, but only up to a point. The Pol had brought him in and had given him a chance to earn and spread his wings, so to speak. Tony was the guy who made sure the bars and restaurants were hooked up with one of the Music Man's fine boxes. Otherwise, though he and Freddie weren't that chummy.

If you needed dough to start up your own joint and couldn't go through the normal channels, Tony was also the guy to see. A lot of prospective bar owners in the neighborhoods weren't exactly the type who were going to be welcomed with open arms by Harris Bank, or by Bohunk S&L on Cermak for that matter. They had to look for alternative financing. Tony had the equivalent of an MBA in alternative financing. And a PhD in debt collection as well.

Tony had most of the West Side wired and was making great inroads throughout the city. He made sure the establishments took on the product and kicked back 20% of the take. He had a regular crew of collection people who were not above filling in as muscle guys when a place said they weren't interested. The owners usually got the message after one visit. A few broken windows or a fire in an entranceway with some minor damage and most people made the right business decision. Sometimes some asshole would have to take a beating before he understood the value of entertaining his clients with the latest tunes. We delivered the jukes and occasionally got an order to make sure that reluctant participants signed on board.

We were loyal to the Pol as well as to Tony and assumed they'd be loyal to us and to each other, but we learned that sometimes the ugly side of human nature overcomes loyalty.

Tony's personality was the direct opposite of the Pol's. Tony was always glad to see us when we came in and would sometimes greet us with a c-note handshake. The Pol would usually greet us when we came in from making our rounds with something like, "Are... are...you sure you made all the stops?"

Yeah, we always made all the stops, but sometimes we'd be a little light. There were guys with genuine reasons or excuses. Some guy was out of town or his old lady was sick, and he'd pay us the next day. We knew our customers and they knew us—we didn't need to take any business classes to know that's what you do. Our stops always came up with their percentage, but the Pol hounded our ass anyway.

Furthermore, instead of slipping us some extra dough on occasion, like Tony did, the Pol wouldn't even give us our envelope until we asked for it every week. You'd think once he'd just have it ready and call us into his office. No, we'd have to ask (beg) every Friday, and then it was like, "Oh….oh…..you guys want something before I go, huh? Heh, heh, heh."

Even though the Pol was the boss, Tony made his entrance into the office like he owned the place. If the old cliche of the tall, dark, and handsome type applied to anyone, it was Tony who fit that bill, and the broads swooned over him. He hired his own "assistants" and there was a lot of turnover. But he was well-liked and respected – much more than the Pol.

Looking back at it, when Tony hung around the office and made small talk with the ladies, that seemed to make the Pol more nervous than usual. Besides that, the Pol's wife, Gina, would come in from time to time and Tony paid a lot of attention to her. I think he just wanted to make his usual good impression, but she seemed to enjoy the attention, and maybe Tony was purposely yanking the Pol's chain. Gina was a good-looker and younger than the Pol. We had the feeling that she'd probably like to get something going with Tony, and we'd joke that it was doubtful that the Pol was delivering the goods at home. I doubt anything was really happening, though. Tony always followed the code, and that includes not messing with a wife or girl friend in the Outfit, let alone your own boss's old lady.

Things went on this way without too much friction for quite a few months after we started working there, until a certain Wednesday. The Pol always went to the track on that day of the week, and Mrs. Pol, which is what we called Gina, had the habit of turning up at the office on Wednesday. Invariably she'd wind up talking to Tony. They'd usually be in a corner knees touching, her skirt creeping up her thighs, and her loose blouse flouncing up and back as she laughed (not like I took much notice or anything).

This particular Wednesday, there had been a fire in one of the buildings at the track in the morning, and the cops and fire officials closed the track for the day to investigate. The Pol suddenly showed up in the middle of the day and spotted Tony and his old lady all tete-a-tete in a corner. He just mumbled something about thinking she was supposed to be shopping and went into his office without a fuss. But we knew Freddie the Pol, and we knew he was in there steaming. Still, although the tension seemed to get thicker, nothing happened.

Tony was a guy who enjoyed breaking balls and would go at everybody in the office, even the Pol from time to time. Most of it was good-natured, but one day he started asking the Pol about Angie, a greaser broad from Tripp Street that he knew the Pol had been banging and gave him a wink. The Pol's face turned red. It seems that Mrs. P. was in his office with the door open and might have caught the reference. Did she or didn't she? Did Tony know she was there or didn't he? We didn't know, and frankly we didn't give a damn at the time. But much later we thought of what Hoffa said in the movie bearing his name.

> *The thing of it is, a guy's close to you, you can't slight him. You can't slight the guy. A real grievance can be resolved. Differences can be resolved. But an imaginary hurt, a slight, that motherfucker is goin' to hate you till the day he dies.*
> Jimmy Hoffa (Jack Nicholson), *Hoffa*

Maybe that slight never left the Pol's memory. His attitude started to get worse. He started carping about whether he was getting all the dough that he felt he was entitled to out of the machines. He complained about how the envelopes were light and was all over everybody's ass who had anything to do with collecting. And there was a load of ice between him and Tony.

Soon the Pol took to coming out of his office after Tony had just left and asking things like, "How does that guy afford that shit?" We assumed he was talking about Tony's suits. "Where is this guy getting it all?"

We could all hear him, but it was like he was questioning the air. He didn't expect an answer. The Pol, being the cheapskate that he was and all, would never understand what Tony was all about. We feared he was looking for a reason to make a move. As the cold war continued, he called Tony in for a sitdown to discuss his concerns about what he saw as a reduction in income.

Tony, who always was a cool customer, left the office that day, knocking over a rack of brand new 45 records, cursing the boss under his breath. Tony was smart and we figured he would never make the mistake of skimming the profits, but he should have been smarter about the way he dealt with this situation. If he had followed Lesson One about not letting anybody know what he was thinking, he might have been okay.

Tony let his anger spill out. He told not only us, but also asked anybody within earshot—"Why am I being disrespected? Who the hell is he that he should question me?"—and shit like that. Of course, these comments also got back to the Pol and must have given him further reason to question Tony's loyalty.

Freddie Polito was a made guy and although he wasn't particularly well liked, he was a good earner and the higher ups respected him because of that. Tony was well liked, but on the "depth-chart" was a few rungs lower. Word is that the Pol went to the boss and said he felt that Tony was disloyal and was stealing from him and the organization. When that happens, some action's got to be taken. If things weren't resolved after a sit-down, then the boss had a decision to make. We were worried about Tony, but we kept doing our jobs and kept our mouths shut.

For the next couple of weeks when Tony came in, there was none of the usual "how you doin'" and hand-shaking. Instead there was tension. He didn't come in as often either, and then suddenly we didn't see him for about a week. This just wasn't like Tony, because in spite of everything he was the kind who was still going to do his job. A few more days passed and still no word. The Pol brought in his nephew, Angelo to fill in for Tony. He seemed more concerned with business than where the hell Tony was. We soon found out he probably knew exactly where Tony was. The next day the cops found an Eldo parked at O'Hare airport. Tony was in the trunk sleeping off the after effects of two bullet holes in the back of his head.

Our sorrow at the wake was real. DB looked like he was going to cry. It had been five years since our friend Jimmy had become Swiss cheese on Cermak Road, but in some deep recess of our minds we had known he was a loose cannon. Tony was somebody we had seen on a daily basis and had looked up to. His sudden departure struck close to home. We realized that although we never went through any ceremony, this was part of the life we had chosen.

It was the Pol who made the biggest impression at the wake though. He made sure everyone who walked in noticed the floral arrangement he sent, the biggest one there. It said, "For my best pal Tony, from

Freddie" He kept yammering, "I'm really gonna miss this guy," and "I don't know how we're gonna keep the business goin' without him," and "Tony was the best." We nodded in agreement but kept looking at each other wondering how he could say this shit with a straight face.

Was Tony disloyal? Did he skim the profits? We didn't think so, but we figured that the perceived lack of loyalty and respect to the Pol and his paranoia about something going on with old lady got Tony clipped. It wasn't until a few weeks later that we learned that his worries were justified. It turned out that Tony thought he saw a weakness that he could take advantage of. He was trying to make an end run (for the business, not the old lady) and the Pol was right on top of it. It wasn't paranoia this time. Being cautious kept him from being taken advantage of and enabled him to survive. We got caught up in Tony's charm and likeable personality, the way a lot of people did. He was working us, and everybody else. He skimmed payouts from the machines, lined his own pockets, and put the word out that the Pol was running a fucked up operation. He didn't have the clout to pull off his power play, got caught lying, and paid the price. The lessons for us were that looks could be deceiving and that in our business you had to see through all the bullshit to find out who had the real power. After all those years of supplying the city's establishments with juke boxes, now Tony was the one playing trunk music. If we still needed any lessons on loyalty, we sure had gotten them, and we were behind Freddie the Pol all the way.

Loyalty is to omerta as sauce is to pasta—it's hard to imagine one without the other. If you are loyal, you keep your mouth shut. Period. Every wise guy on the way up aspires to be called a trusted, loyal lieutenant.

But if "you can't trust nobody" is a fact of life in this thing of ours, loyalty can also be hard to come by. With a lot of money to be made and a lot of power to be gained, the guy under you can be tempted to become disloyal or to try to get to the throne himself. Therefore, bosses surround themselves with people they know to be loyal. They eliminate those who they don't think are loyal.

Lessons on Loyalty from the Movie Mob

In *Godfather II*, consigliere Tom Hagen feels he is being frozen out of the family business. He later finds out that this was only to keep him safe and put him into position for his ultimate task, one which only he could perform because he was the only one Michael knew was totally loyal:

> *You're going to take over. You're going to be the Don. I give you complete power, Tom, over Fredo and his men, Rocco, Neri, everyone.*
> Michael (Pacino) to Tom

That's true trust. But it exists because of the loyalty that creates that trust. Presidents surround themselves with a loyal cabinet. Even a cabinet member who disagrees with the Commander-in-Chief's policy must be ready to fall on his sword in public for the decision once it's been made. The alderman in our ward wouldn't hire anybody that he didn't already know and who he didn't trust to be loyal. And that was just to collect the garbage. "You don't bring in no goddam fuckin' resume in here," he once told some poor moke off the street. Your resume was the people you knew who would vouch for you. Your "fuckin resume" on paper didn't prove your loyalty.

Mafia loyalty is based on business, though; it's not personal. In *The Godfather,* Michael tells Frankie Pentangeli (Michael V. Gazzo),

> *I like you and you were loyal to my father for years.*

But Frankie Five Angels is not happy with the business decisions that Michael has made. He wants certain people dead, "Morte," he says to Michael. Michael explains that he has important business with Hyman Roth. But Frankie doesn't understand the concept and complains,

> *Then you give your loyalty to a Jew before your own blood.*

Michael explains that his father did business with Hyman Roth and respected him. Still, Frankie can not see that business and loyalty have to work hand in hand, and he eventually pays the price as so many others have.

Business decisions and loyalty don't always mesh. Tony Soprano (James Gandolfini) tries to justify his actions by telling his psychiatrist that...

> *Some of us didn't want to swarm around (like worker bees) and lose who we were. We wanted to stay Italian and preserve the things that meant somethin' to us – honor and family and loyalty.*

Tony wants to preserve loyalty, but he also wants a piece of the action. He wants the two to mesh in the moral code he carries around in his fat head, but the conflict he feels when these concepts don't mesh leads to blackouts and visits to the "shrink." Loyalty goes both ways. Tony will be just as loyal to his people as he expects them to be to him. Paulie (Tony Sirico) explains the facts of life to Christopher just after Christopher gets his "button":

> *If you got a problem...This man, right here, he's like your father. It doesn't matter if it's with somebody here or on the outside. You bring it to him, he'll solve it.*

Your business is no different from ours. You're not going to hire some incompetent jamoke just because he knows somebody. Where you make your mistake, though, is to hire somebody just because of a great resume. Yes, your underling has to be able to do the job at hand. But just as important is that he is loyal, at least as far as business is concerned. His resume won't tell you that.

A lot of employers don't even check references. Check references? You should take the references out for dinner and drinks. Only, *you* pick the references, not take the ones the job seeker gives you. Ideally, the references should be known and checked before the guy even comes in the door for the job. How does that work? Somebody sent him that you can trust and that you know is loyal. When he first walks in, you already know everything about him. That's why he came in, in the first place.

We're fools. You know why? Cause we did it. We let Sammy in. We let Sammy in, Frankie, into something that's called this thing of ours.
Gotti (Armand Assante), referring to Sammy Gravano. *Gotti*

How loyal you want to be to your family and your friends, I will leave up to you. Americans tend to be a very loyal people—loyal to country, loyal to freedom, loyal to their sports teams. When it comes to personal relationships, they are less so, certainly less than Italians. At the very least they are more conflicted. They may be more loyal to their careers (business) than to their families. They may move thousands of miles from their roots to further that career. They may spend long hours at work and barely see their wife and kids. They may be loyal to the almighty buck instead of the Almighty.

When being loyal goes against your own immediate gain; when the Feds offer you immunity; when a rival offers you more money—then your choices will determine if you're loyal or if it was only about business. Where your primary loyalties lie, only you can decide. But decide you must. You don't want to realize that you misplaced your loyalties when it is too late, and I guarantee you, one of these days it will be late for you.

When a man comes to this point in his life, he wants to turn over the things he's been blessed with, turn them over to friends as a reward for the friends he's had and to make sure that everything goes well after he's gone.
Hyman Roth (Lee Strasberg), *Godfather II*

6. Friendship

The neighborhood called him Crazy Louie because he would do just about anything. He'd be the first one to pull a fire alarm, rip off a car antenna, or puncture a tire for no reason. If things were dull, he'd pull some stunt just for the laughs. He might have been crazy but he was our friend. Since he would do anything, well, we tried to do anything we could for him.

We could get Louie to do stupid things, but we could not get him to stop. And one senseless thing he'd always do is root for the Cubs. (That's enough right there to earn the name Crazy). We went down to Wrigley a lot ourselves, but with Louie it was like he was brainwashed or something. I wish we could have told Louie what Sonny told "C" in *A Bronx Tale*, after Mazerowski hit the home run to beat the Yankees in 1960. C had read in the paper that Mickey Mantle was crying and C was feeling sad for him.

Mickey Mantle? Is that what you're upset about? Mickey Mantle don't care about you, so why should you care about him. Nobody cares. If your father can't pay the rent, go ask Mickey Mantle and see what he tells you.

I'm sure The Mick would have told a similar Crazy Louie from the Bronx to take a hike. But by the time *A Bronx Tale* came out, Louie had made his final Wrigley appearance long before. Louie had a good run for a while though. In the late 60's the Cubbies broke into winning territory for only the second time in about twenty years. He was in heaven. He felt like Ernie Banks was his grandfather. He revered Billy Williams, who'd talk to him in left field where we usually sat. And Santo! Well, Ron was a god to Louie.

Louie always had money. His old man was in insurance and had locked up most of the neighborhood families with life and auto policies. And if people had businesses, he'd make sure they had "supplemental policies" against fire and the bad things that seem to happen when you don't have enough "protection." After his mother and father split up, what Louie didn't get off his old man, he stole out of his old lady's purse. When we were kids, he was always paying our way into places or buying us stuff, and that helped make him even more of a friend.

Louie lived life in the fast lane and had some health issues as a result. He was the kind of guy—well, let's put it this way—if we had more like him, the federal government wouldn't have to worry about fixing social security. The chance of him ever collecting was very low.

One day Louie must have had one of those premonition things. It was a Saturday afternoon and we were sitting in Ray's on Sheffield across from Wrigley Field, waiting out a rain delay. Brickhouse was on TV telling Vince Lloyd for the 85th time about how beautiful the vines were in the Friendly Confines, when Louie asked us if we'd do him a favor.

"Of course, Don Louie. We are always at your service. Now who do you want us to kill?" I replied in my usual, affectionate manner.

"No, man, shut up, I'm serious. If I ever kick, man, scatter my ashes over the wall in left field." Louie laughed after he said it, but you could tell how he felt about it.

"What, do I have to buy an extra ticket for your ashes? You want me to take a chance of getting thrown out for littering the field with garbage?"

I was almost sorry the moment I said it, even though he laughed. It was all a joke but somewhere deep down I must have known I had made a promise. I have no doubt there are some yuppie jagoffs who've thought about having their ashes scattered at the Friendly Confines since then, and have probably done it, but I'm convinced Louie was the first. Still, I figured, maybe it'll be a long time before Louie kicks.

You can't imagine what Wrigley was like in '69. This was when the neighborhood was still real, before it got all rehabbed and gentrified or whatever the fuck they call it. Over a million and a half rabid diehards, not tourists and suits, made it to the Confines. This was more people than had attended in about 40 years—since back when Hack Wilson (on booze, not steroids) was poking 191 RBI's in a single year and Capone ran the city. By August of '69 the Cubs were way ahead of the pack in the National League, and it was obvious to everybody that they were going to win the pennant.

The Mets finished eight games up. I'm not saying the collapse was responsible for what happened to Louie a couple of months later. Like I said, he did not have a healthy lifestyle, but who knows? Maybe it had an effect. Wouldn't you know, one night in November I got the phone call. It was from this broad, Marcy, who lived in Lake Point Tower. She was in a panic because she had done a number with Louie just a half-hour before, and now he was lying there and she couldn't wake him up. I told her to clear out anything that might get either of them in trouble and call an ambulance. When they got there Louie was a goner. I had always feared getting that phone call but figured it was bound to come one day.

Louie's family wasn't excited about the cremation thing, especially his father. But his old lady went along with it just to piss off the old man. Although she granted Louie's final wish, she said we could only have half of the ashes. So, after a ceremony at Salerno's Galewood Chapel on Harlem Avenue, out where his father now lived, we got a small container with half of Louie in it. And we waited for Opening Day.

It was April 14. The Cubs' home opener was against the Phillies, and we made plans to give Louie his final send off. Before going to the park, we made a stop at the Billy Goat for some drinks and toasts to our dear departed friend. Well, we wound up getting a little fucked up, and it wasn't even noon yet. It was me, Joey, and Buddy C. Buddy showed up with a Cub jersey, hat, camera and one of those belly packs in which he had the container with Louie's ashes. He looked like a fucking tourist and we gave him all kinds of grief.

We grabbed a cab and headed to the park. When we pulled up, Buddy insisted on paying the driver. As he pulled out his money, the container with Louie's ashes opened up and went all over the floor of the cab and all over us. We were cursing Buddy while at the same time trying to scoop and scrape up as much of Louie as we could get back into the container. The cab driver was pissed and was yelling some Paki-Hindu lingo at us and calling for his money. We did the best we could with what was left of Louie, paid off the driver, got out at Clark and Addison and headed around the other side of the park. Suddenly we looked at each other and started laughing our asses off. We knew that Crazy Louie was somewhere doing the same.

We got into the left field bleachers and moved right to the front row. Actually, there were a couple of guys we had to persuade that the view was better a couple of rows back. When Billy Williams ran out to left field to start the game, we called out to him while he was throwing with somebody in the left field bull pen.

"Billy. This is Louie, your number one fan. He kicked the bucket last year."

I don't know whether Billy heard it all or not, but we sent the ashes over the wall anyway. At the same time a little breeze off Lake Michigan kicked up and some of Louie got blown back in our faces and other innocent bystanders in the first couple of rows. But a lot of Louie made the warning track and was dusting the ivy so we accomplished our goal.

Kenny Holtzman and the Cubs actually eked out a 5-4 win that day in Louie's honor, but what's more important, we did what we said we would do for a friend. As we headed back to the neighborhood we had to laugh again. You know how often they clean those cabs? Some of Louie might still be riding around his beloved city of Chicago. There's nothing we wouldn't do for a friend.

Lessons on Friendship from the Movie Mob

We would have done anything for Louie and for each other. You'd probably do the same, but it's just as important to know the difference between real friends and those who are just current associates.

Your real friends might be fewer than you think. That makes them all the more important; just make sure you can tell them from mere acquaintances. You might hang with guys in your crew for years, but the only reason they're there is that they are being paid for the job they do. Any one of them might have turned up in someone else's crew or might turn against you if it is to their advantage.

In our work, if a guy takes an oath, it means that he won't give you up to the cops; but if he perceives you are weak and need to be replaced, or if he sees another crew moving in that might eliminate you, he might have to move against you to save his own skin. If you depend on his friendship, you're confusing allies and business associates with friends. Weak people, who have no self worth, are always doing this. They are so desperate, they convince themselves the people they have daily contact with are their friends when that's often not the case.

> *You see, all our people are businessmen. One thing I*
> *learned from Pop was to try to think as people around*
> *you think. Now on that basis, anything's possible.*
> Michael, *The Godfather*

Michael never mentions "his people" as friends. You've got to conduct yourself the same way. These guys aren't your buddies—you've got your family to give you good vibes, emotional support and all that bullshit. Some of the other topics in this book—respect, loyalty, trust—these are based on alliances and business too, not on true friendship. On the other hand, if you find a true friend, you might be closer to him than to people in your immediate family.

You might not like hearing this, but you've got to be the hard guy. Let me give you another example—the Cardinals of the Catholic Church. These are some of the most powerful "made guys" on the planet. When the Pope makes them, he expects them to be loyal allies to "his thing," not to be his friends. Yet even they can turn against each other when business dictates. In *Godfather III*, a Cardinal tells Michael,

> *I trusted my friend (but) these friends use the good name of*
> *the church to feed their greed.*

Can you believe it? This hymn-singer whines about being taken for millions in the church treasury by "friends." Cardinals are not chosen for their piety. They're supposed to know the score on business, organization, and what makes people tick. Yet it's up to Michael to be confessor/ advisor to this red robed rube and to explain how money and friendship react together.

Civilians often think that *mafiosi* must not have many friends. They think they have more. I doubt that's the case. The way you can tell your real friends is simple. The person who stands with you when he has nothing to gain is your friend. The co-worker who you will see and whose company you will enjoy long after you no longer work at the same place he does is your friend. Others are just your passing acquaintances, temporary allies. Do you really want them in your home? Are you invited to their home because of some mutual interest or genuine connection? Or is it just business?

Will this person turn against you or ignore you as soon as you no longer serve his purpose? Look at those you work with and ask which of them will still spend time with you if your job looks bleak. Which of them will spend time with you if you don't socialize on their terms? Which ones will you continue to see if you no longer work with them? Listen, I'm not saying there is anything wrong with your business allies. To the contrary, without them you cannot be successful. Just don't confuse them with friends.

Those of you who have three, two, or even one solid and true friend can count yourselves lucky. Treat them well. If you have more than three it must mean you make a great friend. Those of you who confuse phony attention, gifts, and happy talk from people who will be gone the moment you are of no use to them, do not know yourselves. You lead lives emptier than that of the mafioso. He is realistic enough to recognize false friendship all around him and he does not succumb to it.

Trying to buy friends is useless. You're just buying a temporary ally. If a better offer comes along, wiseguys will forget you in a Palermo minute. The same truth holds for women. They can try to buy friendship with all kinds of currency. Women who try to buy friendship with their bodies, giving up what they value, wind up in the same situation.

When we supply the public with liquor (like during Prohibition), gambling, broads, loans, or protection, we're just filling a sales niche.

We're not stupid enough to think we're buying friends. We know we're buying customers.

> *Friendship and money boil in water*
> Michael Corleone, *Godfather III*

Want to know whether he or she is your friend or not? Cut to the chase and make a reasonable request of the person. Reasonableness is paramount, because one must be careful about the favors he grants.

> *Favor gonna kill you faster than a bullet.*
> Carlo Brigante (Al Pacino) *Carlito's Way*

But among honorable men, if one refuses (excuses are not acceptable), he is not your friend. If he agrees, you must be prepared to reward him at a future time so as not to be in his debt. Whatever it costs you is worth it, because you have gained something much more valuable.

> *Do me this favor. I won't forget it. Ask your friends about*
> *me. They'll tell you I know how to return a favor.*
> Young Vito Corleone, *Godfather II*

> *When did I ever refuse an accommodation?*
> Don Vito Corleone, *The Godfather*

Maybe the most important lesson you can learn here is to keep friendship and money separated as much as possible. Not only will you get into less trouble, but sometimes you can gain unexpected benefits. A scene from *A Bronx Tale* is one we all have the opportunity to learn from:

> C (Lillo Brancato Jr) (he is now a grown, young man):
> *This guy Louie Dumps over here, you know, he owes me*
> *20 dollars. It's been two weeks now and every time he*
> *sees me, he keeps dodging me. He's becoming a real pain*
> *in the ass. I mean, should I crack him one or what?*
> Sonny: *What's the matter with you? What have I been*
> *telling you? Sometimes, hurtin' somebody ain't the answer.*

First of all, is he a friend of yours?
C: *No, I don't even like him.*
Sonny: *You don't even like him! There's your answer, right there. Look at it this way, it costs you 20 dollars to get rid of him, right? He's never gonna bother you again. He's never gonna ask you for money again. He's out of your life for 20 dollars. You got off cheap. Forget it.*

Know who your real friends are. Then lend your brother-in-law or any other phonies ten or twenty bucks and hope they don't pay you back. They'll avoid you and hopefully you'll be rid of them forever.

If you don't get it early, it kills you.
Sonny, *A Bronx Tale*

7. Ambition

DB and I had seen what happened to guys whose stupidity overwhelmed their ambition. The only bars we wanted to deal with were the ones on Rush Street, not the ones you look through. But we also had ambitions. The big guys on Chicago Avenue, Taylor Street, 26th, or the near west burbs had the cars, the clothes, the women, and the reputations. We wanted to roll that way and—to be honest—we knew we weren't cut out to do real work to get those things. Delivering jukes and 45's for The Music Man wasn't going to take us where we wanted to go either.

Our friend Tommy "Ears" had an uncle who was one of those guys we aspired to be. When his uncle Vito came around you couldn't tell if he was straight out of the movies or if the movies were imitating him. Italian suits, gold chains, a diamond pinky—the whole nine yards, or nine miles to us. Vito wasn't exactly handsome though. He was putting on some weight and had a pocky face that never smiled or frowned. You could read your own emotions into that kisser. If you were scared, you might think he was mad. If you were happy, you'd imagine him smiling with you. We tried to see the smiling Vito, and even though we didn't have any kind of plan then, we were always trying to impress him when we got the chance.

One day Don Vito (as we called him behind his back) was in the Music Man talking to Freddie the Pol when we came in after our routes. We were done but we always had to report in, just in case there were more orders that came in or other jobs the Pol wanted us for. There usually wasn't anything. Couldn't we just call in? Drop off the old 45's the next morning? No, the Pol wanted to see our mugs every day.

"This car has everything," we overheard Vito saying as we walked in. "And I'm sure the fuckin' *mulignan* who was drivin' it didn't get the down payment from his savings account at the S&L."

"Yeah, unless he withdrew it with a z-zip gun," muttered the Pol.

"And Biancuzzo at the Caddy dealer can't get me one for months, even if I decided I did want to buy one."

After Vito left we asked the secretaries who were working in the office what kind of Cadillac he was talking about. They heard it was a '72 Eldo, Biarritz. Cadillac had just come out with the new models and if you remember back in the day, if you were anybody at all you had a Cadillac, or maybe a Lincoln. That was before all the Jap and German cars became the in things. I guess we kind of tucked the knowledge of what Vito wanted in the back of our minds, because neither of us said much more about it. Later I realized we both must have been on the lookout for the car.

More than a month later, though, Vito's Biarritz was about as far from my mind as the French resort town after which it was named. Then late one afternoon we made a jukebox delivery near Greek Town and headed south on Halsted to drop something off for Alderman Keane at Schaller's Pump, a tavern at 37th. This is where the City Council met. Okay, officially they met downtown at City Hall, but everyone knew that all the important decisions were made at Schaller's, a couple of blocks from "Da Mare's" house.

We were almost into Bridgeport when we saw it—a brand new white Eldorado Biarritz. We wondered for a moment who the hell it might belong to. Halsted and 26th was not the greatest location to park such a car, but there it was. We decided to keep an eye on it and came back later that night. Sure enough, it was parked in the same spot.

You might think that jacking a car would be part of the curriculum for graduating from street school on the West Side—maybe even part of pre-school—but somehow we must have been absent that week. We had been joy riding and had sold parts for other guys, but we hadn't been around when someone had gone to the street showroom to pick out a new model. The time Jimmy D ripped off his car, it was easy because the fucking goof who was driving it left it running while he went into a store. We knew we couldn't hope to get that lucky with an Eldo.

Now that we had a real reason to take this risk—that is, to deliver this vehicle to Vito—all I knew was how to drive it and fill it with gas, and not much else. DB was in much the same boat....er, car. We knew we needed help.

As usual, we cased the guys on the street, but we didn't want to bring anybody else in on the job to take away our credit. We just wanted to be pointed in the right direction. Neighborhood clepto, Johnny "Dump Truck" Doyle, had been hot-wiring and lifting Corvettes from Chicago to Carbondale, where he was supposed to be going to school (he told his parents he was majoring in auto shop), but Truck involuntarily transferred to another institution in Vandalia when he flunked not getting caught.

Then there was Mike "the Rug," whose front was a carpet-cleaning business. He was one of the best thieves in the neighborhood, though even a better fence. Mike was a Sears and Roebuck catalogue. You didn't go shopping at the mall in those days. You went to see Mike. If he didn't have it, he'd get it. We helped "the Rug" fill his pockets when we needed new leather jackets, or Italian knits, or presents for the girls. He also had what you might call a car dealership too, only his showroom was the entire world. We knew Mike would give us some shit—"You two assholes don't know how to jack a car? Where you from? Stickney? Lake Pussy Forest?"—and similar stuff, but we figured he'd eventually show us what he knew about our auto venture.

A couple of days after we approached him, "The Rug" told us that the easiest way (for us, at least) on this model, was to break into the steering column to start it. We knew we were going to need some coaching, so we had him come up with a plan for us. Mike decided to take us to an auto shop where he knew a guy who had cars going to the junk yard that we could practice on. He got us a tool and showed us how to punch in the door lock and then how to crack the steering column and get the car started. "But first," he said, "you've got to make sure there's no alarm on the car. That doesn't mean you can't take it—you just have to work quicker. Most people ignore the fucking alarm anyway, but if the owner hears it, you got problems."

DB felt confident we could do this, so we cased the car for a couple of nights to see if any pain-in-the ass innocent bystanders were hanging around. Usually the car was there, but not always. Mike came along on the first night and said it looked like the dumb prick didn't invest in a car alarm. We knew from what happened to Jimmy D that if we got caught, there could be some jail time. If your name was Wesolowski, O'Brien, or Rufus Johnson, you'd probably be able to cop a plea on a first offense. But if you're name is Madura or DiBruno, some of these judges are gunning for you—unless they're getting paid, of course.

This thing had to go down late when no one was around. We finally decided to make our move and headed up there at 2 a.m. on a moonless night. The neighborhood was quiet as we drove up, and, sure enough, the car was there. We parked around the corner. DB was going to be the lookout, while I went to work and drove the car off. We'd meet back in the neighborhood.

I approached the car and threw some change on the ground near it. If somebody spotted me and wondered what the fuck I was doing, it would look like I dropped my money. I pulled out the tool that Mike gave me, and with one quick shot, I popped the door lock on the passenger's side. Very little noise. DB signaled that the coast was clear as I jumped in. I smashed the steering column with a couple of whacks of the hammer, and finally the plastic covering broke off. I pulled out the screwdriver that "the Rug" had given me, stuck it into the opening in front of the piece he said would be sticking up, and pulled it toward me. I was in a sweat by then, but—unfuckingbelievable—the sonofavabitch started right up. DB took off for his car and I switched to the driver's seat of the Caddy and we were gone. Twenty minutes later we were back in the neighborhood, driving cautiously so as not to draw any attention.

The next day we called Tommy Ears and asked him if he knew where his uncle was going to be. He told us if Vito isn't doing anything special he usually hangs out at The Leather Bottle in Elmwood Park.

We wanted to surprise "Don Vito." We had the car stashed in a friend's garage, because we didn't want to be driving it around while the cops might be looking for it. A few items on the car would have to be altered and the vin number etched out and changed first. That would be easy. But surprising Vito would be tricky. Even though our reputation was squeaky clean as far as the Outfit was concerned, a ride to some undisclosed location for a surprise was not the kind of invitation Vito was likely to accept. So we brought the car down to The Leather Bottle and parked it in back between a fence and some dumpsters.

We sauntered into the bar area and after a little light conversation, we told Vito we had something serious to discuss with him. I elected DB to start it off. He sounded a little nervous, a little stilted, like he was doing an impression of Lucca Brasi rehearsing his wedding speech to "the real" Don Vito, Corleone. At least, that's how I remember it. Only problem is this was 1971 and *The Godfather* didn't come out till the following year.

"Uncle Vito, we have always had the greatest respect for you. We're not sure what the future has in store for us, but we know we would be glad to work with you or for you. Whether or not that happy day comes, we thank you for your past advice and support and we have a little present for you."

Vito seemed happy, although a smile on Vito's mug was about as rare as chitlins in an Italian deli. We took him out back, going first so he could be behind us all the way, and took him over to the car. DB handed him the screwdriver and said, "Here's your key!"

At first Vito looked stunned. Shock and awe is how I'd put it today. He walked around the car two or three times, admiring it. Finally he stared in the window. He looked back at us and didn't look as happy, although it was hard to tell. He grabbed open the passenger door, opened the glove compartment, looked at some papers in there (something I hadn't thought to do), and went nuts.

"What the fuck do you two-bit jagoffs think you're doin'? You're gonna get me pinched—and for what? Did I fuckin' ask you to do that?"

We didn't know what to think. Maybe he was pissed because of some of the damage we did while lifting the car—that was the only thing I could think of.

"But Vito," DB tried to say, "the lock and the steering column can be fixed as good as new."

"Get the fuck out of here," was the mildest of Vito's answers, answers that indicated we'd be better off somewhere else. But he kept the screwdriver. Later that night, we went back and the Eldo was gone. Tommy called us the next morning and gave us the scoop.

"The Eldo belongs to an alderman, who's been parking in that spot whenever he visits a certain senorita who lives in the neighborhood. I'm supposed to tell you what's gonna happen to the car," Tommy continued, "and then Vito wants to tell you personally what's going to happen to you. I know you're gonna have to pay for the damage. I just hope it's only gonna cost you money."

"Shit," was all I could think of, but neither of us said anything. Sure enough, a couple nights later, the Eldo was back in its spot, with the door and steering column fixed, just like Tommy said it would be. And we went to our meeting with Vito.

Although we didn't think we had done anything that bad, we drove out to Elmwood Park feeling like so many of the characters we've seen in movies since then. Although you know no one is in the back seat (we checked!), you can't help imagining that wire suddenly being slipped over your head and cutting into your neck—that kind of feeling.

"You guys are major fuck-ups, you know?" is the first thing we heard when we sat down at Vito's table in a corner in the back of the bar. But then he continued. "I might give you a break, though. Maybe you can do me a little favor."

"You name it, Don, uh, Vito," DB blurted.

Within a month, Vito was driving a brand new Eldorado Biarritz convertible – black, not white. Turned out that the one we found this time did have a new anti-theft device on it, called "The Club." As anyone in law enforcement will tell you, locks, alarms, clubs, whatever, will only discourage theft, not prevent it. They're meant to make the thief's job more difficult or make him move on to the next mark. If he's determined, though, you can't stop him. We were determined. I brought our consultant in on the deal, like any good businessman would, and when the car's previous owner came out one morning he found The Club in his favorite parking spot instead of the Eldo. Vito had wanted a black one anyway.

If you're ambitious, sometimes you've just got to act. You might make a mistake, but if you wait till you know everything is perfect, you won't do dick. We never got any money from this venture, but from that day onward Vito looked at us differently.

The importance of the jobs we were given grew and it wasn't long before we were out of the jukebox delivery business. When the time came for us to make good a few years later, Vito was the guy that helped us get the go ahead. Without the ambition we showed, who knows if we would've been able to open and operate our business. As it turned out, this was another "Don" Vito who "knew how to return a favor."

Lessons on Ambition from the Movie Mob

Ambition is like a picture I saw of a gun with the barrel twisted backward pointing toward you as you shoot. Ambition is good, but make sure it doesn't backfire on you.

From the very beginning of the Chicago Outfit, raw ambition has paid off for those who had it and destroyed those who let it get out of hand. Capone and Johnny Torrio moved Big Jim Colossimo out of the picture but then Al pushed Johnny aside, and eventually Al went down.

In New York Gotti had his godfather, Paul Castellano, hit and the Dapper Don achieved his ambitions, for a while at least. In 1940's Vegas Bugsy Siegel was wildly ambitious overspending his budget, knowing it would eventually pay off. Boy, was he right! Unfortunately, his timing was off and he didn't get to enjoy the payday.

The same thing happens on film. When Sollozzo has his hitmen pump bullets into the godfather, Don Corleone, they fail to kill the Don. Sollozzo winds up never finishing "the best veal in the city" at Louie's in the Bronx. The capos who back him, Tattaglia and Barzini, join him in his long dirt nap. If you're going to do something, follow through to the end and make it a success. Our business isn't horseshoes and neither is yours.

Not only should you be ambitious yourself, but you'll also need to be wary of the ambitions of your underlings. Every number two man gets thoughts of replacing Mr. Big. One of them may make a play to get rid of you. You've got to be sure that their ambitions are channeled in the right direction. There are many signs. Do they give you full credit for what you are doing or do they try to take some of the kudos? A loyal staff member will sometimes even see you get the praise for what he has done, rather than stealing some of your thunder.

Do your staff members always report to you? Do they come to you for guidance and for their marching orders? If the answers to these questions are yes, then the odds are you have a loyal crew. Help them reach their own ambitions. Let them wet their own beaks.

What if the answers to these questions are negative? What if Joe Staffmember is always pushing his own agenda or is always trying to bask in your sunshine? What if he starts going over your head when he wants something or doesn't like something? What if he takes your boss's suggestions and guidance directly, rather than getting them from you. Odds are he is going to be a problem. though he may not even be conscious of what he's doing. Either way he's only looking out for himself. Your crew should always follow you up the ladder, not jump over you or step on you on their way up. If such a person does not respond to getting a taste, or is still too ambitious, he will be a threat to you. You must finish him off.

How you get rid of this too eager beaver depends on your situation. It doesn't mean you have to do him physical harm—mental harm will do just fine. Fire him, demote him, transfer him, keep him out of the loop, give him the worst jobs, send him away from the office when possible, weaken him. In our line of work, these solutions are dangerous. They breed resentment. The troublemaker may move on us, either for ambition or revenge. Or worse, they might violate the code of omerta and talk to law enforcement. Hopefully the danger of such reprisals is less in your business, though you can never tell. In any case, do it soon.

> *Trouble is like a cancer. You gotta get it early. If you don't get it early, it kills you. That's why you gotta cut it out.*
> Sonny, *A Bronx Tale*

What if it's *your* capo, though—your boss—that you want to be rid of? If he is keeping you from advancing, sabotaging your efforts, or even if he is being just plain incompetent, he's got to go. It's just business. You may be violating the codes of trust, loyalty, and probably omerta. But...at that point, he's not part of "your thing," you don't owe him those virtues...it's nothing personal, it's just business.

But only you can tell when to make that move. Regardless of how much he needs to be gone, you cannot miss in your attempt to take him out. You've got to make yourself indispensable to the company, ingratiate yourself with his bosses, and insulate yourself from attack. And when you strike at his heart, your case must be the equivalent of an offer that the higher-ups can't refuse. They have no recourse but to get rid of him. Until then, keep him close to you and do not let him know your thoughts.

If you don't follow these lessons, you are better off planting your lips on your boss's posterior. Because if you attack and fail, it is you who will be pushing up the daisies or playing trunk music like our friend Tony, who worked for the Pol.

Another way of greatly increasing the chances of success for your ambitions is by being available.

> *Machiavelli – he's a famous writer from 500 years ago.*
> *Availability, that's what he always said.*
> Sonny, *A Bronx Tale*

What's in it for me? Why should I show up at that meeting, that party, that hang-out spot? What am I going to get out of it? What guarantee do I have that this is going to be worth my while? You should avoid those questions and the losers who ask them. Usually they're not going to ask them exactly this way. Instead, they're going to give some lame-ass excuse for not going somewhere or doing some job. Hell, you can always find a reason for not doing something you don't want to do. The truth is they don't want to take the extra time—they aren't making themselves available.

> *Ask around on the street, the neighborhood, about me.*
> *They'll tell you I'm a man who knows how to return a*
> *favor.*
> Young Vito Corleone (Robert DeNiro), *Godfather II*

When Vito Corleone arrived in New York, he instinctively realized he had to be on the streets and be known. There are two main reasons to make yourself available: 1) to know what's going on so you can nip anything in the bud; and 2) to be able to take advantage of opportunities. In *A Bronx Tale*, Sonny was always hanging around the neighborhood. He was keeping close to any potential rival or enemy, in his own camp or in another, so he could spot any problem that might occur. Better still, he was stopping anyone from even thinking about moving against him. They could see that Sonny was in control, that he was visible. Availability is the key, and Sonny was always available.

Look at what happened in real life in New York. After Paul Castellano took over as head of the Gambino family, he isolated himself at what associates called "the white house." His underboss delivered messages to him but he stayed locked up with his servant-mistress and was rarely seen. In short, he was not available. He soon had no feel for the war that was brewing in his family and he lost respect. Gotti saw this opening and by the night of December 16, 1985, "Big Pauly" was shopping for a harp.

Availability's second charm is opportunity. When it knocks or rings the doorbell, a lot of mokes won't open the door because they didn't even hear the chime. No, I take that back—odds are there's nobody home. They're out with some broad or getting hammered watching the ball game (not that there's anything wrong with either of those, but you've got to make sure you've covered your responsibilities first). Guys like that never make it big because they want a guaranteed short term reward, and the big dough is in long term risk with no guarantees. This is true whether it's Sonny in the Bronx being available to his boys to make sure there are no plots or slackers, or whether it's you making yourself available for an interview, a job, an audition, a contact, or whateverthefuck. When the right opportunity comes along, the losers will say, "jeez, that guy has all the luck. He was just lucky to be at the right place at the right time." You'll know luck had nothing to do with it. You were always there waiting. You made yourself available.

Another way to achieve your ambitions is to know how to handle requests. Treat any request by your boss as a command. You don't turn him down. When the Pol's right hand man, Tony, made a request we knew it was coming from the Pol. We followed through immediately because we knew it was in our long term interest to comply. But—listen carefully—you have to handle requests from almost anyone else the same way. You put them in your debt and you get ahead. Fulfilling a request is like putting money in the bank. Except you'll get interest tenfold. If a deposit goes astray once in a while, who cares. The reverse is also true—denying a request is an insult. If a time comes when you are not willing or able to fulfill a request, it's not the end of the world. Just be aware that you are making an enemy and be cautious.

> *He never asks for a second favor when he's been refused*
> *a first, understood?*
> Tom Hagen (Robert Duvall), *The Godfather*

In *The Godfather,* movie-mogul Woltz refuses Don Vito Corleone's request that Johnny Fontaine be given the leading part in a movie, telling Tom Hagen that he can grant some other favor, but not that one. He insults the Don with his refusal. Not only that, but as we will see in the chapter on respect, Woltz refuses with the utmost disrespect as well. Tom doesn't ask again. He doesn't coax, cajole, or threaten. He simply gets his coat and hat and leaves to give Don Vito the bad news, setting the stage for the "horse's head scene."

You must understand something fundamental about requests and favors. The person who requests a favor is vulnerable. He is taking the risk of being turned down. He is transferring some of his power to you, putting you in control. If you deny him, he will be unhappy, whether he knows it or not, or shows it or not. You must comply with his request if at all possible, because then you have more power. He owes you—he is in your debt. You will have credits to call upon when needed, just as surely as Don Corleone knows that in the future he may call upon those he has helped to return the favor

> *One day, and that day may never come, I will call upon you to do a service for me.*
> *Until that day, accept this justice as a gift on my daughter's wedding day.*
> Don Vito Corleone, *The Godfather*

All good business people know how to achieve their ambitions by granting favors. It's the losers who say, "That's not my job." A good waiter wants diners to ask him for many favors. Each service he or she provides puts the diners further in debt to the waiter, a debt that should be settled at the end of the meal.

On the other hand, if you are the one who asks for a favor and it is a reasonable request, the person you ask must comply or he gravely offends you. You must not ask again. Your first request puts you in his debt or shows a willingness to exchange favors. After a refusal, a second request is begging. A third request would reduce you to nothing—you would cease to exist. The person refusing a request has lost your trust and should be eliminated from your circle. Extenuating circumstances may enter into the situation—the refuser may realize his error on his own (or through some third party) and come to kiss your pinkie, in which case he may be given a second chance. Or he may be supported by someone more powerful, and you can do nothing at the moment. But you will not forget.

Even if you got a family, this is your family.
Lefty (Pacino), *Donnie Brasco*

*A man that doesn't spend time with his family can
never be a real man.*
Don Vito Corleone, *The Godfather*

8. Family

*A*bbondanza—that's the only word to describe Christmas Eve in an
Italian kitchen. On that day Anna, DB's wife Marie, and the other
women in the family would put on a spread that would make the holiday
even more precious to the family, if that was possible. The *nonnas* (our
kids' grandmothers) gave the orders in the kitchen, starting early in the
morning preparing the *mille foglie* (a thousand layers), the hand-made
lasagna with a veal/beef bolognese sauce. The sausage and meatballs
cooked and simmered all day.

Special homage was paid to the Old World tradition of having seven
seafoods as well, and I was looking forward to the calamari, baccala,
jumbo shrimp, clams, octopus, crab legs and cuttlefish that might be the
choices for the night. No Christmas Eve dinner was complete without

pane di festa (feast bread) either, which we would be dipping in olive oil and parmesan cheese that evening, though the aroma during the day made it hard not to dip some bread into the gravy a little early. Sides such as spinach and baked artichokes might make the table groan further, and after dinner deserts such as puffed pastries, cannoli, tiramisu, and Italian cookies would be served along with espresso.

Family would start to show up around four o'clock to sip wine, drink cocktails and munch on appetizers, which the visiting wives would bring. Aunts, uncles, and cousins packed the small house and kids ran all over the place, but nobody complained about the lack of space. Nonna would serve the food around seven o'clock and, after a toast to express our love and appreciation for each other, the feast would begin. Believe me, nobody was bashful and guys would be eating like they were going be executed the next day (not always totally out of the question in some cases).

After dinner, as the women cleared off the dining room table, Uncle Frankie would slip out for a cigar and return as Santa Claus, and the kids got to open their gifts. The older ones knew the deal. They could smell the alcohol and cigar on Frankie's breath, but they kept up the charade for the younger kids. Once the gifts were opened, the new toys were put into action while the men got the cards out for hands of briscola.

The older women hung out in the kitchen and the younger ladies sat around, probably bitching about their husbands. At about 11:30 the wives would try to get everybody ready to head to Our Lady of Angels for Midnight Mass. This was a tradition, but also a struggle. Half the kids would be sleeping on the floor; the guys would be liquored up or losing at cards, so not everybody got out the door to the church.

Though nothing could match this time of year, we found out that our personal family and our business family could clash even on the Holidays. Our personal family was most important to us, but if we didn't earn, we wouldn't be able to provide for them. The two finally collided one Christmas Eve. It was the Madura household's turn to host the dinner and, of course, Anna had done one hell of a lot of work to prepare the yearly extravaganza. The food was just coming out, but before we could sit down to dinner the phone rang.

"Aaah," Anna kind of whimpered, and with a semi-dirty look toward me said, "It's Mr. Polito for you." I got up and took the phone into the hallway.

"Listen, Bobby." Freddie "The Pol" Polito sounded more nervous than usual. There were no preliminaries, no "Happy Holidays," just, "You and DB gotta go up to Broadway Barry's, you know it, on the North Side, and have the owner sign on for a box now." (Freddie still hadn't replaced the recently departed Tony Frangione after his untimely demise. Tony usually would have done this kind of work).

Now, for any of you that still don't know the rules by now, a request such as this is not questioned. Even guys like us, who didn't have to do much enforcing and weren't primed to be made guys or anything, when we heard the bell, we didn't ask questions, we got in the ring and started punching. But I was thinking, "Geez, the whole family is here and it's Christmas Eve, I can't believe this." Besides, it had just started to snow. So this one time....just this one time.....I hesitated.

"Freddie, listen, can't we go over there the first thing on the 26th? The whole family is here, and the food is almost ready."

There was silence on the other end of the phone. Maybe it was only five seconds; it felt like five minutes. Then I added, "Besides, it's snowing like a motherfu....."

"You're going to go over there and give this cocksucker a Christmas he'll never forget," The Pol's seething voice interrupted. I could tell he was trying to hold his temper. "You're going to meet me at Ferndell's in five minutes to get the details and I don't want no fucking weather report." And the phone went dead.

Christmas, the baccala, and Santa were put on hold and we went to work. Naturally we didn't discuss any of this around the tree. I just gave DB a nod and he knew to get up without my saying a word. He had been watching my expression on the phone. We excused ourselves with a simple "We'll be back soon."

We met the Pol at the local coffee shop he had suggested off North and Pulaski and saw a side of him we hadn't seen before. It seems he had sent his nephew Angelo in to see the owner of Broadway Barry's. Freddie was just trying to give Angelo some needed work that he thought would be easy, Barry had not only told Angelo to fuck off but when Angelo mentioned his uncle's name, the guy said Freddie could fuck off too.

Even with this provocation, the lesson the Pol wanted to send could have been postponed to the 26th, but he was in no mood to wait. He was so hot we thought he was going to tell us to clip this bar owner. Thank

God he backed off and just insisted that we "do whatever you have to do" to make sure he "gets on board." Neither one of us had ever put a guy away and didn't plan to (and can you imagine breaking your cherry on Christmas Eve?). We stopped off at the Music Man to pick up some ski masks and two .38 caliber snub-nosed Smith and Wessons the Pol had locked up in the safe as he instructed. I just wanted to go up there and give this guy a beating, but DB had another idea.

"Since we're giving up our Christmas, let's make it worth our while and rob the joint. Maybe we can come up with some jewelry, watches, rings, and stuff from the clientele."

"Joey, it's Christmas Eve, for chrissakes," smiling after realizing what I'd said. "It's the season for giving, not taking."

"Hey, what kinds of guys are hanging out at Barry's on Christmas Eve? They can't have much respect for their family, so they can pay for messing up ours."

In for a dime, in for a dollar—a robbery it would be. We made the drive and parked around the corner off Broadway, lit up a couple of Luckys, and walked down the street. It was a cold night with snow whirling around, and there wasn't much activity. We figured we could get in and out without a lot of trouble. It felt just like a movie. Broadway Barry's had a couple of pool tables and some foosball machines and on an ordinary night it was usually packed. Apparently Barry had told the Pol's first messenger that his clientele wasn't "up for no tunes." Well, his patrons were going to be in for a melodious 1973, whether they knew it or not. A look in the window tonight showed about six or seven people sitting at the bar and Barry, serving drinks.

We gave one last look around, slipped on our masks and burst through the door.

"This is a stick-up," yelled DB and the feeling of unreality got stronger. How much do the movies imitate real life and how much do people like us say and do what we say and do because we watch the movies?

I ran behind the bar, gave Barry a crack in the head, and put the gun to him.

"Everybody relax, and you won't get hurt. We just need some Christmas money and presents," DB told the customers. He went one by one down the bar and had the few lonely drunks dig into their pockets and give up their wallets, watches, rings, and jewelry they had, which wasn't much. In the meantime I made Barry clean out the register. He stuck everything in a bag we brought along and the place was dead quiet for a moment. Barry wasn't coming across as the cocky jagoff he apparently was earlier and seemed ready to do whatever we asked, so I didn't give him the beating he deserved, just a couple of kicks in the ribs. Then in a low voice I schooled him on what needed to happen.

"You should really liven this joint up with a jukebox, Barry. We've got friends in the music business who can take care of that for you. They'll install it and service it every week. Not only that, but they'll include insurance to make sure that the bar is protected against fire, burglary, assaults, and other mishaps, like this robbery here, for instance. You can't be too careful."

"Yeah, anyway, if this place ain't more lively, I'm gonna have to come back," added DB.

Barry looked kind of out of it for a moment but then his light bulb finally turned on, "Yeah, music might be a good idea."

So we gave everybody a hearty "Merry Christmas."

Barry called to order a jukebox on December 26.

That's the thing about our business. You've got loyalty to two families, but one has to take precedence. When a soldier enlists, he goes when his Outfit is called, whether it's Broadway Barry's or Baghdad. His other family's got to wait for him.

Anna and Marie heated up the food for us when we got back. DB got lucky at cards, whereas Uncle Frank caught his ass at poker and left all pissed off. I took a pass on Midnight Mass, but was hoping that our work that night would pay dividends for us up the road, and that the prayers Anna and Marie were saying for us would pay dividends even farther up the road.

Lessons on Family from the Movie Mob

Who is your real family? Family usually means your wife and kids, your parents, brothers, sisters, cousins, and so on down the line. But in Mafia movies and in real life, close business associates are family too. A basic rule is to keep those two groups separate. But then to which family do we owe our first allegiance? Who is our real family when the stuff hits the fan? One opinion is that your mob family comes first.

You swore an oath of blood......that you would always put
the family above everything else in your life.
Don Corrado Prizzi (William Hickey), *Prizzi's Honor*

You might think that's harsh. After all, few concepts or images
pierce the human heart more than one's natural family. This is true in
all nationalities, but (although I'm sure other nationalities will disagree)
I have to say family is more important for us Italians than for anyone
else. For centuries our ancestors considered it not only honorable, but
an obligation, to pursue a vendetta for even the slightest perceived insult
against one's family. Today, we might not go out and kill someone who
gets our sister pregnant, (but then again we just might), but we still
believe in keeping the honor of the family intact.

The "super-bond" that Italian families have gives movie writers an
ideal way to humanize and idealize even the most violent Mafia figures.
It allows moviegoers to identify with characters even if those same
family men kill or maim.

But if you think that using the family is just an excuse for Hollywood
to romanticize Mafia figures, just look at the fractured nature of the
average family in the U.S. today. The husband is working late, the wife
is working too and then maybe she goes to the health club. The son is
holed up in his room playing video games, and the teenage daughter
is out—God knows where—they're lucky if they ever are at home at
the same time for a frozen dinner together in front of the tube. And
this is in the rare instances where there actually are two parents in the
household.

That doesn't happen in the Italian family—or so the movies portray.
We always come home and *mangia* with the family, unless our thing
takes us elsewhere. Frankie Saggio's 2004 book, *Born to the Mob*,
describes one New York mob family. He explains how his relatives
knew his uncle Phil "Lucky Philly" Giaccone's (one of Bonanno's right
hand men) had met foul play. It was because it was six o'clock and he
wasn't home for dinner.

Uncle Philly always came home for dinner by 6 P.M.
every night he was alive.

That says it all for me. Family ties are a big reason films about our people are so popular, not just to young men, but to the public at large. Look at the old style Mafia family, even the ones in America. When Mama Corleone sets the table, everyone wants to be sitting at it, teasing little brother Michael while passing the bracciole and, of course, "never talking business" at Sunday dinner. Imagine a still photograph of the Corleones around the dinner table in *The Godfather*, and you'll see a stylized portrait that touches the strongest chords in the soul. Nothing romanticizes or idealizes the Mafia better than these family scenes. The American public is so guilty about not living up to this ideal that they eat this shit up.

Oh, sure, modern lifestyles are changing the Italian family thing too. The Soprano clan is a good example. Family is very, very important to Carmela and Tony. But look at the way they eat. Tony is grabbing some gabagool out of the refrigerator and Meadow wants to take off and get out of the house as soon as possible. At gatherings, people are milling about with little plates as if they are at a cocktail party or a backyard barbecue. Guests fall asleep during the meal and the kids smoke pot in the basement. A.J. mouths off to his mama or even to the old man, who'd beat or kill anyone in his crew who talked that way to him. At the end of season three you saw a little of the old traditions. Junior was singing old Italian songs in a darkened restaurant. But still, Meadow was drunk on cosmos and throwing some crap at him. She eventually ran out into the street symbolizing that she wants to get away from the family. And A.J. doesn't get it:

> *Why do we call all these people uncle when we're not*
> *even related.*
> A.J. (Robert Iler), *The Sopranos*

It's this breakup of the family that contributes to the breakup going on in Tony's mind.

In films, love of family is real to the characters and is also a way for the filmmaker to romanticize them. Most of the passion expressed for the family by the lead characters is sincere and well intentioned. But let's see what happens when their natural family and their Mafia family clash? You remember that Mama Corleone instructs her son, *you can never lose your family,*

but Michael's answer,

Times are changing,

...suggests it might be otherwise. Today, for all the talk of family, when push comes to shove (or when punch comes to shoot), business often comes first in America, even for us Italians. Why are there so many television commercials that show the old man struggling with his business schedule just to make it to his kid's soccer game or ballet recital? Because this is an ideal a lot of American men are not reaching. There's a limit to love of family in Mafia movies as well:

1) When Michael's brother Fredo betrays "our thing" (out of weakness of character rather than greed), he's not long for this earth. Michael keeps him around for a while only because he doesn't want to devastate Mama Corleone.

2) At the end of *The Godfather*, one of the most famous montages in film history cuts scene after scene of contract murder into the tender family portrait of the baptism in which Michael is Godfather to his sister's first child.

3) Tony Soprano suffers more angst about his family than major characters in feature films, but when Christopher becomes a made man, we hear the code he must follow.

> *This family comes before everything else—everything!*
> *Before your wife and your children and your mother and*
> *your father.*
> Tony Soprano, *The Sopranos*

Tony is telling Christopher that his business family comes before his other family. That tells it like it is. A man's "gotta do what he's gotta do" to be a man. If he didn't take care of business, he wouldn't be able to take care of his family or hold his head up. This extends to Christopher's fiance too in the end.

Consider the ironic example of FBI agent Joe Pistone, aka Donnie Brasco. He's told by his mob mentor,

Even if you got a family, this is your family.
Lefty (Pacino), *Donnie Brasco*

Whether Pistone realizes it or not, Lefty is a prophet. Pistone gives up his family for ten years while infiltrating the mob for the bureau. He follows the Mafia code to the extreme, neglecting his real family more than the mob figures he is pursuing neglect theirs.

He isn't much of a man according to Don Vito Corleone's dictum about spending time with your (natural) family.

Even after coming out of the FBI closet, agent Pistone says in his book *Donnie Brasco* that he had to testify for at least six more years and that

> *...there was more fear in my family when I came out, than when I was under.*

Business came first for Pistone. Would he do it again? He adds in his book,

> *I don't know whether that loss (10 years) was worth it.*

It is easy and simplistic for the movies (and for you and me for that matter) to extol the virtues of family. But when the love of family is in conflict with who we are and what we do with our lives, which do we choose? How much do we sacrifice family for "our thing," our business, whatever that is. Do we follow Lefty's decree: "This (business) is your family"? Do we go off to war and leave our wife and kids if we're sent? Do we go to Cleveland for the meeting or Boise to see the buyer if we're sent?

We have to.

Mob leaders may owe loyalty to their mob family, but one of the most important goals of the men I respect is that their biological, emotional family have the chance to be legit—to have their sons and daughters go to college and become lawyers, doctors, businessmen, politicians, whatever. That's what members of "our thing"—both in the movies and in real life—want as our legacy.

Sure, there are a few lowlifes who don't want to see their kids become better than they are. But for the most part, from Vito Corleone to Tony Soprano, they'd rather have their children getting bumped up the ladder in the business world than taking the chance of getting bumped off in the mob world.

Sometimes, they're not successful:

> Kay: *It made me think of what you once told me. "In five years, the Corleone family will be completely legitimate." That was seven years ago.*
> Michael: *I know, I'm trying, darling.*
> The Godfather

Sometimes they don't care. John Gotti Jr. was facing indictment at the same time his dapper dad died in prison, and the old man was proud when Junior got his button. And both Gravano and his son were in prison while we were writing this book.

> *Natural law—sons are put on this earth to trouble their fathers.*
> John Rooney, *Road to Perdition*

But more often than not the sons of mobsters have been successful. It's just that you don't hear those stories. The new legit generation isn't going to publicize the past and how the family got its start. But the success stories are all around you whether you recognize them or not.

One story is about a big shot in the 1920s. He was a bootlegger and had "his own thing" going, dealing with Frank Costello and other mob bosses. He muscled his way into the movie business. He was such a master at phony stock manipulation and insider trading he would have left today's corporate criminals green—with envy, instead of money.

This godfather almost never discussed where his money came from with his wife, sons, and daughters. He set the kids up with trust funds so they could not only be legit—but would never have to work regular jobs; instead they could concentrate on achieving power. Though he personally may not have had anyone whacked for trying to stop his enterprises, those he associated with did. Though his stock frauds were not all illegal at the time, they were surely unethical, not to mention immoral. Many were made illegal in later years. Though his liquor-smuggling would surely be excused by most of us today, it was certainly illegal during Prohibition. He did it to achieve power and wealth. And broads? Let's not even go there. Suffice it to say he had plenty, including famous actresses.

Not only did this boss become legit, he became ambassador to England and held other posts in the U.S. government. He had three sons who became senators, and one who became president—John F. Kennedy. Does somebody out there want to quibble about romanticizing mob bosses in the movies? Give me a break. For decades JFK's picture was second only to that of Jesus in millions of homes in the U.S. and abroad.

Could the success of the descendants of Joseph P. Kennedy have been achieved otherwise? Could he have scrimped and saved in a menial job to send his kids to college. Sure, it's possible. Some people have made it that way. But most strivers, the ones we do not hear as much about, have failed miserably and been doomed to stay in the underclass. The Corleones, the Sopranos, and many in the movie mob chose a different way, the same way as the boss of the Kennedy family. They chose it because of a key part of the American dream—a better life for their children.

Vincenzo, when they come, they will come at what you love.
Michael Corleone, *Godfather III*

9. Love

We didn't even get a greeting from Christoforo "Chris" Cristaldi, the bartender at Bottoms Up, when we made our weekly stop. He simply reached into his shirt pocket, unfolded a twenty, and set it on the bar demanding, "Take a look at this."

"Yeah? So? Are you buying? Thanks, Chris, this'll set us up for the night."

"Look closer. Will it pass?" he asked as he leaned down the bar drawing us a couple of drafts.

I never knew much about counterfeiting, and neither did DB. But I understood its appeal. Like gambling, the lure of money falling into your lap is hard to resist. If your old man ever harped that "Money doesn't grow on trees," there was a reason he did. You *want* it to grow on trees— everybody does—trees in your own back yard, that only you can go out and prune. Twenties that you could crank out in the garage. Or Benjamins you can reproduce in the basement. Your own ATM that never runs low. It all evolves around the magic of machines spitting out cash for you. It was no different in ancient times, when guys in robes, sandals, and Bin Laden beards would keep trying to figure out how to make gold from everyday junk metals.

"This is pretty good work," said DB picking up the bill and inspecting it like he knew what the hell he was talking about. "And just who is the designer of this fine work of art?"

"You don't want to know that now, but you know I wouldn't give you no monopoly money, Joey," replied Chris. "I'm getting it directly from the source. And don't worry, I never pay you guys with any of this."

"Hah! I know you're too smart to do that, Chris," I said.

"I know you're stupid, but nobody's that stupid," is what I was thinking.

What I was also thinking, though, was that it was a shame we couldn't get in on this bogus bill deal. No way could we ever go into business with Chris, though. We had known him as a kid and liked him but he was another screw too loose to be counted on to keep a project together.

Bottoms Up was a shot and a beer joint owned by his brother Ray on the Avenue. It had been called The Friendly Tap before Ray bought it and most people still called it The Friendly or just The Tap, and now sometimes just Ray's. It was not as friendly as it used to be though. The previous owner had set up a little train that ran on tracks close to the ceiling and chugged around the entire perimeter of the bar. He'd dress the cars up at certain times of the year—you know, little Santas sitting on the locomotive in winter, American flags in early July, that kind of stuff. Guys would bring their kids into the bar to see it. Ray kept that touch, but little else. The back rooms were for smoking reefer, but rumor was harder stuff exchanged hands, and I'm sure rumor had it right. Bottoms Up was just a bit more on edge than when it was The Friendly.

Chris, though, seemed to me to be well suited to his current occupation and career choice. He was about my age and had graduated from Ryerson (mainly because the teachers didn't want to get stuck with him one more year). He had done a stint at Montefiore (reform school), and had been in the Chicago Avenue Jokers. People liked him, and his brother Ray seemed to look out for him. He aspired to bigger and better things, and the reason he did was summed up with one look at the love of his life, Patti McGhee.

Most women, especially ones this hot, can be trouble. Patti was different. She seemed to accept Chris exactly the way he was. It was Chris who didn't accept Chris as he was. He felt he had to be something much more to deserve Patti. And when he felt inadequate, he did strange things. There was the jukebox incident for instance.

The Friendly had always been a neighborhood institution. Ray continued the tradition of sponsoring 16-inch softball and bowling teams, putting up entry fees and paying for uniforms, now with "Bottoms Up" on the back. Female supporters of the teams formed informal cheerleading squads. Their only routines were screaming at what they thought were appropriate moments, and wearing little shorts with the bar's name stitched on the rear.

Of course, after a game the whole gang—the players, their girlfriends and relatives, and any assorted hangers-on—repaired to Ray's, ordering as many pitchers of beer as they could consume into the wee hours. This meant good crowds in and out of season. As a consequence, we hung out there a lot ourselves. I liked Ray, but knowing him from the neighborhood, I had always imagined that the train chugging along in his brain wasn't making all its required stops. Obviously I was the one off track. It was his brother Chris who had the loose wheel.

One July night, Ray's current sponsorees, a dysfunctional softball group aptly named the Maladroits, were pounding down the suds after having whipped another local ten (there was a short-center fielder). Chris's girl Patti was there, all red tank top, no bra, and cut-off jean shorts. Most of the guys didn't give her more than a look because they knew who she belonged to. Chris had already threatened a couple of patrons who had talked to her and chased one guy into the street because he thought the guy had taken some of the cash Patti had on the bar. Turns out she later found the ten dollar bill he thought the guy had picked up in her back pocket. Those jeans were so tight Chris probably could have seen Alexander Hamilton's profile through them if he had just looked.

The "Droits" were sliding quarters into the juke (provided by the Music Man and yours truly) that night, keeping a steady stream of Marvin Gaye, the Temps, the Miracles, and even an occasional Frank or Dino song flowing over and around, and sometimes drowning out, the rousing discussions of how a line drive had hit their third base coach in the head when he was looking into the stands, and how the Cubs did that day.

The Droit pitcher, a guy nicknamed Mudcat, had been cruising through every Al Green 45 on the juke until he got to "Love and Happiness." He played it twice even though it kept skipping after the first few bars. On the third try his buddies started kicking the box to help the song along. I remembered this because I'm responsible for these boxes. Even though Ray would ultimately have to pay damages, the Pol didn't always see things logically when I gave him bad news, like someone broke one of his boxes. And the fact that I was actually there witnessing this destruction was not going to help. The Pol was known for shooting the messenger—figuratively, that is; but I didn't want to take any chances.

Ray had just brought me another Old Style and was hanging around when I happened to notice Chris further on down the bar talking to Patti and looking steamed. Mudcat had just put another quarter in and was staring in their direction, but mainly at Patti. His pals started shaking the box again, I guess thinking they could catch the song before the skip. Maybe it was the fact the a/c was on the fritz and all the tap had going for it was a large fan in the doorway; maybe Chris snapped for some reason; or maybe it was just Chris being Chris; but I'll always think Patti had said something and Chris wanted to be the big man. Just as I glanced toward him, he was bringing out the .38 he had tucked away under the bar.

I had been considering intervening myself to stop these guys from doing damage to the box, but I didn't think a measure this extreme was necessary. Still, I thought he was just trying to scare them. Suddenly "Boom!" a blast sounded that sent customers diving under tables and left me with the fleeting image of Bottoms Up staring back at me from backs and butts as I hunkered down on my side of the bar. I barely had time to realize the guys near the box were okay when two more blasts came from Chris's gun and the jukebox was a goner. The first voice I heard was DB's from under the pool table, "The Pol isn't going to be happy about this, but the skipping problem is solved."

When the Tap cleared out, which took only a few minutes, DB and I walked up to Ray and Chris and I said, "We'll see you tomorrow at noon," and we left. I was giving them three hours while the banks were open.

The next day Ray had the money for the box before we even told the Pol what had happened. We were able to bring our boss the cash for a new box, with a substantial mark-up, and music instead of gunfire was again heard at Bottoms Up by the end of the week.

I don't know if Ray took care of the whole cost or had Chris working it off, but Chris's desire to make some extra money must have led him to jump at being part of the counterfeiting scam. And he was asking us to be part of it too.

For us the decision to get into a new business—counterfeiting—was one we would have had to make on our own. We couldn't have told the boss. He would either have squelched the idea or taken a lion's share cut for himself without any of the risk. Going it alone, we still would have had to get the bills checked out by someone more knowledgeable. Then we'd have to meet the source, adding one more person to the roster of potential rats. And then there was Chris, who was a general fuck-up in the first place. And would I believe he could keep what he was doing from Patti? I doubted it. That's at least six people who would have known our involvement.

Furthermore, most of these people had to get a cut of the proceeds. Twenties are harder for the cops to track than hundreds, but you've also got to move five times as many of them to make the same profit. Pay for your groceries once in a while in a strange neighborhood and they'll never get traced. Paying for a new car with a thousand new twenties isn't going to work. Deposit them in a bank? Mmm, I don't think so. Run around buying things all over the city? It may not be worth your gas and time, and a traceable pattern starts to develop. Travel the country? You'd better be ready to stay on the road for a long time. Even then you start to leave a trail. Give them to your wife to spend? You've made your love into an accomplice. Counterfeiting is not as easy as it seems, and it's a federal rap to boot. Still, there's that image of the leaves on the trees—rectangular leaves with pictures of Old Hickory on them.

As you can guess, we passed on this money-making opportunity. Unfortunately, this put Chris into a funk. Not with us, but just in general.

"You guys,....." he just trailed off. "What the fuck am I gonna do?"

"Whaddaya mean, what're you gonna do? What's wrong with what you're doin' now?" answered DB.

" I want to marry Patti and she wants to get the fuck out of here."

"Get the fuck out of where?"

"Off Chicago Avenue! Are you fuckin' blind? It's changin' here. I don't think it's safe for Patti. These guys are always lookin' at her like they'd like to....."

"They've been moving in for years. You can take care of yourself," I interjected, and then added, "And Patti can too."

"Ah, I'd just as soon move to Elmwood Park or further if I could afford it."

"Well, there's lots of things you can do, man," said DB.

"Like what?" he answered.

"I don't know. You've just gotta go out and start doin' them. Start tryin' them," DB continued. "Maybe get a job with the city."

It seemed as though Chris, only in his mid-twenties, saw this time as his last chance to make something out of himself and impress his love. Or maybe he was trying to impress himself and feel like a man. Patti seemed impressed enough already with Chris. She didn't look like she needed any encouragement where he was concerned, and she seemed quite happy living where she was, but we weren't going to violate his trust by talking to her.

All the messing around in school, getting into trouble, and never "applying himself," as the nuns used to say, was coming home to roost in the back yard of Chris's psyche. Actually, I identified with him. Luckily, I had found a niche, had the support of a loyal wing man, and had a woman who loved me. Chris didn't seem to be that much worse off. But that's not how he saw it. Bottoms Up wasn't enough. Maybe Ray didn't give him as much support as it looked like on the surface. And having the affection of the hottest chick on the Avenue could have its downside. It apparently made him feel more unworthy and nervous than confident.

So when we turned down his offer, Chris decided to do what any desperate lowlife would in his place. He turned to the only person he knew wouldn't say no to him.

It was late September and the afternoons were finally cooling down (the a/c never had gotten fixed in the bar). We hadn't been in for a while except to make collections in the mornings when Ray was usually there working on his liquor orders or his books. We dropped in to watch the last Cub game of the season on the new TV Ray had installed. When Chris had a minute off from the bar he came over and joined us.

"Say hey, woulda been, coulda been, shoulda been partners," he greeted us as he started to pour an Old Style for me and a Dewars and water for DB. "This first one's on me."

"How's Elmwood Park?" needled DB.

"Gettin' there, gettin there. That's just it. This takes time, but you guys'll wish you had gone in with me on this."

By early evening, in between scooting down the bar to take care of thirsty patrons and our runs to the men's room, Chris described how Patti had been passing the 20's everywhere she could. First she concentrated on shopping downtown, buying stuff they needed. They figured people came to the Loop from all over the city so she'd get lost in the crowd. And the busier the store, the harder she'd be to remember. They'd end each trip with her picking up a small deli item at Stop and Shop and then some caramel corn at Garrett's on Michigan Ave. In the middle of the day, when Chris wasn't working, they'd go out to O'Hare and she'd buy stuff at stores there. She'd do the buying and Chris would keep counting the change.

When I saw the wad of real money that Chris flashed, I had that momentary surge of greed that makes you do stupid things. It's the same instinct that kicks in when you've seen guys making money off the stock market for years and years and then you finally jump in too, just before the crash. Or when your pals come back from Vegas bragging about how much they "won," never mentioning how much they lost, either this time or on previous trips. You're constantly looking in that back yard of your mind, dreaming those trees will sprout. I took another sip of Old Style and let the surge subside.

A couple of weeks later I was back at the Tap and Chris was making plans for the place in the burbs. The excitement that he felt of plucking money off those branches was palpable. His face was flush and I thought I could almost see or feel his heart racing. One of the reasons he was so excited was that I was one of the few people he could talk to about his success. It's like I heard someone once say—"It's not that good doin' good, if nobody knows you're doin' good."

Between the main lines of his story, though, I started to pick up the details of what they had been doing. I had been afraid they'd eventually get tracked anyway, but they were getting downright careless. Patti had been going to Jewel's and stores all over the city, and then to nearby cleaners and gas stations. She'd been changing twenties for ten-cent candy at Walgreens and then buying a newspaper on the corner. She'd buy separate tickets for a couple of bucks at different windows for the bleachers at Wrigley. Every time they wanted a hot dog and soda, she'd buy them, one item at a time. And every transaction, they'd be banking 17, 18 or 19 bucks of legal tender in a wad they kept in Chris's apartment on Racine. They were passing paper so fast it had become an addiction.

I was surprised it was going on as long as it was, figuring if nothing else Chris would spill the story to his cronies, and they'd start telling "the secret" to their best friends on the condition that they wouldn't tell anyone else, who'd in turn tell their best friends on the same condition, and so forth. That's what usually happens—everyone tells only a trusted few people—the secret is supposedly kept, except everybody knows it. But Chris's lips seemed to stayed zipped.

I wasn't there when it came down, but it happened right at the bar. Ray later filled us in with the details. Plainclothesmen came in and ordered a drink. The doofuses waltzed in with jackets and ties, while just their general demeanor made them stand out. They hadn't even touched their drinks before they asked Ray if a woman named Patti McGhee was in the bar. Ray tried to give it the "what's this all about" and "who's asking" routine, but when they showed their IDs, he had to point her out. Chris was watching all this, as was just about everyone in the bar out of the corner of their eyes.

"Are you Patti McGhee?" the first dick asked as they approached her. When she responded, they told her that her father had been picked up and was being held in Cook County jail. "He wants to see you bad," said the second cop. "Can you come with us?"

Patti was a pretty fast thinker, but not fast enough. She made a move toward her purse, then hesitated and reached just over it to the purse that lay next to it on the chair, and started out with the cops. One of them noticed that flinch, though, and asked to see her ID in the purse. As she started to look through it, she pretended to gasp, "Oh, I took the wrong purse. I must have left mine at home."

"Maybe you just mixed them up, they look so similar," one of the officers retorted. Patti's purse on the chair was a small red one, while the one she had "accidentally" picked up was a black bag twice its size. He picked up the little red purse and asked the two women who had been sitting with her at the table if it belonged to either of them. Although their mouths were open, no sound came out from either. Since no one was claiming ownership, he looked in the purse, fishing through the few odd cosmetics and then pulled out two or three cards with Patti's name on them—and two envelopes. One was stuffed with tens, fives, and singles. The other held just five new twenty-dollar bills.

It's not likely that a successful purse switch would have done anything but delay judgment day for Patti. What had happened was that her father had been pulling 20's out of her purse for weeks, spending them at Riley's saloon on Grand Avenue every time he went out. Seems he had lately become quite a favorite, buying rounds for the whole assemblage with a sudden generosity. When Riley's bank started bouncing the bills back, tracing them back to old man McGhee was such child's play, even for Chicago cops, that they took the collar for themselves before they informed the Feds. McGhee lasted about a Chicago minute before he gave up his daughter.

Whether it was love or whether it was omerta, Patti was true grit. She told every story she could think of rather than give up Chris—stuff like she thought she broke a hundred at Margie's Beef Stand last week and maybe that's where she picked up the bad bills in her purse. And she didn't know where her father got his. Nothing she said held water for long, especially when the other twenties started surfacing. Vendors who at first could not remember who gave them a bill a week ago, started to pick Patti out of a series of pictures. Young male clerks in particular picked her out, because although she tried to blend into the big city, she never hid most of her sleek and slender charms.

The Feds had enough to indict her and a trial date was set. Chris had been in denial, hoping her stories would work. He was in denial that they'd lock up such a sweet "innocent thing." We dropped in at the Tap as often as we could to give him support.

Finally, Chris decided to do the right thing and turned himself in. What he hadn't figured on was that Patti wasn't buying his sacrifice. She wanted to take the rap all by her lonesome and save him the grief. "The judge will be easier on a woman," she said, but I doubt she believed it. The Feds had been pressing her to make a deal and name her accomplice and her source. They figured all along her boyfriend was involved and threatened to throw the proverbial book at her. Chris couldn't let this go on or he wouldn't have been able to look at himself in the mirror, let alone show his face in the neighborhood once word got out. But she wouldn't give in either. They were at a standstill until a week before the preliminary hearing for the trial when he called the FBI.

It's not too smart to turn yourself in without cutting a deal, and I guess we thought all along that lack of smarts fit Patti and Chris's profile. It turned out we should have been examining our own IQ's.

"Did you hear? Chris and Patti got a suspended sentence," one of our fellow jukebox colleagues announced when I got to work one morning.

"Who the hell was their lawyer?"

"I dunno," said Carlo, "maybe he's a friend of the family or something."
I had asked about the lawyer kind of rhetorically, but then realized I really

wanted to know. We found out later that day that it was an Irish guy, name of Dave Halloran. None of our guys had ever heard of him.

Somehow, love had conquered all, or so we thought. It wasn't until years later that we learned a lesson the hard way. When someone around you gets let off mighty easy by the courts, be suspicious of the reason.

Lessons on Love from the Movie Mob

Patti and Chris were trying to prove some ideal of love to each other. I'd call bullshit on it although they finally did make it to the suburbs. Chris got a good deal on the engagement ring, courtesy of Mike, the Rug, of course, and they're still together. Can I really give you any advice about love though? I could try, but who knows what I've learned myself. And who can figure out women anyway? What's more important, I doubt you're going to listen anyway. Most people don't hear so good when it comes to this subject. So I'll just let the films speak for themselves.

> *Rico, listen, I love her. We're in love with one another.*
> *Doesn't that mean nothin' to you?*
> Joe (Douglas Fairbanks)
> *Nothin' – less than nothin'! Love – soft stuff. The way*
> *she's got you, you ain't no good for anything.*
> Rico (Edward G. Robinson), *Little Caesar*

Rico probably knows he is wasting his breath, but he's a realist. Of course, he's also an unadulterated bad guy. Decades later, gang chief Sonny in *A Bronx Tale* shows "bad guys" can also have a soft side.

> *Let me tell you somethin', when you're alone late at*
> *night, in bed, just you and her under the covers, that's*
> *all that matters. C, you gotta do what your heart tells*
> *you to do.*
> Sonny (Chazz Palminteri) to the young Calogero

On the other hand, in *The Last Don*, Pippi Delana (Joe Mantegna) divvied out the toughest advice of all. He tells his son Cross to trust no one, not even him, his own father. When he sees Cross with his girl friend, Athena (Darryl Hannah), his counsel is just as harsh:

> *Love is not a reliable emotion, no matter how deep. Love does not ensure gratitude. Does not ensure obedience. Does not provide harmony in so difficult a world.*

You can say that in the end maybe love conquers all, if you want to call love what you feel when you looked at Patti. I still hear Al Green's words on that juke box-skipping song, *Love and Happiness,*

> *Something that can make you wrong,*
> *Make you do right*

Personally, I'd stick with Rico. Beware of the *soft stuff.*

The head of a big industry throws out 50,000 employees. It's just business. Cigarettes kill thousands of people. What'a you gonna do. People are going to smoke.
Pippi Delana (Joe Mantegna),
The Last Don

Yeah, Johnny, I know that. I understand. This is a business, Johnny. This is a business and it has to be run like a business. If there's a guy doesn't cooperate, then out he goes.
Al Capone (Rod Steiger), *Al Capone*

I got sent for. In our thing, you get sent for, you go in alive, you come out dead and it's your best friend that does it.
Lefty (Al Pacino), *Donnie Brasco*

10. Business

Dominick Santoro had been running Thursday and Friday poker nights in the neighborhood for a couple of years. Thursday was "friendly game of poker night"—ante was fifty bucks a hand and it was a chance to socialize. Friday was high roller night, where he'd try to pull in the big shots through word of mouth. Politicians, corporate types, athletes, entertainers, and other high-class degenerates who wanted action were his usual clientele. Betting was no-holds barred on Friday. We played on Thursdays, but occasionally on Friday, when Dom needed an extra player or had a mark he thought we could beat. He'd stake us.

One Thursday August night the game was at Dominick's house. Sometimes he needed to move the game around, but there hadn't been a hint of a raid for months, and his house had the best a/c. By the time the black and white Felix the Cat clock on Dominick's kitchen wall meowed twice, the rubber band on the roll in my pocket was pretty loose. I had been doing more losing than winning for the last six months, and this muggy night wasn't any different. Five of us were left and the smell of sweat and cigar smoke was taking its toll. We were ready for one last hand, but that was it. The Pol expected us in early to do some "accounting"; always paranoid someone was skimming him, he wanted to tally the summer's take with us nearby in case he had questions.

The games were almost always five-card draw. Dominick dealt the cards down to each of us after we anteed up. Richie Accetura was up the most dough and had a smug look on his face as he picked up his cards. I wanted to smack his fucking kisser. That sometimes happens after five hours of a friendly card game. If everyone is quiet and poker-faced, the night stays calm. If one guy has an attitude you don't like or says something that rubs someone the wrong way, punches could be thrown—or worse.

I looked at Richie before I looked at my cards, intent on kicking his ass this last hand. DB got his cards first, and just said, "Check." Probably a bad sign for him because he wasn't much of a bluffer. Tommy Numbers, a good accountant but a bad gambler, bet $50 and it went to Richie. He eyed his cards, looked up at me, glanced down again, and called. Was Richie intentionally trying to piss me off, I thought, as the bet went to me?

I had been caught up with Richie's antics and hadn't even looked at my hand. When I did, I had to do my best Pacino, something like when Kay asks him if he had Carlo killed. If DB isn't much of a bluffer, I'm not much of an actor, but I was motivated this time and I think it worked. Pairs of kings and nines and a trey meant I was going to squeeze this prick and get a bunch of my money back.

"Ah, fuck, last hand, I'll raise it $50," I yawned, trying to nonchalant it. Dominick folded and focused on his dealing. I later learned that DB was holding a Queen, Jack, 10, and 8 of clubs, looking for a straight, a flush, or a straight flush. Two of those nines, including the club, were sitting in my hand as he threw in a hundred bucks to call. Tommy called and now Richie decided to raise it another $50.

"You can't fucking do that," yelled Tommy, "You called the first time around."

"Yeah, I'm afraid he can, Tommy," said Dominick. "He might have called but other people at the table bet and raised after that, so he can do what he wants." Was Richie trying to slow-play us from the beginning or just enjoying pissing us off? Everybody called, including Tommy who I could see was fuming. That of course meant he didn't have much of a hand and would be looking for big help. I was looking at about $850 sitting on the table as the four of us studied our cards. It was DB's turn to draw. He asked for one card and did his rub-it-around-the-table-for-luck bullshit before he peeked. When he murmured "motherfucker" everybody knew he didn't catch his one card and would be out. Tommy Numbers drew three cards and wasted only one of those syllables: "Fuck." One more man down.

Richie had a calm look on his ugly mug and took his time before saying, "I don't need shit, I'm good." Damn, I thought, I may really need to draw something unless the bastard is bluffing. I asked for my card and stole a look. Now I really had to go to acting school. I had picked up the 9 of hearts and could beat any straight or flush Richie was holding or any crap he was pretending to hold. I just needed to get as much of Richie's money as I could. DB and Tommy checked for the hell of it, but we knew they'd quietly fold as soon as the next round of betting started.

Richie opened with $50 and looked smug, knowing he had stood pat and I had been looking. But when I bumped him a c-note, he got a bit more serious. He took one more look before he said, "I'll see that and bump it up another hundred." Now it was my turn to get a bit more serious. If this had been on film, they'd probably be doing a close-up of little beads of sweat starting above my upper lip. Did Dom turn the air off or something?

I could have called and ended it there. I was getting sick of all this bullshit. It was hot, I had been losing more often than winning all summer, I had to see the Pol tomorrow morning. Where was I going? Where were DB and I both going? And then there was Richie. He ran with another crew and always seemed to have more dough than we were making. I hit him with another hundred. This time he didn't hesitate and hit me back.

His raise sobered my urge to get as much of his money as possible. He knew I wasn't going to fold at this point, so he must be holding something strong. I thought. I was down to my last hundred and didn't want to use a marker, not with this asshole. The $1550 sat there waiting to be pulled toward me and spent.

"Call," I said.

Now this prick broke into a smile and ran his cards over and left me staring at his own full-house, queens over sixes. It's all I could do to keep from punching him in the face as he drew the pile of dough over, laughing like Paul Newman beating Doyle Lonnegan in *The Sting*. I sat there stunned, and looked over at Dominick and said, "You dealt this fucking guy a full-house? He didn't even have to draw for it?" Richie shrugged and mumbled, "tough break" or something when I turned over my unlucky cards. My instinct was to show them I wasn't bluffing, to increase my credibility for future games, but I felt somehow that not only was the night over, but these games would never be the same either.

I lost that week's earnings after busting my ass hauling those jukes around and wondered what look I'd get when I got home. On the way home I started to wonder. Dominick and Richie were tight. And he dealt him a full house. Nothing I could prove. Nothing I wanted to prove, because there would have been nothing I could do about it anyway.

Dealing with the Pol the next morning was the last straw.

"How come this account is so sh-short" He had questions about almost every stop we made, and stupid comments about the ones he didn't question.

"That guy closed up last month," I explained, "I told you at that time."

"Oh, yeah, dumb Ricans don't even know how to run a bar."

The questioning went on and on, and I didn't always know the answers. I was being straight and I knew DB was too, but I couldn't remember every detail of what happened. If we couldn't remember what happened, we'd sometimes even come up with the money ourselves rather than put up with his bullshit. If he really thought we were skimming, we would have been out on the street, maybe with a price on our heads, and not a big one at that. He knew we were straight. He just liked to keep sticking it to us. I felt I was losing it and wanted to take out all my frustrations—losing money, smart-ass Richie, the fucking humidity and heat, the Pol's questions—I wanted to take it all out on him. Something had to change before I snapped.

DB and I had talked about what we wanted to do for maybe two years now. Something my old man had told me a long time ago had always stayed with me. He wasn't much on history, but I think somebody told him the story. Of the dreamers who went out to strike it rich in the gold rush of 1849 in California, only one in ten, hell, maybe one in a hundred, struck it rich. The rest went broke, and became farmers and laborers, if they lived through it at all. But the shopkeepers who equipped them; the provisioners who fed them; the managers of bars, whorehouses, and gambling dens who entertained them—they all got rich enough. We were the dreamers, but all we had accomplished so far is to be laborers for the Pol.

DB's Uncle Roman had just bought a store down the Avenue. Roman was a success. He owned a men's clothing store, which he named DB's after himself. We'd buy our Italian knits, our baggies, hats, and such when we didn't buy from The Rug or go down to Maxwell Street or Smokey Joe's. Now he had bought a second store which had been a grocery store that had folded after the Jewel's opened.

"I think I might try to re-do the grocery store as a laundermat or sometin,' I'm not sure."

We thought our idea was better. We'd open up a social club. The rotating poker games could now be in one location. But that would only be a start. With all the juke collections we had been making, we had contacts all over the city. We'd start out as an Italian social club, but then we could expand. Puerto Ricans, Mexicans, Jews, Polacks, crazy Serbian and Ukrainian fucks—you name it—they were already our clients. What's more important, we knew them. Even if it wound up that we didn't get a city-wide audience, there were plenty of degenerate gamblers living right in the neighborhood waiting to fill our pockets. We'd be the ones getting rich, providing them the services they lived for, instead of working our asses off, and dreaming about striking it rich.

"Do you think he'll rent it to us?" I asked DB. "Let's find out," is all he could say.

Uncle Roman DiBruno was always a good guy to talk to, but when it came to business, his attitude changed, or so it seemed to us at the time.

"Youse guys got a plan?" was the first thing he asked.

"A plan? Sure, we're gonna corner all the gambling in our hood," answered DB.

"That ain't a plan, kiddo. That's just a wish. How you gonna do it? How you gonna deal with Dominick, who's running the card games now? What're you gonna tell the Pol, who you been workin' for? Is Mr. Big gonna give his okay on it? How you gonnna operate?"

"We'll work those things out, Uncle Roman, we've got ambition." DB tried to sound confident.

"Yeah, well, when you *work tings out*, come see me. Listen, kid, I'd do anything to help you. Your father was like a brother to me. Matter of fact he was my brother, ha, ha." Roman had a weird sense of humor sometimes. Then he directed the phrase at us, that we'd only heard in the movies up to that time. "Sorry, guys, I like you, but this is business. It's not personal."

We went to work using Roman's philosophy in jumping over, or just plain obliterating, each of the hurdles he shined a light on. We knew that using logic and reason with Dominick or The Pol was a waste of time. We'd have to show some power, but also appeal to their business sense. It was a couple of years before that we had stolen the Eldo for Vito. We had done it on a hunch, some intuition that it would pay off down the road. Now we were turning the bend on that road. It was payoff time. We'd need Vito to talk to the big Boss to see if we could get his backing for the operation.

"He don'ta say 'yes,' and he don'ta say 'no,'" was the answer Vito finally brought down from on high, mimicking some of the boss's paesans that he kept around for protection. My first reaction was my usual, "What the f....." DB set me straight immediately, although I would have seen it soon enough.

"Fuck, man, that's a green light. That means he'll be behind us if we can pull this off," DB interpreted.

"That, she'sa sound right," interjected Vito, keeping up the shtick. Then he dropped it. "The Boss can't go against the Pol, and he sure don't wanna piss off Dominick if you guys don't get off the ground. He's gotta be able to deny he ever gave you his okay. But he'll back you. It's up to you to use the power this knowledge gives you. It's just business..."

"I know, it ain't personal," I finished the mantra before he could.

In reality, Dominick was penny ante and merely scratching the surface of the deep gambling itch on Chicago's West Side. Freddy Polito, on the other hand, was a business kingpin for the organization. But we weren't directly threatening Freddy's operation the way we were Dominick's. So a different strategy had to be devised to bring each of them over.

With the Pol we were direct. We indoctrinated two youngbloods to take our place and taught them the works. Their job interviews (they didn't know the interviews were happening) consisted of us taking one of them on a particular run where "strong salesmanship" was continuously necessary to keep the stops in line and the money flowing. After the guy passed the run test and seemed to know the city, we checked his background and family. One last test was to put extra dough in an envelope that he was supposed to collect and see if the full amount showed up at the end of the day.

We went to the Pol with these two guys in our pocket and told him how they'd do our jobs for less. We dropped the fact that a jukebox in our new place would generate three or four times the revenue of other stops —we'd guarantee it—and told him he'd be an honorary member of the club. In addition, we'd connect him with customers who had a bad streak of gambling luck and needed loans to tide them over. After Tony's untimely nap in that car trunk, the Pol's income in that particular sector of his balance sheet had gone south. I don't know if he checked with anyone above him, but without much discussion, we were suddenly unemployed. I think he was glad to get rid of us. We knew too much— not just about the business—but about him personally.

Dominick was a tougher nut to crack on the outside, but it took a lot less planning. With the Pol we had to pretend we were asking for permission. With Dominick, we talked like what we were doing was a done deal, hinting at the fact that higher-ups had made some decisions on this. We were ready with the old Louisville Slugger, but before he could get too pissed we threw him a carrot. He'd be our head dealer once the club got going. He could train new guys, and come out with at least what he was making off the poker games. And of course we ended by explaining it was nothing personal, Dominick, just business. He said he was in. So we figured he was.

When we went back to Uncle Roman, we had the rest of the set-up figured. For starters, poker and craps, along with "91," a gin rummy game for the Mustache Petes. We'd start with the guys we knew and then put the word out through all our juke stops. We'd put out a nice spread with Italian beefs from Margie's, *sangwiches* courtesy of Fontano's, and lemon chicken from Tufano's. It would all be comped, like in Vegas, so nobody would have to leave to get something to eat, and the booze would help ease their concentration. Ten percent of the pots at the poker tables would go to the house. We named it the St. Francis Social Club, knowing that the godfather of all Franciscans was also Roman's favorite saint. And as we became more and more successful, he could raise the rent accordingly.

This kind of business couldn't really be open to the general public. Enjoying the services of St. Francis's was like getting a job with the Outfit—patrons had to know somebody to get in. People we didn't know did walk in off the street now and then in the day time. We'd give them a cup of coffee, tell them about the things our club did for the neighborhood, get their names, and send them on their way. Later we could check on them and decide whether we wanted to invite them back. It took a couple of months to set things up, but within a couple of weeks of opening, St. Francis became the place to be. We still needed the imprimatur from the Boss, but all the signs from Uncle Vito were positive.

As our fortunes seemed ready to soar, though, Dominick's spirits seemed to plunge. While we felt on top of the world, he was acting like his world was coming to an end. We were sharing our good fortune with him, but it wasn't enough. He was bitching about everything from the food not being cooked right to the seat cushion he was using being too lumpy. "Dominick, what's up with you? Your attitude will drive people out of here." I finally told him at the beginning of his shift one day. "Talk to me."

"Yeah, I'll talk. I'll talk to you later." he muttered as he readied his table for the next game.

"No, let's talk now." I couldn't wait another second, so I had Fat Tony take over his table. DB had been ready to go home from his shift, but I had told him to stick around, and I signaled to him to come over as I told Dominick, "Let's go out back and tell me what's up."

He got up slowly and the three of us made for the back of the club and stepped out the rear exit door into the alley.

"I'll tell you what's up, I'm getting fucked here. You guys are cleaning up and I'm getting chump change," he blurted out immediately with rage in his eyes.

DB jumped in, "Hey dick-head, this is the arrangement we made and you're making more than you ever did. You should thank your lucky stars."

"Fuck your stars. It was my game you turned into this casino. I'm not getting my cut. I'm not getting near what I deserve." Somehow Dominick had gotten the idea that he was working with us, not for us.

"Dominick, this is the deal you made. What do you want me to do? I said.

"What I want is one-third. That's fair."

"You know goddam well what your cut is in all of this. It's not no one-third. It's just what it's been these ten weeks. You work for us and you get your pay."

"I was showing you punks how to run a game before you knew a joker from the back of your ass, and you said we'd be partners in this operation," he said through clenched teeth."

Did he really believe this? Did seeing all the money coming in convince him of something just the opposite of the truth? I didn't know and I didn't care. "You're playing a jack high hand as if you've got a full house, Dominick," I said in a monotone, trying to pick words he'd understand and looking straight at him. I tried to be as serious and threatening as I could when I finished. "You'd better fold 'em."

He didn't get it and started again with some half-assed story about us being from the neighborhood and partnering up and all.

I stopped him, "You're right about all you said about us being from the same hood and you teaching us shit, Dom. But understand—this is not personal, it's business. This meeting ends now. You come back in tomorrow and I don't ever want to hear another word on the subject."

Dom never brought up the subject again with us, but we heard stories from other guys in the club that he was still bitching and complaining. Then Richie, the guy who had beaten me with the full house dealt by

Dominick in his final card game, started showing up more often. And started winning. And winning. And usually at Dominick's table.

You've got to understand—a professional card dealer like Dominick can deal up almost any hand he wants unless equally sharp people are watching him. Casinos today videotape every hand and study what every dealer is doing. We didn't have that kind of technology then and we probably wouldn't employ it now. If Dominick was running up pots for his partner to win, it meant he was also setting up our real customers. If they got suspicious that our games were not on the up-and-up, our business would be ruined, at the least. Dominick would not only be guilty of cheating the customers, but of cheating us.

We knew we had to do something, so we consulted with Vito. "That ungrateful prick," was Vito's first reaction and then, "Keep Dominick around tomorrow night after closing and I'll stop by. We'll have a little sit-down."

Although Vito knew of our suspicions about Dominick's dealing, we were surprised that the meeting was entirely about Dominick's position and his cut. We thought Vito knew that Dominick could not be reasoned with and was out of line. Vito listened to both sides and then said, "Dominick, even though these guys have built up a nice business, you've got some good points. You're the one who got the games started. I'm going to talk to the boss and work something out to make sure you get what you deserve."

Vito was in his best godfather mode ending with "Boys, this is just business. Dominick must get what he deserves. I have spoken." He stared at us as he spoke and then got up and walked straight out without giving anyone a chance to say another word. An unconscious smirk crept across Dominick's face and made me want to belt him right there. I felt betrayed, but there was nothing we could do about it. This was the business we had chosen and Vito's decision was the way it was—there were no debates, no negotiation.

The next night Dominick was a no-show and Fat Tony had to fill in again. "Hey, save some of the beefs for the customers, will ya," DB harrassed Tony, wondering when we were going to see Dom again. Maybe he was exercising his muscle after the sit-down and letting us know he'd make his own hours. The thing is, though, he didn't post the next day, nor the day after that. Vito came in on Friday with a couple of marks and we mentioned Dominick's absence.

"Who knows, maybe he took a trip to Vegas to celebrate. I'm sure he'll turn up. He'd want to come back to protect his interests here wouldn't he?" said Vito. And then slowly, while looking straight at us, he added, "He was awfully determined to get what was coming to him."

We never saw Dominick again. We didn't have to pull the trigger ourselves, but Vito taught us this was serious business. Maybe we had been kidding ourselves about doing it our way and nobody gets hurt. Then again, the body never showed up. So maybe Dominick just got smart and moved to the West Coast or something. Vito might have just scared him off. Then again maybe he's playing five card stud with Hoffa up on some farm in the Upper Peninsula. We didn't ask. What we did know for sure was that he wasn't taking a cut out of ours or Vito's profits at St. Francis social club.

> *It's not personal, it's business.*
> Michael Corleone (Al Pacino) *The Godfather*

Life Lessons on Business from the Movie Mob

In the 1970's Ford Motor Company let dozens of people burn to death in their Pintos, instead of fixing problems with the model's gas tank. They figured it was cheaper to pay off the lawsuits on behalf of the dead people than fix the problem with the car. "Hey, nothing personal, you family members of the mangled dead people, it's just business."

In the 1980's Union Carbide decided to operate an unsafe and polluting chemical factory in India, rather than spend the money to plug the leaks and clean the plant. When poison gas leaked in, thousands of people died. "Nothing personal, you cow-worshippers, just business."

In the 1990's tobacco executives refused to admit, under oath before Congress, that cigarettes cause cancer. Tens of thousands had been dying. It's business.

When disco owners lock the fire exits to keep out gate-crashers instead of hiring security; or when they pack two to three times as many patrons as the joint is supposed to hold and hundreds die, what do they say? It's just business?

I could fill pages with more of these stories and so could you. The bosses of all these outfits say they're running honest businesses. And then do-gooders say that our business is crooked!? Maybe some of it is, but give me a break.

Americans would rather deal with "honest crooks" any time rather than with phony politicians or lying businessmen. Americans prefer to confront people directly and "honestly," rather than destroy them through deceit and lies behind their backs. It's no wonder the movie Mafia holds a certain romantic sway with the public. It is what it is. Take it or leave it. Get involved or don't. Compare that with a crooked corporation that pretends to be honest, but then acts like a criminal conspiracy, stealing millions from old retired folks. They're hated by everybody, including us.

> *This is family business and that comes first, before anything else—anything else, and that means getting laid, love, your mother, god, and country.*
> Pippi Delana (Joe Mantegna), *The Last Don*

Give the people what they want. Capone said it and most successful businessmen will tell you the same thing. DB and I decided to do likewise. Once we made that decision, we had to live with it and its consequences for the rest of our lives. One thing I don't like to hear is civilians bitching all the time about their jobs and what they have to do. What a fucking waste of time. If you don't like what you do, quit. You should be happy that you have that option in your job. We don't always have that choice in ours. When we feel like bitching about our business we reflect on...

> *When I heard about it (Moe Green getting a bullet in the eye), I wasn't angry. I knew Moe. (But) when he turned up dead, I let it go and I said to myself, 'This is the business we've chosen.' I didn't ask who gave the order because it had nothing to do with business.*
> Hyman Roth, (Lee Strasberg), *The Godfather*

One of the greatest writers of our time, Arthur Miller, has his salesman, Willie Loman, say it in just as few words: "It comes with the territory." So shut up and suck it up.

On the other hand, if you're the one doing the hiring in your business, you should be using the same principles. They work whether you need to snuff someone or let an employee go in the more traditional way.

"Sorry, I have to let you go, Joe, I really like you, but it's just business."

Managers say that hundreds of times a day around the country. It's the same as Tom Hagen (Robert Duvall) saying,

Can't do it, Sally,

...when Sal Tessio asks for a break from his one way car trip in *The Godfather*. That's Sal's only weak moment, a very human moment. He catches himself immediately and wants Michael to understand:

Tell Mike it was only business. I always liked him.
The Godfather

The execution of Pussy on *The Sopranos* at the end of the second season is masterful in showing the importance of business over personal. Pussy is a lovable figure. He's godfather to Tony's son, for Pete's sake. And Tony, as we all know, is a sensitive guy. He has shed tears for ducks in his pond and has cried in front of his psychiatrist. (Nobody's saying *The Sopranos* is realistic.) But do you think for a second he's going to have a breakdown because he has to kill one of his best buddies? No way. On the surface he, Silvio, and Paulie remain cold as they do their job.

After a dramatic buildup, the moment they choose to start pumping bullets into Pussy is almost random. They can't risk a ceremonial sendoff that might touch them in a more emotional or sentimental way than it already does. Pussy, after doing his frightened best to cop a plea that he was using the FBI rather than vice versa, simply asks, "Not in the face, Tone." Tony Soprano, the mafioso with the conscience of a Shakespearian tragic hero, starts shooting, without a word. Later it's going to affect him in other ways—such as imagining Pussy's face on the head of a fish talking to him. But at the moment of truth there is no choice. Pussy has become a rat, turned FBI informant in order to beat a drug rap that would have meant long years in the pen. He has broken the law of omerta—now, what is done is done, and cannot be undone. This is nothing personal. It's strictly business, and Pussy has broken the rules of the business.

When someone makes the decision to buy into "our thing" and knows the rules of the business, he has an implied contract, a contract that stipulates that as a made man he can be eliminated if he breaks the rules or becomes a "business competitor." (In which case, another type of "contract" is put out on him.) He's more like a soldier who, once he's in, can be legally court-martialed and even executed for treason or dereliction of duty, on the battlefield or off.

If you understand that, then even murder doesn't seem so bad. It's part of the business all along, a move that is understood by all the players. The cops and Feds have known this for decades. Except for big crackdowns by occasional crusaders or prosecutors wanting to make a big name for themselves in their own business—politics—their attitude has usually been to let the mob guys kill each other. The general public goes along with the program too. In return, our code has gone along with their program: Don't kill a cop. Don't involve civilians (ordinary citizens). Don't bring extra heat on ourselves. Heat ain't good for business.

Compare the mob business environment with the one which allowed the CEOs (Bosses) of most of the leading tobacco companies to tell Congress, under oath, one by one, that they did not believe there was a link between smoking and cancer. Which business leaders do you think are more honest? Which leaders are more hypocritical?—Murder Inc. or Tobacco, Inc.? After all, the Tobacco Gang said, "People are going to smoke. What'a ya gonna do?" In effect, the Corporate Criminals were telling thousands of dead and dying smokers: "You knew the score. You chose to participate. Now die, to us it's just business."

It's no surprise then that a Mafia character like Michael Corleone becomes an idealized and sentimentalized character, compared to corrupt businessmen or politicians. One destroys with a gun, out in the open, punishing those who go against the code or the business. Corrupt businessmen and politicians destroy almost anybody, and they do it behind closed doors.

How closely *The Godfather, The Sopranos,* or other movies represent reality is one question. The morality of what they portray as fiction is another. Their film code seldom includes the business of hurting civilians.

Oh, sure, Soprano bad guys hijack trucks, steal from casinos and legit business, extort politicians, put muscle on labor union contracts, and so forth. Most of it is immoral and we all pay the "mob tax" (higher prices) for it. But we also all pay a "corruption tax" to our politicians and a "lobby tax" to corporations and an "accounting tax" to those who bankrupt companies after they've bled them dry for tens of millions of dollars. One illegitimate business doesn't justify another, but let's put them into perspective.

The other basic rule of business is......Survival. That is, you do what you have to, to stay in the game.

> *You just learned the first rule of law enforcement. Make sure when your shift is over you go home alive.*
> Jimmy Malone (Sean Connery), *The Untouchables*

You can talk all you want about your touchy-feely crap such as love the work you do, fulfill yourself, or my personal favorite—"Be all that you can be" (and get your ass shot off). The fact is, you go out to work every day, and you've got to survive another day to put bread on the table, bring home the bacon, keep the roof over your head or whatever damned cliché you want to use.

Maybe you're a construction worker who has to take care of the foreman to get hired on the next contract. Maybe you're a cop who has to look the other way while your buddy pulls some shit. He's going to have your back when you walk into that next alley or building in the projects. Maybe the boss in your office is an asshole, but you're going plant your lips on his butt anyway. Maybe you're a soldier—Patton told his men, "Don't die for your country, make the other bastard die for his." Whoever you are, you've got to decide whether you want to be a survivor or a martyr.

The second rule of survival, no matter what business you're in, is to know your enemy (competition), how they think, how they breathe, what their likes and dislikes are, what their strengths and weaknesses are. Successful corporations study their competition more closely than they study their own operations. Today, corporate spying is more important than spying on countries.

I was very happy this house never went to strangers. My father taught me in this room. He taught me, keep your friends close, but your enemies closer.
Michael Coreleone (Pacino) to Frankie Pentangeli, *The Godfather, Part II*

In personal matters, if your enemy does not know that you know that he is your enemy, you can keep him close to you while watching his every move. Guard against the natural, emotional inclination that "an enemy is someone distasteful so I will shun him." Ninety-eight percent of people feel this way. Instead, stay close to that enemy and know him—you will be in the two percent that have a great advantage. Use reason instead of emotion to know your enemy intimately.

In short, survival means not only not coming home dead; for you it may mean not coming home fired or otherwise unemployed. Suck it up. Survive.

Surviving in business also means controlling your anger, rather than letting it control you.

Never show your anger. Tell nothing of yourself.
Pippi Delana, *The Last Don.*

For instance, few words anger people as much as personal attacks on their nationalities. The only outrage guaranteed to spark a comparable rage or anger in the person being attacked is an attack on his family. But anger is a losing proposition whether in business or personal affairs. In *The Godfather*, consigliere Tom Hagen meets movie mogul Woltz (John Marley) at his studio, and seems to react quite matter of factly to Woltz's insults:

Woltz: I don't care how many dago, guinea, wop, greaseball, goombahs come out of the woodwork.
Tom (calmly): *I'm German-Irish.*
Woltz: Well, let me tell you something, my kraut, mick friend.
Tom's final response, later: *By the way, I admire your pictures very much.*

Later at a meeting in Woltz's home, Tom endures more slurs about "olive oil," "guinea charm" and "goombahs," and replies,

Thank you for the dinner and a very pleasant evening. If your car can take me to the airport...

This scene recurs in *Godfather II* when Senator Geary refers to Michael's "oily hair, silk suits," and "your whole fucking family." (See the next Lesson on Respect for more of Geary's comments). Ethnic slurs like these are a request to be shipped one-way in a concrete box to depths unknown off Catalina Island (or Mackinac Island, in our case). We won't even comment on the reference to "your whole fucking family." But Michael shows no anger other than what we can read in his eyes and know from his heritage. He sticks to business. He simply states, calmly and coldly, the details of his new business offer:

Senator, you can have my answer now if you like. My offer is this—nothing.

Both Woltz and Geary get their just rewards for showing such contempt and bad manners. Neither one is killed, either in anger or otherwise. Their punishment is much more effective than what might have been done in anger and much more wise for the business. The Corleones strike at what Woltz loves, and he winds up in bed with the head of his beloved thoroughbred horse, along with a fear that will make him give the Corleone business whatever it wants. Senator Geary winds up in bed with a very recently deceased prostitute and the Corleones know they now own him and will get all the political help they need.

Don Vito and Don Michael are not interested in revenge against Woltz and Geary. Revenge would have been bad for business. Few people in Hollywood could be as powerful as Woltz could be in helping Don Vito. In the case of Sentator Geary, his death would just bring a tremendous amount of heat and investigation, and someone else would take his place anyway. Woltz and Geary are much more valuable just where they are, playing ball with Dons Vito and Michael. Anger? No. Revenge? No. This is business. It's not personal, it's business. What would you have done? What would Sonny Corleone have done?

We would fight and argue, but I never doubted his love. He would do anything for me. But his temper—too much—clouded his reason.
Michael talking about Sonny, *Godfather III*

Never hate your enemy. It affects your judgment.
Michael, *Godfather III*

I was born in Sicily where society and government were the enemy. I could (be) as a slave....without dignity or hope, or I could (be) ....a man who commanded respect.
Don Clericuzio (Danny Aiello), *The Last Don*

One day some of the kids from the neighborhood carried my mother's groceries all the way home. You know why? It was out of respect.
Henry Hill (Ray Liotta), *Goodfellas*

11. Respect

St. Francis Social Club earned for everyone involved from day one. At the start we hired only guys we knew personally. Buddy C. had been with us from grammar school. Fat Tony Torelli had gone to St. Mel with DB. Augie "Buts" Ronzone was a fellow Joker and an Austin High dropout, who got his nickname because he ended every sentence with "but," like he wasn't really sure of anything he was saying—there always was the other side. Paulie Gasparo we had met at Bottoms Up through Chris. He was known as one of the best softball players in Chicago and would show up as a ringer for any team in the area who'd pay him.

Then there was Carlo. Mutual acquaintances had introduced us to Carlo Gianluca in Mategrano's on Taylor Street at a memorial lunch after a funeral. His family had been in the restaurant biz since they arrived, and he was destined to be invaluable at the club, brokering the food deals with Tufano's, Fontano's and other eateries and years later easing our own entry into the culinary world.

Danny Haggs, who used to pour booze at Erin's Isle, was put in charge of our bar. His attitude was a lesson all by itself. He'd always buy a round of drinks at Erin's after you bought one. Then somebody else would buy a round and he'd buy another one. You couldn't spend ten bucks in there. Whether he was absorbing some of the cost or whether the owner was footing it, I don't know, but I'm sure the place made money one way or another. It was always full. Not like these places today that have computers measuring the amount of booze that gets poured to last tenth of an ounce. Treating customers right paid off for Danny. We gave him a raise and he'd seldom be charging anyone for drinks any more.

Two years later, after his probation was over, Chris Cristaldi talked us into taking him in. He hadn't wanted to go back to the Bottoms Up with his brother, and had been working on a delivery truck, while Patti worked in an office downtown. Two card dealers came to us (highly recommended, of course) and helped train the rest of the guys.

These stalwarts of the area had friends and connections that helped get the club rolling as well, though we hardly would have needed it. Think about how much legal and internet gambling is around today. Thirty years ago very little of that was happening. People were as thirsty for prohibited gambling as they were for alcohol during Prohibition in the '20's. Gamblers also knew that they would get a fair shake at our club, they'd be safe, and they could *mangia* on the kind of food they liked. The more they ate, drank, and hung around, the more dough they'd drop.

Our success meant we'd be getting a visit from the Boss real soon. One day Vito called me and said he wanted a meeting and that I should make sure DB was there too. He didn't tell us anything else. We knew not to ask. At the appointed time, a black Lincoln pulled up in front of St. Francis and a couple of underlings jumped out along with Vito. They opened the back door and the Boss got out.

The first time we had ever seen the Boss in person was a night we were coming out of Mother's near Rush Street. It was late and we had been pounding down quite a few cocktails. We were headed over to the Lodge across the street and as we started to cross Division, a Chevy

Malibu sped along in front of us and almost got clipped by a black Lincoln pulling out of the alley. The two guys driving the Malibu jumped out of their car and started to macho it up, like they were looking to kick the guy's ass who cut them off. To our surprise, out of the Lincoln stepped the Boss. He was alone, wearing a shark skin suit, silk tie, and shiny pointy-toed Italian shoes. We had only seen his picture before, but we immediately knew it was him.

The Boss showed no concern as these two goofs cursed and headed toward him. When they were only a few feet away, he simply parted his jacket and rested his palm on the butt of the piece stuck in the front of his belt. His left hand reached into his jacket pocket at the same time.

"Holy shit," was all I could whisper as we stood in a doorway on the south side of the street.

"Are you fuckin' kidding me?" was DB's only reply as we stood rooted to the spot, wondering what would happen next. This looked more like *Gunfight at the OK Corral* than *The Untouchables.*

Though this movie seemed to be unreeling in slow motion, it all probably only lasted a split second. There seemed to be an invisible glass shield in the middle of the street that the Malibu guys hit and pivoted away from when they saw that gun. They jogged back to their car and were gone in seconds. The Boss seemed to smile, got back into his Mark IV and drove away. Our respect for him before had been based on reputation and position. It accelerated to a new level, watching him handle himself. It wasn't the gun—it was the confidence he displayed in what was going to happen that made these pricks turn tail. If they had been drinking, they sobered up on the spot.

Sure, a lot of people are going to say that's fear, not respect. But sometimes the two go hand-in-hand. Even as a young guy, The Boss had a rep as someone not to be fucked with, in large part because of the muscle he provided. Yet he was a guy who still often did his own "heavy work," instead of leaving it all to members of his crew. That might have explained why he was alone that night.

Word also was that the Boss was fair. He made the rules and if you abided by them, you got rewarded. You got to keep a decent percentage of the swag you brought in, you were protected, and new "markets" were offered to you. If you didn't follow the rules, he dished out punishment fairly. He always listened to both sides before making a decision. And we never had any trouble with him.

Later, we'd see the Boss visiting his Chicago Avenue turf and he always made one hell of an impression. His suits didn't come from Maxwell Street, Irv's, or DB's (Uncle Roman DiBruno's place) where we bought our crap; he'd have a year-round tan and there wasn't a hair on his head out of place.

The Boss was also respected because, though he lived in a mansion in the near west suburbs, he gave back to the old neighborhood. If the church or school needed anything, they knew they could count on him. He wasn't soft by any means; he was a benefactor. People in his position didn't have much to do with guys like us though. It was like we were individual parishioners in his flock. That is, until the club started to take off. Now we'd have our first face-to-face sit-down with him.

This must be the way an audience with the Pope feels, I thought, except I'd never met with *Il Papa* either (Today, I don't know if I'd want to, what with a Polack and a Kraut muscling in on what was exclusively an Italian racket for centuries). Though Vito had given us the unofficial go ahead to operate, we knew that we'd have to pay the price sooner or later. We hoped that this was just a negotiating session. DB had the details about how much we were taking in, how we planned to expand, and other details on the club. We were ready.

We didn't need to be. The Boss's methods and words were simple. He got out of the Lincoln, walked over, shook my outstretched right hand with both of his, and said, "Let's go inside and talk."

I guess this is what a big job interview feels like, I was thinking, except I didn't know because I'd never been on one. The Boss was not asking any questions, nor was he taking any resumes. And the personal references had all been checked long before. The interview was short.

"I hear you boys are doing pretty good for yourselves," he said and took a sip of wine that we had provided.

We were puffed up, trying to look calm and tough at the same time, while saying things about our loyalty and respect for him.

"You're from down the Avenue and now you're out west here" he continued. I was thinking, "Yeah, so what, what's the point?" but I didn't say a word.

DB started to confirm what the Boss said but he was not interested. He cut him off continuing in his same mild tone, "Vito tells me that you're good for the neighborhood and that I should sponsor you and keep you under my protection. My insurance is going to cost you. I'll let Vito work out the details."

That was it. He didn't even finish his glass of Spadina, and a minute later he was out the door. We were relieved. We had been ready to plead our case depending on the percentages he wanted, but this meant we didn't have to. We'd only be asked to pay the street tax. We've been figuring on a 20% kickback as part of our operating expenses and Vito'd already been collecting that. Besides, having the Boss behind us meant that if anybody tried to fuck with us, he'd have our backs. It was a good deal all around.

We started feeling pretty good about ourselves. We had been paid a visit from a very powerful man, and we knew we'd arrived. A couple of days later Vito came back in broad daylight with a couple of muscle heads. They held the door open for him while he strolled around the club looking all around the room. I was thinking, "What the hell is he checking for, roaches?" Vito pointed his goons to different spots along the walls in the backroom next to the kitchen, saying, "Put one over there, two over there and two over there." The two Schwarzeneggers left and were back in minutes wheeling in five quarter slot machines.

"This will help all of us earn," Vito mumbled. He was clearer as he said "20% of the profit from the machines goes to me. Keep it separate from the card games. We got them set up so the players will win 70% of the time. That will keep them playing. We'll see how things go, we can always adjust the number later."

We were allowed to run St. Francis's any way we wanted, but we always knew who was in charge. We kept it open twenty hours a day seven days a week to accommodate all the business. We worked in ten-hour shifts, the place being closed for four hours to clean up (that meant getting the money out of the machines in addition to throwing out the trash and wiping everything down.) High stakes poker was in a separate back room on Monday nights. Soon, we were grossing 30 G's a week. We were taking the cash out of there in garbage bags and had to figure out how we wouldn't attract attention. Later we never closed.

Vito did eventually adjust the slot machines after a while so that they were paying out 60% to players instead of 70%. The only thing wrong was that he also adjusted his take to 30% of the profit instead of 20%, so we were actually making less. By this time, we knew our way around a little. I called a guy at Seeburg who got us two new machines and put them in. We would put an out-of-order sign on Vito's machines from time to time so players would have to use ours. When we felt we had earned enough, we put his back in operation so he'd get enough to keep him satisfied.

Vito always picked up the envelope, and when the Boss came around he'd give us a nod as if to acknowledge our role in his operation. He showed us respect in backing the St. Francis Social Club, and we responded in kind.

That is, until years later when the cops knocked the joint over and I got pinched. At that point, we got deserted like we had the plague. But we knew that was the deal. The only message sent down was the one you already know from the omerta chapter, and you can bet I kept my mouth shut. As a result, I got to live another day. You got to respect that.

Lessons in Respect from the Movie Mob

The concept of respect is different in Sicily than in the U.S. of A. In America people might respect those with the courage to stick to their principles even if it means suffering, losing money, or being pushed aside. Many Italians do not respect such a person. We respect the person with the power to impose or defend his principles. Weakness and respect do not go hand-in-hand. Others might disagree with what I do, but they will respect my power to do it. If what I do is good, then I am a man of honor as well.

When Bonasera comes to Don Corleone at the beginning of *The Godfather*, it is not only for justice, but to keep his own self-respect. But he is taught by the Don that true respect goes both ways:

> *...now you come to me and you say, Don Corleone, give me justice. But you don't ask with respect. You don't offer friendship. You don't even think to call me Godfather. Instead, you come into my house on the day my daughter's to be married and ask me to do murder for money.*

Bonasera still doesn't understand: *Let them suffer, then, as she suffers. How much shall I pay you?*

Don: *Bonasera, Bonasera, what have I ever done to make you treat me so disrespectfully.*

In twenty-first century America, if someone murders your wife or rapes your sister the "respectable" thing to do is to call the cops. If you take your own revenge on the perpetrator, you'd better do it fast—while he is still on the scene. You'll probably get off with a light rap. But if you think about it for a day or more and plan your moves, you will be guilty of pre-meditated murder. You might not get the chair or the needle, but you will be punished.

Life and death where our parents came from followed a quite different code for centuries. The rule of law?—Fuhgeddaboudit. The national government was far away and had little effect on the lives of our people. When the national government did do something, it usually hurt us rather than helped us. Call the local *carabinieri* (cops) and you would get help if they were allied with your family. Otherwise, they likely would not interfere. You had only one option to keep the respect of the people in your town—find justice by handling the situation yourself. You avenged the transgression by using your full power against the one who had insulted your family. Anyone who did less was not respected. Though the rule of law has become stronger in Italy today, in many places the situation is still not much different.

Thus our code—the Mafia code—became one that equated violence or the threat of violence with honor and respect. After a while, it sometimes didn't matter whether that violent power was used for good or ill. Americans of 21st Century sensibilities have a hard time understanding that we were reared not only to fear power but also to respect power. And we were brought up knowing that those who were supposedly enforcing the law were just one more enemy gang.

It was with this defensive attitude that most Italians came to America, viewing government and authority as oppressors—bad guys—against whom a respected and honorable person fought. Those with the power to fight against an oppressive government were the respected ones.

Mario Puzo describes how "a true Mafioso" was respected:

His men loved him not only because of his charisma but because he valued honor above all. A true Mafioso

was strong enough in his will to avenge any insult to his person or cosca. He could never submit to the will of another person or government agency and in this lay his power. His own will was paramount. Justice is what he decreed justice to be.
Omerta, Mario Puzo, Random House, 2000.

Committing violence to avenge one's family honor can easily lead to committing violence to salvage your own personal honor or self-esteem. When you come to a new land with nothing and everyone is exploiting you, you have to react any way you can to save your job, your respect, and sometimes your life. See the film *Gangs of New York* –the Irish did the same thing.

When you first arrive you're a nobody and you want to be somebody. In one of the first gangland movies, *Little Caesar*, Rico (Edward G. Robinson) exclaims,

Hey, I can do all the things that fella does and more, only I never got my chance. What's there to be afraid of? When I get in a tight spot, I shoot my way out of it. Why sure, shoot first and argue afterwards. You know this game ain't for guys that are soft. Money's all right, but it ain't everything. To be somebody. To look hard at a bunch of guys and know that they'll do anything you tell 'em. Have your own way or nothin'. Be somebody.

Marlon Brando's prize-fighter character, Terry Malloy, in *On the Waterfront* fails at the same goal when he says with a mournful wail

I coulda been a contender, I coulda been somebody.

Equating power with respect and honor is supposed to be against the polite tenets of modern society. But look a little deeper and you'll notice the popularity of the vigilante or revenge movie. When a cowboy, a criminal, or even an average citizen wants to exact revenge for a wrong, the public is usually with him.

You can understand respect even better by looking at its opposite— disrespect. "Dissing" a person is one of today's cardinal sins. In a scene near the opening of *Godfather II*, Nevada Senator Geary (G.D. Spradlin) meets with Michael and his associates concerning a Nevada gambling license. Geary is not willing to give the Corleones the license on their terms. This is a decision Michael could respect—after all, it's only business. He then would have had a decision to make. Do I have the power to force the senator to meet my terms? If not, should I accept the senator's terms? In either case, both he and the senator would have left with their respect and honor intact. It's just business.

But this outcome is never in the cards. Hints of a lack of respect are given at the very beginning of the movie when the Senator mispronounces their last name, "Corli-on" in front of the crowd. He even pretends to mispronounce "Vito" calling him Anthony "Vie-toe (Michael's son's middle name and of course, Michael's father's name). Nobody's that stupid, not even a senator. Once he meets with the family behind closed doors, he shows his true face.

First, the senator insults Michael by speaking down to him,

> *I intend to speak to you...maybe more frankly than anyone...has ever talked to you.*

...then with disrespect,

> *Ya, well, let's cut out the bullshit. I don't want to spend any more time here than I have to.*

...then threats,

> *I intend to squeeze you.*

...and ends with ethnic slurs and insults to the family.

> *I don't like your kind of people (in this) clean country with your oily hair, dressed up in those silk suits, trying to pass yourselves off as decent Americans. I despise your masquerade...and your whole fucking family.*

This scene whets your appetite for what is going to happen to the senator. If there are different levels of hell, as a famous Italian described them hundreds of years ago, you know that this insulting bastard who has no respect or honor is going to wind up in the lowest level, and that Michael is going to send him there soon. You don't know how it will happen, but you respect Michael's power to make it happen.

It's Geary's penchant for kinky sex that brings him down. He winds up in a whorehouse, where the prostitute servicing him suddenly and inexplicably dies. Police and news reporters will surely be on the scene in minutes, but Tom Hagen, the Corleone family consigliere, materializes at that moment and offers to make sure this all goes away—an offer that Senator Geary so clearly cannot refuse, it is not even spoken. Now he'll need to do anything the family wants. A little respect would have gone a long way.

Even Fredo looks for respect by going outside the family and gives information to those who are against the family.

> *Take care of me? You're my kid brother and you take care of me? Did you ever think about that? Send Fredo off to do this...to do that. Let Fredo take care of some Mickey Mouse nightclub somewhere. Send Fredo to pick somebody up at the airport... It ain't the way I wanted it. I can handle things, I'm smart. Not like everybody says, like dumb. I'm smart and I want respect.*
> Fredo (John Casale), *Godfather II*

Fredo thinks that respect is gained by words, not deeds. He's wrong. Your boss respects what you accomplish, not what you talk about. Your spouse respects what you do for her, not what you promise. People respect what their elected officials do, not what they promise in their campaigns. Countries respect the deeds of other countries or the power used by them, not their treaty and negotiation talk. Instead of respect, Fredo ends up with the opposite from his younger brother,

> *You're nothing to me now, Fredo.*

Michael lets him live only until their mother dies to save her the pain of losing another son. Do not show someone respect and they may turn against you unnecessarily.

> *I say to all of you I have been treated this day with no respect. You will not give, I'll take.*
> Joey Zasa (Joe Mantegna) tells the "Commission" in *Godfather III.*

How far you need to go to earn respect only you can answer. But you'd better be ready with the answer. Sometimes your test comes in a split second—say someone suddenly confronts you and your woman. Other times it comes hidden—a co-worker wants you to turn on another. Or you may have years to pass or fail your test, such as when a corporation involves you in slowly killing people.

For us, growing up on the West Side of Chicago meant being ready to fight to keep respect. If a guy was taking abuse, everyone would watch to see if he would step up and take on the wiseass who was punking him out. One of the older guys on our street even organized battles for his amusement. He would instigate some trouble between a couple of kids and then make sure lines were crossed. Unconsciously, he was playing an ancient role, testing the youngbloods to see who made the grade.

If you fought—if you stood up and showed you wouldn't back down—you'd gain respect, even if you took a beating. Some guys would talk a good game, but when confronted, would wimp out and immediately lose respect.

Passing these street tests was more important than most tests we took in school. Many straight shooters passed these tests right along with those who didn't follow the conventional path. I like to think they work for companies that spend millions to treat their customers with respect, especially those who call in to complain. These companies regard a dissatisfied customer as an opportunity, not as someone to insult. Often the complainer is just looking for a little respect.

A smart restaurateur gives a dissatisfied diner a free dinner if he views the diner as sincere in her complaint about the food. That diner is more apt to become a repeat customer because she was treated with respect, than to refuse to return because of the food. But at least she won't leave disgruntled and tell all her friends about the shitty meal she had. Or worst still, threaten to sue because of food-poisoning.

Lawyers in the U. S. make tens of millions of dollars every year from real, valid legal disputes. But they make hundreds of millions because one party (or both) in a suit disrespects the other. Divorce suits are some of the most difficult. The people involved know each other so intimately that they often find it harder to treat each other with respect. There's a break even chance you'll be in a divorce. If you treat her with respect, it may mean thousands of dollars in your and her pocket instead of the lawyers' pockets. Do you ever wonder why the United States has ten times as many lawyers and lawsuits than other modern countries? It's a lack of respect.

Assert your rights respectfully and you might get upgraded to first class. Whine, complain, disrespect the ticket agent, and you may be waiting a long time and wind up sitting in the back row (which doesn't recline).

Be respectful when dealing with our Outfit and you'll go home happy. Be disrespectful and you may be reclining permanently. Respect—if you will not give, we will take.

You can't trust nobody. Not Billy, not the family, not your father.
That's right son, not even me. You can't trust nobody.
Pippi Delana (Joe Mantegna) to his son, *The Last Don*

12. Trust

"I can just feel when I'm gonna have a winner." The high-pitched voice I had never heard before came from one of the tables at St. Francis's at about 4 a.m. one night. I had been doing some counting and was getting ready to lock up in an hour or two. "Yeah," I thought, "just what every mark thinks. Keep bringing them in, boys." A bit later I see this pint-sized guy talking to Chris. They seem to be arranging a little advance, and I figured I had it right, another sucker for the night.

The first chance he got, Chris came over with the guy's chit. "Carmen DeFavio, $1000" it said on the slip, and Chris whispered, "Hey, Bobby, catch this new guy's patter for a while. It might be worth something."

Within a few minutes, I had all the covert intelligence I needed to realize two things: number one, this guy was losing his ass at our table, just as I thought; and number two, the winners he was talking about were the horses he was riding at Sportsman's Park, not the poker hands he was hoping to get.

When the club closed that night, the little paesan-jockey was still there, so I gave him all the welcome mat I could. He didn't want much to eat. I guessed that figured, so I started thinking about the shortest women we had on call. Then again, maybe he'd prefer a tall blonde, who he wouldn't ordinarily attract. We wanted to keep Carmen happy. Besides the money he was losing at the club, those winners he was talking about intrigued me as well.

In the next few weeks, Carmen became a regular at St. Francis. We'd break his balls regularly concerning his size, and he always took it and gave back as good as he got. He seemed to be a regular guy, and somebody you could trust. And he must have been making good dough, because he was losing it regularly but kept returning. He seemed to want to become a friend and I was all for encouraging that. I wasn't sure what the upshot would be, but knowing a guy who was an insider at the track had to have an angle. And his luck was so poor at our tables that I figured he must be having better luck on top of the horses.

Sure enough, Carmen continued bragging about all the winners he was bringing home and when we checked the papers, we saw that he usually wasn't bullshitting. I decided that the next time I heard "I can just feel when I have a winner," I was going to discuss those feelings with him.

"How can you just feel when you have a winner, Carm?" I asked.

"Listen, you got a dog or a cat? If you do, you know his moods and his daily activities. And he knows yours. When you come in the door, your dog is right there. He knows you. But if the mailman tries to come in, he'd better be wearing a steel cup. Your dog don't know him. Horses are the same way. They tell me how they feel. They talk to me."

"They talk to you! What the fuck!" DB who had been eavesdropping chimed in.

"Hey, listen, I don't mean they actually talk. But, for instance I've ridden this horse a bunch of times, Dixie Commander. He tells me how he feels the morning of a race, tells me if he's feeling' friskie, if he had a good night's sleep, stuff like that. And me and the trainer talk and I get a good idea if I'm understanding correctly what the horse is saying to me."

"And what did Dixie Commander tell you last time you rode him?" asked DB.

"Well, that's why I remember him specifically. He was telling me he felt great." Carmen stopped.

"Yeah, yeah, and so what the fuck happened in the race?" I blurted, getting impatient.

"Actually, he came in second."

"Well, what good is….." I started out, but Carmen interrupted me

"But he ran his fastest time. It's just that he went up against a great horse. I mean, if I could have put some dough on him, I would have."

"Okay, Carmen, let's talk again about this," I said and told Chris behind the bar to keep Carmen happy through the evening.

DB and I had our late evening beef *sangwich* that night and talked it out. What Carmen said seemed to make sense, but I wasn't so sure. Only, I wasn't even sure why I wasn't sure.

"Do you really think his horses are telling him something?" I asked, sounding stupid even to myself.

DB thought he had it figured out. "Most of that is bullshit, or should I say horseshit. Sure they're talkin' to him. But then every one of these dwarfs is having a gab fest with his ponies. Carmen's got other inside information and this is his way of telling us. And if he's willing to bet on a horse, I say that's the sign he knows something is going down."

"Then why did that horse come in second?" I asked.

"He's just telling us that this ain't no sure thing. Don't bet the house on his say-so. But it's obvious he wants us to put some money down for him. And if he's pretty sure, I'd say we could put a small wad down too and see what happens. You know how it is. We don't want to draw too much attention and push the betting line too much out of whack."

"Sounds good," I agreed, "but this is getting fucking complicated. I'd like to go with a sure thing, not some bullshit about this horse talking good. Can we trust this guy?"

DB said not to worry. We'd bet small at first and see if things worked in our favor. We didn't have to wait long because the tiny paesan had been piling up a bunch of markers at the club as well. There was also some talk that he was popping greenies to keep his weight down and might be into the nose candy and that he owed some people for that too. We told him we'd put some dough down for him and give him 20% of our winnings if he could line us up with a sure thing. He said he'd have a pretty good idea if he had a winner by the time the horses head out of the post parade and go toward the starting gate. He'd let us know with a signal.

We settled on this scam: when they parade the horses out, we'd stand alongside the fence. If he held his whip or riding crop, whatever the fuck you call it, high in an upright position as he rides by, we should get down. If not, we just pass.

In past years we had gone to Arlington or Hawthorne a lot, but since the club opened, we had hardly been at the track. Now, we started taking turns going to Sportsman's when Carmen was riding, which was most days. After only a couple of visits, DB happened to be there when Carmen held his whip up for the first time. We had decided to bet light so he put a hundred across the board (win, place, and show) for each of us, besides some dough for our little friend. Six hundred bucks would not move the odds or arouse suspicion, and we wanted to see how sure a thing this was. Sure enough, Miss KatieO, the horse he was riding, won. We got excited as hell at the prospects of having developed a new business venture.

Carmen showed up at the club late that night, and we gave him his share and encouraged him to give us more of these "tips." We also agreed to clean the slate on some of his gambling debts if he kept coming up with winners. We invoked the law of omerta on all of us as part of the deal too. Race track betting is tricky, as is all sports gambling. If you start telling every Tom, Dick, and Tony what you are doing, they'll want to get in on the action and pretty soon the odds are driven down to nothing. What's worse is that officials and pros at the track will sense something's wrong with the betting line. Small action won't affect the line that much. When the track officials get suspicious, all bets are off (so to speak).

As the weeks went by, Carmen came through most every time that he gave the signal – usually with a winner, and sometimes just in the money. In the meantime though, his gambling debts kept right in line with his track winnings. We had to straighten him out a couple of times as he kept piling up IOU's and was late with the juice. He decided to go for a bigger score to take care of all the people waiting in line for a piece of him. Exactly what was going on and how it was being managed— was it the trainers? were the other jockeys involved?—we didn't know, and frankly we didn't care, as long as we got results. Then again, do you remember Francis, "The Talking Mule"? I do. Maybe Carmen did have a special gift.

The Sportsman's meet was drawing to a close in a couple of weeks, when one day Carmen came in and told us he was riding a long shot in the 5th the next day, and he thought he could bring the horse in.

We got to the track the next afternoon in plenty of time for the 5th race. We both wanted to be there this time, so we let Chris and Tony run the club. They were a little amused that we had the bug for the track again, so much so that we'd both be out of the club. The 5th was a claiming race, and we were there to claim a big part of the prize. When OurPappaJoe first came out, the odds on him were 50 to 1. As Carmen pulled past, sure enough, the whip was straight up. Joey went up to the window and loaded up, betting 800 to win and 800 to place. By the time the race went off, the odds had dropped to 30 to 1.

OurPappaJoe started in the middle of the pack, but as track announcer, Phil Georgeff, called out "here they come spinning out of the turn," he was right there and Carmen was whipping the shit out of this horse as they headed to the finish line. We were going fucking nuts as he was neck and neck with the horse next to him. At the finish line we couldn't tell who had won. Now we had to wait for the photo. After what seemed like an hour the results were posted—OurPappaJoe, the winner, paying out $62 to win. We collected around 32 G's that day, 24 large for the win and 8 for the place bet. There was one hell of celebration that night and when Carmen came to the club, he got his end (a little over 5 grand). With this and the 10% of the purse he got for bringing home a winner he was able to pay off most of his debts.

As we've noted more than once, Carmen was a shitty gambler. He had the disease and couldn't stop. It wasn't long before he was again up to his asshole in debts with us and with guys on the outside as well. He even took a beating from somebody after leaving the club one night.

One day Carmen came in and told us he wanted to set up one more hit and move on. We felt like this thing was probably running its course anyway and the meet was almost over, so we agreed and got ready for one last score. Besides, like I said, you can only bet so much and move the odds so much before somebody starts getting suspicious. And you can't really share the knowledge of your good fortune with many people.

Almost a week went by before the little guy quietly announced at the club one night, "Tomorrow's the day." He had something solid. "There's no need for a signal this time," Carmen said, "I'm going to be riding Ancient Mariner in the last race. He's very fast, and he'll be the favorite, but he's not going to win. Bet the house on Awesome Deduction. Get me down and I'll meet you guys tomorrow night for the split."

The sun was dipping in the sky that next day as DB went to the window and laid down 3 G's to win and 3 more to place on the four horse, Awesome Deduction. This was the first time we were betting on Carm to lose and it felt a little strange. Looking back now, I can see that our mob films are filled with characters who place trust in each other, such as the way Don Vito and Don Michael trust Tom Hagen; but it's also filled with those who "don't trust nobody." Now we were putting our trust in this gambling degenerate of a jockey, but something in the way he looked at us or up to us told us to trust him. So we even got a little exotic and combined our sure thing in a trifecta key. DB put Awesome Deduction in first and hit the "all" button for second and third, meaning any combination of second and third finishers would win for us—another $1800 well invested, we hoped.

When he got back with the tickets we walked down to the finish line and lit up a couple of Cubans. We watched as the horses rode out and thought we saw Carmen give a little nod of recognition in our direction. We were confident, but still we were holding our breath. As the race started, Awesome Deduction went off at 6-1.

Awesome Deduction was either second or in the lead from the get-go. He looked great and we were feeling like we had the world in our hip pocket. As they made the far turn and headed for home, Carm's horse, Ancient Mariner was in about 3rd or 4th along the rail and we figured he was doing a good job holding the horse back but making it look good. Suddenly the horses ahead of Mariner drifted off the rail opening up a "dream trip" (as jockeys call it) for the favorite. He took off and in seconds was challenging Deduction for the lead, charging hard on the inside. Mariner was gaining fast on Deduction. They were dozens of yards away and people jumping up in front of us, but later I remembered seeing Carm grimacing, trying to hold Mariner back. At least I imagined I saw it—maybe I just recognized his cap and the yellow and green colors he wore.

In the few seconds it took for them to reach the finish line, a dozen thoughts shrieked through my head. What is going on? It looks like

Deduction can't hold on. Mariner has too much. What is Carm doing? Is this a "Sting"? Is the joke going to be on us? Are we just imagining it, or is Carm really trying to hold Mariner back? Is he fighting him? Suddenly, a fact many people ignore—racing is a dangerous sport— became obvious. There was Carmen falling off Mariner and bouncing down near the rail. It looked like he was being trampled as the bulk of the field passed by him and over him, and a jockey-less Mariner crossed the finish line.

Before we could make a move to cash our tickets, the automatic inquiry light went on and we had to wait out the judges upstairs. Did they see him hold the horse back? Will they hold up the money? Will they know some kind of fix was in? Five minutes later, the light went off and the board announced that the final results stood. We learned later that if something wasn't kosher there wasn't much they could do anyway, except investigate and prosecute.

I don't want to say we forgot about Carmen in our excitement in winning, but we saw paramedics with stretchers and medical stuff taking Carm off the track while we were moving down to collect our dough and while Deduction went to the winner's circle. (A.D. paid $14.20 to win and $6.60 to place, while the trifecta we had covered paid $460 on a dollar, making the total winnings a bit over 35 grand, not bad for a day's work.)We tried to get down to the paddock to see how he was, but by the time we got there a trainer told us they took him to Loretto hospital. We asked the guy about Carmen's condition, and he just gave us a weird kind of smile and moved away from us. Maybe he thought we were news reporters or something. The other jocks were packing up pretty fast too.

"You didn't have to try to kill yourself for us out there," DB said after we arrived at the hospital, walked into his room, and saw he was all right. He wound up with a couple of bruised ribs, a broken arm, and a lot of scratches. "We would have taken care of that for you." The nurse looked at us as if we had dropped in from another planet but Carm just laughed. When she walked out we gave him his envelope, which he told us to put under his pillow for the moment.

"Listen, I wasn't scared of you guys, I figured you could see what happened. At least I hoped so. But I knew there was a good chance I'd be facing the State Racing Commission anyway, and incurring injuries might help get me off the hook. I mean a jockey's not going to risk his life for a lousy bet, is he?"

True to his word, Carm left town after the meet and that's the last time we saw him. A few years later we got word that he surfaced in New Jersey. He was tried and convicted for race-fixing. Apparently his scam there would have worked too except he sent a young guy to the window to pick up his substantial winnings. When the cashier got suspicious and asked the guy for I.D., it turned out he was underage. After a few questions, the kid gave up Carm. He got banned from racing for life.

I don't know when he got out of prison. In the 90's a jockey's body was found floating in a creek in California, and we got a sinking feeling for a moment until we saw the name was Ron Hanson, famous for race-fixing. Carmen never surfaced, though. Maybe when it was his turn they couldn't identify the body. Maybe he's in another hole in the Jersey Meadowlands. Or maybe he just retired. If you're reading this, Carm, give us a call.

Lessons on Trust from the Movie Mob

We knew enough not to trust Carmen immediately and to be more wary as the stakes got higher. But when we started to win, we started to trust him more and more. True trust can exist, but it is as unusual as true friendship. Michael Corleone's feeling toward Tom Hagen in the lesson on loyalty was a rare example and maybe is the exception that proves the rule:

> *I'm trusting you with the lives of my wife and my children*
> *and the future of this family.*
> Michael to Tom Hagen, *Godfather II*

Another exception is Marlon Brando (supposedly playing Carmine Sabatini but actually continuing his persona as The Godfather) making the following statement. He is believed and trusted instantly to keep his word even though this is a comedy and a caricature.

> *Every word I say is by definition a promise.*

Carmine Sabatini, *The Freshman*

We have tried to make it clear to our crew that in most situations wiseguys, even "made men," can trust no one. They are loyal first to their business, their family, and their own interests. This point is made by a father teaching his son when young Cross (Jason Gedrick), tells his father, Pippi Delana (Joe Mantegna), about his friend Billy, in *The Last Don*,

> He's a friend pop. He's like a brother to me. I gotta trust somebody.

His father answers…,

> You can't trust nobody. That's right son, not even me.

For a long time the traditional requirement for becoming "made" in the Mafia was to commit a murder. Why? Because committing a murder was proof positive that you weren't an undercover cop. Furthermore, the odds are you'd never rat on your brothers because they had the goods to put you away too. Once you murdered, you were "trusted" because you didn't want to spend the rest of your life in a cozy federal flat at best, or fried at worst.

Even this rule has changed in the last few years though. The U.S. and Italian governments now offer immunity even to murderers in order to get convictions of other kingpins. Look at Gravano. He committed 19 murders. Still, he got immunity by giving up Gotti and other bosses. The Feds talk about us using immoral means. Nineteen murders and Gravano was appearing on TV bragging about his murders and writing books.

The judge in Gravano's case called his decision to testify, "the bravest thing I have ever seen," according to Peter Maas's book, *Underboss*. The judge wondered why Gravano was called a snitch or a rat, because he turned in criminals, asking whether we would apply the same name to someone who turned in a terrorist bomber. Brave? I don't think so, Judge. He turned on his own people to save his skin.

If the participants in "our thing" ever did trust each other (doubtful), that trust has eroded to nothing. Sonny, the mob boss in *A Bronx Tale*, says it all. When Calogero (Lillo Brancato) remarks,

That's a horrible way to live (without trusting anybody)

Sonny answers,

For me, it's the only way.

When the same boy tells his father, Lorenzo,

You're wrong, Sonny trusts me,

his Dad confirms what Sonny has said.

*That man can't trust anybody. The sooner you know that
the better.*

Most of you civilians would be better off following the same advice.
If you trust too easily it shows how separated you are from the reality
of life. You see trust as a virtue, so when you say you trust someone it
sounds like a noble quality in yourself. But listen to me—in the vast
majority of cases you use it as a weakness, an excuse, a copout. When
you trust someone, you are setting up to blame that person, not yourself,
when things go wrong.

"I trusted my financial advisor." "I trusted my stockbroker," you'll
whine when you lose your shirt in the stock market.

You should have been watching your own wallet. And you'll whimper
when you catch your old lady stepping out and finding someone else to
fill her needs, "But I trusted my wife." Maybe you shouldn't have been
working all those long hours or hanging out somewhere else.

I went to the police like a good American,

says Bonasera (Salvatore Corsitto) to Don Corleone at the beginning
of *The Godfather* after finding that the two men who beat his daughter
received no jail time. He trusted the system and got screwed.

Trust does exist. But it's a special quality like a rare gem or a good
friend. And it can seduce you into giving up "your thing" to someone
else. Or it can kill you if it is placed in the wrong person.

All this stuff doesn't mean anything. Money—this doesn't mean anything without trust. I have to be able to trust you with my life.
Ace Rothstein (DeNiro) *Casino*

Ronald Reagan was a good *capo di tutti capi* of the United States in the 1980s. When he was asked how we can trust the Russians to keep their end of a treaty, he answered, "Trust, but verify." He said it diplomatically, but his words really meant, "Don't trust! Verify!" I'm sure in private he told his crew something like, "Don't trust nobody, especially those bastards."

Care and caution are not the first concepts that jump to your mind when you think of "this thing of ours." But they were essential for the most successful movie don of all time, just as they are in real life. You cannot be careless about concerning whom you trust:

Women and children can be careless, but not men.
Don Corleone, *The Godfather*

You can view that statement as sexist if you want. But if you got this far in the book, why quibble now? The Don is making the point that a person dealing with life and death issues cannot afford to be careless; those with lesser agendas can. If you think you are not dealing with life and death issues if you work in an office, think again. We all are.

I hope you don't mind the way I keep going over this Barzini business,
Don Vito Corleone, *The Godfather*

Carelessness is unthinkable to the Don—it's a matter of life and death. He warns Michael that Barzini will set up a meeting with someone Michael absolutely trusts—that is the person who will betray him and assassinate him. Yogi Berra might have said it if he had had the chance: "If you can't trust someone you have absolute trust in, who can you trust?"

The answer, you already know: "You can't trust nobody."

Therefore, you have to be careful in all your actions and relationships. Do you trust your company pension program, the U.S. government, social security, your lawyer, your doctor? Be careful. Use caution, check things out yourself, consider all the angles, get a second opinion.

> *The difference between winning and losing is being able to read your opponent. That's why I'm still here. A number of times the only thing that kept me out of a satin box was I could size up the other guy, maybe a half second quicker than he could me.*
> Carlo, *Suicide Kings*

I know it was you, Fredo.
You broke my heart. You broke my heart.
Michael, *Godfather II*

13. Betrayal

"The IRS called today. They want you to bring in your books next week," announced Tommy Numbers on the phone one evening. He was our Polish accountant from the neighborhood. His last name had so many z's and y's and letters I don't think I've even seen before that we used to call him "Letters" but changed that to "Numbers" when he started doing our books. Before I could even think of a reply, he reassured me, "Don't worry, I'll be there, I've got you covered, I'll take care of it."

We had been running St. Francis's for a number of years, but Tommy had W-2's still being issued to me at The Music Man, and he had DB making good money at one of Roman's clothing stores. Of course we were making a lot more than that from the club, but how would the fucking IRS know that?

"So, what do you think is going on?" I asked when we sat down with Tommy for a Maxwell Street Polish the next day. His office was downtown so I figured I'd meet him more than half way.

"Who knows for sure?" said Tommy, "Could've been some sore loser put them on to the joint. That's all it takes. Then the Feds start paying attention to the money you're spending. They can't prove how much you're making, but they can try to track what you're blowing it on. Then they ask you where it came from. Bunch of fags, they come at you from behind."

I was surprised at first that anyone who came to the club would betray us. We were careful who we let in. Our clientele was mainly Italian, but we had almost every nationality at one time or another. We only discriminated on the basis of who vouched for you and "Who brung ya?" as DB would often ask. But I guess it only took one guy who had it in for you.

Tommy went with me to the IRS audit and had enough answers, showing the auditor the phony earnings I had and saying I also won a lot of money at the races and in Vegas, and like maybe I didn't always keep good track of it. He showed we were reasonable and we compromised and paid some back taxes. Surprisingly, they didn't ask anything about the club. I guess they made their numbers and moved on to the next file. Apparently we weren't big enough fish yet for them to come after us with full tackle.

"We were lucky this time," said Tommy when we met with him over some Buona beef sandwiches the next afternoon. "Besides our little cup of coffee with the IRS, Mike "the Rug" got popped early yesterday morning. Coppers busted into his apartment with a warrant at 5 a.m., and him dead asleep. Hauled out a truck load of hot goods. If they've got inside information, they're gonna have their radar stuck on you. You're gonna need some watchamacallit, a front, a phony business, a plausible way to explain where the money is coming from if they come snooping again. If they can't nail you directly, they'll try to get you for the taxes or for lying about the taxes or something under oath. Doesn't matter if your last name is Capone or Madura."

Tommy set us up as a corporation, M&D Enterprises. M&D was supposed to be in three businesses: travel agencies, real estate, and restaurants.

The travel agencies existed on paper only. We didn't really own or operate them, but we made deals with a few agencies in the burbs. They were happy to arrange group or individual trips to Vegas mostly, but sometimes Atlantic City or the Bahamas too. They'd get us a lot of cheap deals and we'd pass these on to a ready-made clientele who already gambled with us. On our books though, we'd be selling what might have been a $249 trip, for hundreds of dollars more, sometimes thousands. The difference was the profit from the club which would provide a paper trail if the IRS wanted to look. A guy gets a brochure for a trip to Vegas for $1199, including all kinds of special services (which usually don't occur and he knows it), and we give him a discount down to $299. He pays in cash and we issue a receipt for the $1199 we supposedly took in. Sometimes the trip was actually free as we learned the ins and outs of getting guys comped. No doubt Tommy did more with the travel end that I never even understood.

I knew even less about how the real estate operated, but here we were dealing with tens of thousands of dollars, instead of hundreds. There was more room for creating imaginary cash flow. All kinds of un-real transactions flowed through the company on paper, and after a while a lot of actual ones as well. People in our neighborhood didn't usually advertise when they sold their houses. This could bring in the wrong element if you know what I mean. They sold privately and a lot of it went through our books, whether we had anything to do with the sale or not. Tommy didn't take those accounting classes at Circle Campus for nothing. At least we were getting a little payoff from U. of Illinois/ Circle, which had eliminated a lot of the original Italian neighborhood close to downtown and replaced it with cold concrete.

It was the third leg of M&D Enterprises, that I got hooked on, the restaurant business. Tommy had us buy out one of the remaining Italian spaghetti and pizza places on Taylor Street. The former owners continued to cook the pizza, while Tommy cooked the books. We enjoyed it so much we opened a second and more serious *ristorante* called Napoli's in Highwood. It seems as though other entrepreneurs like us had been doing the same thing—this was long before Taylor Street was getting hot again. The middle of the North Shore burbs was the perfect location. Money was spilling out of guys' pockets in the "greed is good" 80's, but they had nowhere cool to go, unless they went all the way into the city. There's miles of rich but boring suburbs, and suddenly in Highwood is this little strip of Italy, with pasta to match.

We didn't even care if we saw a profit, as long as lots of our real money flowed through the restaurant books. We paid Simone Pavone, a native of Sicily and one of the best chefs in the city, to run the joint. He made Napoli's do pretty well on its own merit, but on paper it was really dynamite. It must have looked like the most successful pasta palace in the state.

On weekend nights people were usually waiting in the bar, the foyer, and outside. Instead of hoping the waiting clients would build up Napoli's take at the bar, the girls would circulate taking orders for half-price wine and drinks, and Simone and a waiter would come out with complimentary little bowls of his tantalizing minestrone for everyone who was waiting. At the same time his operatic voice would sing out, booming across the restaurant, "Minestrone for the Sicilian soul," a phrase that wasn't lost on us.

We had our own fun with the restaurant. DB paid a visit to one of these restaurant critic-guys at the *Trib* one day. He offered this guy a meal he couldn't refuse—I mean he really did. He got Mr. Gourmet to tell him his favorite foods and dishes. When the guy showed up at Napoli's, Simone was ready and gave him the meal of his life. We also sent a case made up of some Montepulcianos, Brunellos and some Calabrese wines for good measure and a case of EVOO from Sicily to his house. Mr. Reviewer was no dummy—Napoli's got 4 forks out of 4 in his next column (well deserved, mind you) and Mr. Critic went away happy instead of with a serious heartburn.

All three businesses were successful on their own, but Tommy's enhanced accounting methods had them making astronomical profits. As far as I was concerned this could have gone on forever.

Sixteen months later, though, everything changed, including my career path. I didn't find out why until later. I was sitting in the back of St. Francis's one evening when four cops came to the door. When they identified themselves Fat Tony, following our longstanding instructions, didn't hesitate in letting them in.

In the old days, if some do-gooder did go to the law, Officers Boylen or McCann would call to warn us. Then when they did their duty and conducted their so-called raid they found a few old-timers playing a friendly game of gin rummy. We had wheeled the slot machines out the back door and stored them in a garage down the alley. These two upstanding Irish cops would pick up their envelopes afterwards and by the next day the slots were back, and it was business as usual. I don't call them "upstanding" lightly. They kept our neighborhood safe.

This time it was different. We had had no warning, and Boylen and McCann were nowhere to be seen. About twenty players were in the club and it was obvious they weren't octogenarians from a nearby nursing home. There was no money on the tables, just chips. But the slot machines were just sitting out there, like if you had five naked hookers in your den and your wife came home unexpectedly. What're you gonna say? They put everyone against a wall and pulled everything out of our pockets and tagged it all. I had fifteen grand on me, whereas DB wasn't in the club. One of the players, who owned a car wash, was holding eight grand.

When the fuzz asked who was in charge, I stepped up. They knew anyway. Sure enough, they gave me an itinerary of my movements from my house to the club, from the club to the track, to Rush Street, to my girlfriend's apartment, back to the club, etc. for the last month. They took out the slot machines and busted them up Ness-style, after first taking the money out. We eventually got back every dime that they took from us, but we never saw the money from the slots again.

I was in the holding cell downtown (cops always said, "we're taking you downtown") for about a day and a half and actually made some money running a card game in there. When DB finally came to bail me out, he found it had been taken care of and I was on my way home. I knew Vito or the Boss had my back. They told me what lawyer to use, and he arranged a plea bargain. A month later the judge agreed and I went into Cook County Jail. Ninety days later, Bobby Madura walked out and had to start a new life.

St. Francis Social Club had had a good run but now was no more. I could accept that. Things change, the neighborhood was "undergoing ethnic displacement," politicians sometimes put pressure on, and nothing goes on forever. But for my own curiosity I wanted to know exactly why we got busted at that particular time. After all, the cops could have closed down the club any time they wanted to start an investigation, but too many were getting a taste, and they got few complaints from the public. I started to think maybe it was a situation where they were pressured to take action. Maybe society in general had changed. People want "sin and vice" one minute and then want to show how holy they are the next. In the end, though, I figured it was some cheese-eatin' rat, but I didn't know who.

Then one day I got a call from Gino Spoeri, the lawyer who had gotten us the plea. "I just got a call from Dave Halloran, who's representing Chris Cristaldi. Did you hear that Chris got picked up for dealing drugs?"

"You're shittin' me," was the first thing out of my mouth. We had kept in touch with the guys who worked the club and had no warning that anything was going down.

"Yeah, apparently it wasn't the first time. I've got a source in the prosecutor's office who says he's been at it off and on since he worked at his brother's bar. The only reason he hasn't been picked up before is that he's been working with them, providing information on any, shall we say, questionable activities in the area. But he wouldn't stop dealing and the Feds stepped in. I thought you'd want to know."

There it was. Betrayed by Chris Cristaldi. Betrayed by our own overconfidence in how well the club was doing, we had hired him because we knew him—or thought we knew him. He was going to do whatever it took to get off the Avenue, whether it meant counterfeiting or drugs....or becoming a rat. We had thought that Chris and Patti had been too stupid to cop a plea ahead of time, after getting caught with funny money. We should have known those suspended sentences meant they hadn't copped a plea, they had made a deal. They had gambled their lives for a chance to pluck that money tree. And they had given us up when they got caught.

Ten years before we might have gone to Vito, or we might even have done the deed ourselves. Now we would just wait. Chris was behind bars and we'd see what happened to him. You're angry any time someone you trust betrays you, but that's what betrayal is all about—mistaken trust. I had been curious about why we got busted, I had wanted to know, and now I did.

Life Lessons on Betrayal from the Movie Mob

Because of previous successes, we had started thinking we were smarter than we were. We had started getting careless. We had been setting ourselves up for betrayal.

> *Without trust, you can't have betrayal.*
> Sammy the Bull, *Witness to the Mob*

He ought to know. In the real world, though, it hurts not to be able to trust anyone. But as strong as your emotional inclination to trust someone close to you is, that is all the reason more not to trust them. Being betrayed by a good friend or relative will hurt much more than being betrayed by a stranger or acquaintance. Avoid trusting and you take away any chance of betrayal. Regarding the people you know, the decision is yours alone. Just don't come back later and whine, "…but I trusted him or her. They betrayed me." You are the one who trusted— you'll have to take the rap for your mistake.

Michael Corleone follows President Reagan's dictate, "Trust, but verify." He wants to live in a world where he could trust his own brother, but he knows his brother's weaknesses and watches him carefully. In *The Godfather* Fredo betrays the family's interests by taking Moe Green's side during the meeting in Las Vegas.

> *Mike, you don't come to Las Vegas and talk to a man like Moe Green like that.*

Michael actually gives him another chance, but in *Godfather II* he finds out that Fredo has been talking to Johnny Ola and has been trying to get a piece of the action for himself. Michael never fully trusted Fredo so he is not surprised. Still, this is his own brother—he has a right to feel betrayed and shows it,

> *I know it was you, Fredo. You broke my heart. You broke my heart.*

Each lesson in our book strikes to the heart of the code. That's because one lesson cannot be completely isolated from the others. They are all vital organs that cannot fail. Without business we have nothing. Without the law of omerta, likewise, we fall apart. We must command respect and honor or why would we want to live. Likewise, trust and betrayal are such strong qualities, they are like life and death. If you betray your woman, your friend, your family—you are worth nothing.

If you don't have honor or if you aren't worthy of respect, you will be found out—when the rubber hits the road, when the shit hits the fan, when the going gets tough. Ever wonder why there are so many of these cliches? It's because the importance of honor, respect, loyalty, and trust need to be emphasized in so many ways—they're that important. A person can skate for years, but eventually everyone has his moment of truth. Will he be loyal or will he betray?

> *The Feds, they see the guy…they always smell out the*
> *guy with no parameters. They move right in. This whole*
> *RICO statute bullshit is designed by the rats for the*
> *rats.*
> John Gotti (Assante), *Gotti*

Some wiseguys are expert in gaining trust and later betraying:

> *I know guys who could talk the Virgin Mary into posing*
> *for a centerfold and make her think it was her idea in the*
> *first place.*
> Carlo Bartolucci (Christopher Walken), *Suicide Kings*

You've also got to know where your information comes from so you won't be the one who is betrayed:

> *I come from out there where everybody out there knows*
> *everybody lies. Cops lie. Newspapers lie…but one thing*
> *you can count on, word on the street. That's solid.*
> Carlo, *Suicide Kings*

You will hear people say that Mafia movies romanticize this thing of ours. I say, bull. How romantic is betrayal? To see how strong the emotion of betrayal is, look at just how romantic Nicky's (Joe Pesci) reaction in *Casino* is when he finds out that Ace (Robert DeNiro) has gone over his head to the bosses to try to remove Nicky from Vegas.

> *Get this through your head, you Jew mother fucker, you.*
> *You only exist out here because of me. That's the only*
> *reason. Without me, every fuckin' wiseguy still around*
> *will take a piece of your Jew ass. Then where you gonna*
> *go? You're fuckin' warned. Don't ever go over my fuckin'*
> *head again, you motherfucker, you.*

Nicky is a bit miffed you might say. That's because he feels betrayed.

The heat would've been the first thing you noticed.
Hell is hot. That's never been disputed by anybody.
You didn't go to hell, you went to purgatory, my friend.
Paulie, *The Sopranos*

Psychos who kill for pleasure, cannibals, and degenerate
bastards that molest and torture kids go to hell.
Tony, *The Sopranos*

But, what a wicked world it is that drives a man to sin.
Don Clericuzio, *The Last Don*

14. Religion

You've been with us from burning down our first garage, to our
success on the Avenue twenty years later, to my going to jail. My
ninety days dragged by, but they did give me more time to reflect on life,
family, and religion than I had since I was a *bambino*. Sister Annunciata
at OLA had been right when she said I should be careful or I'd wind up
in jail some day.

My three months were spent in Cook County Jail at 26th & California.
I'd seen the prison movies, with the strip searches, gangs, fights, drugs,

improvised weapons, constant noise, inedible food—they're all true. I
had visited guys there before and had talked to them after they got out, so
I thought I was prepared. I wasn't. I figured I could do ninety days, but I
sure didn't do them standing on my head. The number of non-Hispanic
and non-Blacks in the jail seemed under 5%. On the other hand, I can't
complain. I had it better than most. I had money to buy food at the
commissary and was able to bribe guards to buy more than my share and
give some of it to the toughest group inside to protect me.

The ninety days gave me time to think. Was it worth it? What would
I tell my daughter about going to jail? How am I going to earn when I
get out? Those three months might have had a bigger influence on my
life than anything else, I don't know. Guess I'd have to consult a shrink
or a priest to find out, and I don't think either one is going to happen
real soon. Besides being violent on occasion, guys in jail spent a lot of
time reading the Bible, including my cell mate. That made me think
back too.

My sentence gave me time to conjure up an event that happened
before everything else you've just read. When we were kids we got
the big picture about religion, the church, and God from our parents of
course. Pictures of Jesus and Mary and crucifixes were hanging all over
the house. Growing up Catholic subjects you to violence under the best
of circumstances. Passion of Christ? I'll say. It was more like Torture
of Christ when you look at the details. Don't tell me *Reservoir Dogs* is
brutal. Try getting a knife stuck into your side and then hanging on a
cross with…..well, you know the details.

But on the crosses in our house, Christ looked more like he was
sleeping, just resting his head. Or the way my old man used to look on
Christmas morning, nursing a hangover. In her bedroom, my mother had
a very nice symbolic, silver cross, no body on it or anything. But it was
a special crucifix with a secret compartment containing holy water, a
candle, and other such necessaries a priest could use if somebody in the
family was ready to check out. Ma was ready for anything. Meanwhile,
you felt like you were supposed to genuflect every time you went into a
different room.

Our mothers would have gone to Mass every day if they could have,
and on many mornings they did. Sundays go without saying, and there
wasn't any of that new Saturday afternoon, Saturday evening bullshit

either. You'd go on Sunday like it's always been. Our mothers would do stations-of-the-cross, novenas, rosaries, you name it. If it was some kind of church ritual, they had it down cold; if the church had a ceremony, they were first in line; if sacraments were on the program, they were attending.

We learned by example from our fathers. They usually made it to church only on the big holidays like Christmas and Easter. They'd work in a few Sundays too when the mood was right. A lot of their teaching was "do as I say, not as I do." Fat chance that was going to work. At ten and eleven years old, though, we were hardly questioning what was going on about religion. Nevertheless, we found out the hard way, it was about life and death.

In those days Catholic parents would send you to Catholic school mainly to make sure you got the religion. The fact that you were going to get discipline from the nuns was taken for granted. Sure, you'd learn a lot too, but I think that came in a distant third to religion and discipline. We attended Our Lady of the Angels on Hamlin and Iowa. And we spent the rest of our lives remembering it.

Our parents truly believed that once the good sisters got a hold of us, we would turn into decent, God-fearing, respectful, young men. Yeah, right. Number one, these nuns hated boys. Their order was the BVM's or Black Veiled Monsters. They'd crack us with rulers or just with the back of their hands. If they didn't have a weapon on them, they would grab you by the face and squeeze your cheeks together hard. They could get a good grip and drag a kid by the cheeks across the room and out the door into the hall – impressive! We usually deserved the physical abuse we got, but taking hits from the BVM's just inspired us to pull more antics. It wasn't like we'd go home and tell the old man. You know what he'd do and it wouldn't be pretty.

We did our best to be creative in our attempts to get back at them. For instance, we had to go to Mass every day of the week—I mean the entire school had to go. That was the smiley-faced "Have a nice day" start to your morning in the Catholic '50s of Chicago. The penguins paraded us in and our whole class would have to wait until everybody was lined up in front of their pews. The nuns had these little metal clickers, kind of like a metal frog I once had that would click twice when I squeezed it. Sister would click her clicker and everybody would genuflect at the same time, like a military drill, and we'd file into the pews. This went on for each class as you walked in.

Sister Clare was our teacher and our goal was to make her cry. One day my friend Buddy C stole the clicker from Sister Clare's drawer in the classroom before we left. "Where's my clicker?" she mumbled to herself as she put her hand in the drawer. "Where is that clicker?" we heard a second time, with what seemed like a note of panic. "I can't find my clicker," she exclaimed loudly the third time.

Finally we heard Joey Bartolomeo from the back of the room, "Between your legs." Joey was a master at saying things just loud enough so most of us could hear it but the teacher couldn't. Old Clare's "Where's my clicker?" question stayed famous in the neighborhood, even after the tragic events of that year.

She couldn't spot her clicker (let alone lay a finger on it), so by the time we had to leave there was nothing she could do. When we got into the church that morning, it was Buddy's turn to run the show. As classes started to file in, he started clicking before they got to their places. First and second graders were going into the wrong pews. Third and fourth graders were bumping into each other. Fifth and sixth grade guys were banging into the girls line on purpose, just to create more havoc. Kids were genuflecting all over the place before their teachers gave them the signal. Even some of the other nuns were obeying the wrong clicks or were off schedule on their own clicking. So much for the holy, solemn atmosphere—after what happened in class and now this, we were laughing so hard we were doubled up on the kneeler.

The nuns, of course, were really pissed off. As usual Buddy didn't have enough sense to know when to stop. He was making too much of a good thing, and after the 5th or 6th click, Sister Canice, who always had the evil eye out, caught him and dragged him out of the church by his hair in front of the whole school. I guess the life lesson in religion that Buddy learned that day was "Don't fuck around in church."

One of Buddy's other coups came about a month later. Some of the nuns would put the biggest jerk-off kid in the front seat so they could keep an eye on him. Probably something they learned in nun school. It was not smart—especially when it came to putting Buddy up there. Buddy had been working on a plan to tie the cords hanging from the end of Sister C's robe to the lectern when she wasn't looking, something he really couldn't have done from anywhere else in the room.

One day the class was remarkably quiet after lunch, and Sister Clare was reading out loud some poem about Hiawatha or something from her book on the lectern. She wasn't looking up at all. Buddy turned around to us to give us the "shh" sign and he started to tie those cords to the metal pole that held the flat part that she had the book on and was leaning on. When he was finally successful, he gave the signal to his accomplice, Johnny DiPasquale in the back of the room to cause a commotion. Johnny pulled teacher's pet, Lucille Guarino's, hair and she screamed. Sister C. seized on the opportunity to attack just as Buddy figured. As soon as she made her move, the lectern got pulled down along with part of her penguin suit, including the headpiece. She was in tears and so were we, but ours were tears of laughter. The bonus was that this was how we discovered that Sister Clare was a brunette.

We lived for pulling off shit like that. I remember both of those events clearly because they took place in the fall of 1958, and because they both involved Sister Clare, who was my teacher then. Life and death and religion weren't always fun and games. Most people who lived in Chicago at that time remember why.

It was a Monday, December 1, 1958, the first day back in school after Thanksgiving. I was still sleepy from lunch that afternoon and was dozing off in class. Our Lady of the Angels was an old school, two stories high, with a basement. There was just one fire escape in the whole school and no smoke detectors, sprinklers, and other safety stuff that buildings have now. Catholic schools didn't have those rules about class size back then either. Maximum class size was determined by how many kids Sister could control and how many chairs could be brought into the room. Some rooms had 40-50 kids jammed in.

Around two o'clock on that day, Sister Clare went over to the door. It sounded like there was some commotion out in the hall. Knowing Sister, we waited with the strange glee we felt when she was about to yell at some outsider. She probably knew we were sleepy from lunch and it was safe to turn her attention from us. But she didn't open the door at first. We saw the smoke start to seep from under the door and smelled it at the same time. This time I was glad Sister was the kind of person who moved quickly. I guess other nuns thought it was just burning leaves or something and kept teaching. She opened the door, felt a blast of heat and smoke, and knew we had to get out of there. (Man, I'm glad she wasn't tied to the lectern that time.) She told us to file out in an orderly manner, but within seconds kids were rushing out the door. It was obvious the fire was spreading quickly. I didn't read about it again till years later and found out the fire had been smoldering for a half-hour maybe. Panic set in as kids were pushing and getting knocked over as they headed for the exits.

When I remember the scene now, I imagine myself flying down the stairs barely touching them, running through smoke, dodging or darting around kids, like Willie Galimore heading downfield, but all in slow motion. I finally hit the door, got outside, and spotted my cousin Joey (his DB moniker didn't come until the Chicago Avenue Jokers pinned it on him years later) standing across the street. We hugged and although we didn't say it then, we must have known we were lucky to be alive. Kids and adults alike were screaming and we saw some jumping from the windows on the second floor. It was a choice of sure death by burning or inhaling smoke, or hoping for just broken bones by jumping.

Most of the 89 kids and three nuns who died were on the second floor, where there were only four high windows in each classroom. Some of the small kids couldn't even reach those windows to jump out. Later we heard that Sister Davidicus who was in charge of the key to the back fire escape had left it in the convent that day so everybody had to go out the front door. I guess they kept the fire escape locked because punks like us would mess around with it if it were unlocked. When the firemen got there they got the ladders up to the windows and started pulling kids out and dropping them; there was no time to use the ladder steps. Kids were jammed in the windows trying to get to the ladder. Father Joe and another priest were helping the firemen.

We wanted to help too somehow, but adults kept pushing us back across the street. The whole building went up fast. A lot of the kids who did make it out got burned up bad, spent time in the hospital, and were never the same. The fucked up thing about it is that we heard later that Sister Seraphica kept her 5th grade class in their seats, telling them that "we're going to pray the rosary." I guess the heat was so intense when she opened the classroom door, it blew her back. But lots of kids from that room got out. The ones who stayed and prayed didn't. I guess Sister thought that Jesus was supposed to come in there in a fireman's suit and get everybody out. They found those 27 kids dead in the back of the room. Like my Uncle Frank said at the time, "I woulda said 'My ass!'

and jumped out the window." I heard later that that's what a girl named Charlene did. She was about 11 years old, but she knew the only way out was that window. She went against the word of Sister Seraphica, fought off people trying to hold her back, climbed on the ledge, and jumped. Others followed her. I hope that DB and I would have had the balls that girl had.

Screwing around in school was never the same after that cold December day. And we listened a little more intently when the priests talked about religion and life and death. The priests, with Father Joe leading the charge, did the best job they could holding things together. He had regular meetings with our classes to help us "keep the faith," and a lot of people hung their hat on the hope that these "little angels" were up in heaven with God. Man, I hope that's right.

I can't tell you that the experience had a big effect on what I did later with my life, but I know it had some kind of effect. I tried to pass down that effect to guys in my crew who had never been through something like that. They needed to think about the bigger things. Just because you're supposedly not always on the right side of the law doesn't mean you're any different from anybody else as far as life, death, or religion. Our guys didn't always go to church, but they were believers. Being Italian, we remained believers too, even if we didn't always follow the rules. We knew that God might have you check out at any time—no one knows the hour. If we had any shot of getting into heaven we wanted to take it. We wanted that edge just in case.

Lessons on Religion from the Movie Mob

You can't avoid religion if you're going to feature Italian culture in a Mafia movie. Yet seeing an old don's wife crossing herself with her rosary beads is one thing; actually dealing with what goes on inside that don's mind is another. Remember the last scene in *The Godfather* when Michael's godchild is being christened in church while his crew is assassinating his rivals. Baptism and murder are intertwined in cut after cut. What does it all mean? What's going on in Michael's head?

One of the things unique about *The Sopranos* is that it touches on some of these subjects—things the general public has always wanted to know but was afraid to ask. What do the children of a mafioso think about their father's occupation? How much do they know and when do they know it? What rationalizations does the wife make? And how do they all feel about religion and God? Are mobsters afraid of burning in hell for their sins?

Actually, the answers are simple because mob guys are no different than you. Are you not afraid of burning in hell? Oh, excuse me, I suppose you lead a perfect life, right? You don't fib on your income tax, you don't take supplies and other company stuff home from the office, you don't pad your expense account, you wouldn't screw around with the new secretary if nobody would ever know.

Why do *you* do that shit? I'll tell you why—because you figure if you do it in small enough increments you won't get caught. Would you pull off bigger stuff if you thought you wouldn't get caught? You tell me. Do you stick to small stuff because you have such a great conscience or are so religious? Or is it because you don't have the balls to do bigger jobs? Are those lying, killing tobacco executives worried about burning in hell? Maybe they are, but probably not any more than me and you. Quit thinking you're so damn different and superior. You're not.

Unfortunately religion and sin are closely related in most people's minds. Religion should be more tied to good deeds and the family and how you treat your friends and strangers. My associates and I, and our families, think about religion no differently than you do. We wrestle with it and debate it, maybe more than you do. Each person's attitude toward religion is his own. If any disrespectful jamoke is ready to cast the first stone, he better be without sin, or I'm going to stone him.

In *Godfather III,* Cardinal Lamberto (Raf Vallone) tries to convince Michael to confess:

> Cardinal: *When the mind suffers, the body cries out....I hear the confessions of my own priests here. Sometimes the desire to confess is overwhelming and we must seize the moment.*
> Michael: *What is the point of confessing if I don't repent.*

In *The Funeral* Ray (Christopher Walken) rationalizes to his wife Jean (Annabella Sciorra) after he has just ordered a hit on the guy who he thinks killed his brother:

You wanna get deep on this shit. All the Catholic scholars say everything we do depends on free choice. At the same time, they say we need the grace of God to do what's right. Now follow that Jeannie. If I do something wrong, it's because God didn't give me the grace to do what's right. Nothing happens without his permission. If this world stinks, it's his fault. I'm only working with what I've been given.

Paulie Walnuts of *The Sopranos* worries about how things are going to turn out for him when he gets to the Pearly Gates:

Father Felix: *Your problem's a spiritual matter.*
Paulie: *Maybe, but irregardless, I shoulda' had immunity to all of this shit. I shoulda' been covered by my donations.*

And Paulie tries to instruct Christopher (Michael Imperioli) after Christopher has had a near-death experience:

Paulie: *Purgatory – a little detour on the way to paradise.*
Chris: *How long do you think we gotta stay there?*
Paulie: *Now, that's different for everybody. You add up all your mortal sins and multiply that number by 50. Then you add up all your venial sins and multiply that by 25. You add 'em together and that's your sentence. I figure I'm gonna have to do about 6,000 years before I get accepted into heaven, and 6,000 years is nothin' in eternity times. I can do that standin' on my head. It's like a couple of days here.*

And in *A Bronx Tale* the young kid, Calogero, goes to Confession because he feels guilty after lying about what he witnessed when a man was killed in the street:

Calogero: *Bless me father for I have sinned. It's been one month since my last confession and these are my sins. I*

missed Mass on Sunday twice. I lied about witnessing a
murder once. I ate meat on Friday once.
Priest: *Wait a minute, can you back up a little bit and say
that again?*
C: *I ate meat on Friday once?*
Priest: *No, not that one, back up a little more.*
C: *I lied about witnessing a murder?*
Priest: *Yeah, that's the one. Do you realize what you
said?*
C: *It was only once, Father.*
Priest: *Do you know what the Fifth is?*
C: *Yes, father, I know what the Fifth is. The Fifth is that I
refuse to answer on the grounds that I might incriminate
me.*
Priest: *The fifth commandment!*
C: *Thou shalt not kill.*
Priest: *That's right. Now I want you to tell me what hap-
pened.*
C: *No, father, I'm not tellin' nobody nothin'.*
Priest: *Don't be afraid, my son, nobody's more powerful
than God is.*
C: *I don't know about that, father. Your guy's bigger than
my guy up there, but my guy's bigger than your guy down
here.*
Priest: *You got a point. Five Our Fathers and Five Hail
Mary's for your penance.*
C: *For a murder rap? That's not bad, father.*
Priest: *What did you say?*
C: *Bye, father.*
C reflects back and speaks in the background in the voice
of the older Calogero: *It was great to be Catholic and go
to confession. You could start over every week.*

Sure, there are some crazy murderous fucks in organized crime.
They are wild men who seem to have no concept of religion or sin. And
you've seen them depicted in a number of movies. But the rest of society
has them too. Most of us are interested in business and try to avoid trouble

whenever possible. We're soldiers in the army of life, we scrap for whatever we can get. Most of us didn't start with the connections or education to be able to sell stock options for millions of dollars while the company is destroyed. So maybe we collect on the insurance while the company is destroyed by a suspicious fire. We are small potatoes compared to big time corporate swindlers. Are they worried about going to hell? Why should we be any more worried?

> *Soldiers don't go to hell.*
> Tony, *The Sopranos*

You can have whatever opinion you want about the religion and morality of what our Mafia movie characters (or real life guys for that matter) do. But "irregardless" you have to admit that we live in the moment. Shakespeare gives us about an hour—

> *Life is but a walking shadow, a poor player who struts and frets his hour upon the stage and then is heard no more.*
> *Macbeth*

Anthony Quinn's character, on his deathbed in *Gotti,* gives us less time:

> *This whole fuckin' thing only lasts five minutes.*
> Neil Dellacroce, *Gotti*

In any case it's short. Ask anybody older and they'll tell you—when they were young it felt like it was going to last forever. Now they feel it's all going by very quickly.

> *Time, that's the real hit man.*
> Cozzamara (Ignazio Pappalardo), *Johnny Stecchino*

My last lesson for you is simple. It's so simple that it's an overused cliche that soon goes in one of your ears and out the other. Advertisers tap into our unconscious with it —"Just Do It!" "Go for the gusto!" and "Go for it."

But the fact that it is an often repeated cliche doesn't make it any less true. Appreciate your family and friends, they'll be gone all too soon. Do the things that are important to you today, time will run out on them all too quickly. Don't sweat the small stuff. Very often…

> *Happiness comes from knowing less.*
> The Don, *The Last Don*

I'm not saying you shouldn't make plans for the future too—you probably should. But enjoy making them and enjoy putting them into effect. Don't just suffer through them to get to some far off goal. You'll find out that struggling to get the goal is where the fun is—reaching it is secondary. The journey is more important than the destination, as they say.

When the Feds finally shut the club down and I was incarcerated, I had the goal to get out and be free. But ironically, that's when I first realized I could think for myself and make something out of every day I was behind bars. Later, when my "good behavior" got me better conditions, I started writing this and was even allowed to see movies. When I got out, of course, I knew I could get all the films I wanted. By the time I started writing *Minestrone for the Mobster's Soul*, I knew its publication wasn't what would make me happiest. Happiness came each day I worked on it. I hope the same is true in your "five minutes."

EPILOGUE

One thing that hadn't changed was that drive along Lake Michigan. Oak Street Beach still had the sand, the water, and the sun-bathers, though traffic moved a lot faster now and you really couldn't see much over the concrete wall. The high rises that backed the other side of the drive were unchanged, their long shadows not arriving on the beach until later in the day. More importantly, the habitues of Chicago's best known strand hadn't changed either. The same dancers, strippers, and stewardesses lay out working on their tans in the late morning and early afternoon sun. Their blankets staked out the spots they had last week and last year, and they took turns putting lotion on each other's glisteningly moist brown skin.

Or maybe these were the daughters of the women we remembered. Granddaughters? Let's not think about it. Whereas we once would have been helping to apply the protective, enhancing oils to those smooth backs and soft crevices, now we usually wound up watching. Still, I could only look out the window and smile. Life had been pretty good. Tommy Numbers had done a decent job in making our investments pay off (except for that Lucent Technology tip he gave us, for which I felt like doing a number on his head).

Napoli's had finally closed. Tastes changed. It would have needed an overhaul inside and out and a new re-launch. Instead, Carlo opened up his own restaurant south of Milwaukee and named it after himself. Napoli's chef Simone opened up a new Napoli's in the northwest suburbs. After a trip back to Sicily, Carlo decided to import wine and invited me into his business.

I still had my full head of brown hair, using just enough Grecian Formula to leave a little gray around the temples. DB, never getting into that bullshit, was more white than gray. Still, we had run into an old friend, Jennifer and her gal pal Laura at the Snake Pit the night before, and they said they'd be at the beach. Doubtful, but it was worth a shot.

As we drove up and down the undulating Lake Shore Drive overpasses that cross Addison, Belmont, and then Diversey that particular morning in '07, Joey was still wasting his 8-speaker system listening to sports talk, trying to find the Cub score. He switched to Dave Kaplan at GN (WGN), but still no luck. We had been working on the book for about a year, collecting the quotes you've just read from our favorite films and examining what we could learn from them.

The stories and the lessons were just about finished, but now a second part of the book—the list of movies—would have to be added.

We continued to argue as we drove. Should *On the Waterfront* be included? If so, it had to be close to the top. We agreed it had all the necessities, what with Brando fighting the mob, but we thought that it wasn't totally mobbed up. When we saw it again, we realized it was. Who played the best Capone? For that matter, who was the all time greatest mob movie actor? Who were the top ten? The top twenty? Where do we put in TV movies, or series such as *The Untouchables?* Where does *The Sopranos* fit in? Have we seen all the mob films that are out there? How many are there? There were numerous alleys we had to run down.

As if on cue, the theme from *The Godfather* beckoned me to my cell phone. It was Jennifer, the blast from the past whom we hadn't seen for some time until the night before at the Pit. She really was going to be at the beach, just like old times, and wondered if we were coming by. By this time we had just passed North Avenue and were practically yards away from her. But we were also six lanes and two barriers away. Parking and walking over would be more than a few minutes.

"Hi Jenn, this is Joey," my alter ego said, snatching the phone. "We gotta take a rain check. I just got a call from the Boss and we've got a job to take care of. We'll hope to run into you again at the Pit next Friday."

"Okay. Bye. Be safe," she said according to DB when he gave me the phone back. Jennifer was someone who had an inkling about who we worked for back in the day, and had always seemed excited by it. Although we hadn't talked to any "Boss" in years, we were only too happy to let her imagination continue to exaggerate the dangers we might be facing. "What the hell do you think you're..." I started.

DB interrupted, "There's always next week. I've got her number now on caller ID. The book's what we should think about."

It was my turn to interrupt, "Well, think about it while you're driving. We should hit New York sometime this month," I said all ticked off. "And watch for the kids when you're backing out."

"Okay, Clemenza," DB answered, catching on even to this obscure Godfather reference immediately. We both knew we had another mission. We had new challenges. Jennifer would have to wait, and so would Carlo's wine importing business. We'd have to go to the mattresses,--well, at least the couches. We'd have to find a safe house and hole ourselves up with VCR's and tapes, DVD's and players. We'd need to write down every mob film we could think of and scour the internet for ones we couldn't. Then we'd have to find a copy of every film, seeing every old one again, and watching others, like *Ghost Dog* and the British *Gangster No. 1,* for the first time.

And we had to start—no, we *wanted* to start—now. What we came up with follows.

100 ALL TIME MOB MOVIES

INTRODUCTION

Readers Digest has its top 100 TV shows, and *Rolling Stone* Magazine gives you its top 100 songs of all time. The American Film Institute has numerous 100 best film categories, but they've never catalogued mob films. So here is *Minestrone for the Mobster's Soul: Life Lessons from the Movie Mafia*'s top one hundred.

These top 100 films are connected to "this thing of ours," *cosa nostra*, in one way or another. Deciding on the ultimate list meant having to come up with parameters, reasons, and rules to judge what deserves to be on the list and what doesn't. Movies like *The Godfather, Goodfellas, Casino, Capone* and *Witness to the Mob* need no explanation. You know they belong, it's just a question of where to rank them. Other films fall into a so-called gray area. We confronted three major issues in deciding what should be on the list: 1) how organized is the criminal activity that the main players are engaged in; 2) how does the ethnicity of the main players factor into their inclusion on the list; and 3) how mobbed up is the film.

First, if the word "mob" means anything, it means you've got a whole lot of people involved in something. How many does it take to make a "mob." Five? Ten? Twenty? It doesn't matter because here we're talking about *the* Mob, rather than *a* mob. The Mob refers to an organized group, rather than gangsters acting out on their own. So, even though we love our old heroes—guys like George Raft, Bogie, Edward G. and Cagney; and even though there are some great scenes in their movies and some great quotations from them, most of their films got deep-sixed, because they feature criminals who are not tied to any vast conspiracy. That leaves out Cagney's *White Heat, Dillinger,* and hundreds of others, like *Bonnie and Clyde.*

Second, just because a group of guys gets organized and pulls some capers still doesn't mean they're a part of "organized crime," *capice?* According to Undercover New Jersey Police Officer Bob Delaney in his 2008 book, *Covert,* "organized crime" has to be an "ongoing conspiracy." Often the conspirators choose their fellows because of ethnic ties. And often those ethnic ties are assumed to be Italian. This is both true and untrue. There's no denying most of the Mafia was (and still is) of Italian descent and achieved a special notoriety or fame in America. In addition, the movies helped instill this as an ethnic stereotype.

However, plenty of other ethnic groups have been involved with the Mafia and/or have organized their own "ongoing conspiracies" for money and power. In the movies, they qualify for our list if they follow or affiliate with, somewhat at least, the Mafia structure of capos, soldiers, oaths, *consiglieres*, and other patterns of the old order. This means that Irish, Jewish, Black and Cuban mob movies are on the list. Most of their organizations played ball with the Mafia and were part of the scene. And as you already know, we're not prejudiced. Micks or Spics, Hymies or Lymies, it's all the same to us as long as they follow the rules.

Irish gangsters such as Bugs Moran in Capone's Chicago and the hell-raising Irish mobsters of more recent decades, such as the lead characters in the *Road to Perdition* and *The Departed,* are just as much a part of the story as Gotti and Corleone. Dutch Schultz and Meyer Lansky supplied a lot of the brains to the key Mafia families of the last century, and many fictional Jewish mob figures were based on them. *Hoodlum* and *American Gangster* feature some of the many African-Americans who function like the Mob and with the Mob. *Miller's Crossing*, which features Irish mobsters clashing with an Italian crew over a conflict with a Jewish bookie, is a good example of a film that puts it all together. (Interestingly, societal stereotyping, much of it a creation of the movies, has on occasion helped mobsters beat a rap in court—see *Find Me Guilty*).

Then there are individual examples. Even though the lead character in Pacino's *Scarface* is a Cuban drug kingpin, it's on our list because it is a remake of the *Scarface* of the 1930's, which in turn was based on Al Capone's life. You'll find an occasional British mob figure on our list and a few assorted hitmen from other lands. One you usually don't find is the so-called Russian mafia. They show little pride in, or respect for, the parameters—values we believe in—such as the virtues of loyalty, respect, and omerta as set forth in Part I. In the 2007 film *Eastern Promises,* the Russians adopted enough mafia codes—rituals, lessons, and organization—to warrant inclusion. The senseless brutality they displayed toward civilians almost got it knocked off the list.

Furthermore, this book is mainly about the movies. The film industry and other media are not always about reality. A lot of their money is made through stereotyping and exaggerating for entertainment purposes. They usually don't choose to make films about Fiorello La Guardia, Enrico Fermi, Joe DiMaggio, or the hundreds of other great Italian-Americans. In real life, individuals must be judged on their own merits and not stereotyped.

Third, there are films that have a definite mob element in them, but are not totally mobbed up. Some feature kids (*Gloria* and *The Professional*); unions (*Hoffa* and *On the Waterfront*); restaurant owners (*Dinner Rush*); and women (*Bella Mafia, Wisegirls,* or *Bound,* whose lead characters do things Thelma and Louise only dreamed of). These films focus somewhat on areas other than organized crime. Still, in any of these—if there were no mob, there would be no movie.

Naturally, a few films still wound up on the bubble. Quentin Tarantino has at least two great creations that exist in their own world. You want to put *Reservoir Dogs* on the list, we've got no beef with you. We didn't, however. I had a guy tell me I got to put *Pulp Fiction* on the list, but just because a movie has some great hit-men like Travolta and Samuel L. doesn't mean it gets a pass. *Key Largo* goes on the list because Edward G. Robinson runs a mob out of Milwaukee and Bogie (who plays a good guy) runs off an impressive list of Johnny Rocco's accomplishments. You just know this is a made guy. *On the Waterfront* belongs because it's obvious the mob is running things down on the docks and that workers have to kick some dough back upstairs when they get work. The mob element is sometimes visible, sometimes implied, but it is always the driving force. Plus, Brando is the star, and that alone counts for something. These are just some examples and hopefully you get the point. I mean, you can argue a lot of these, but I'm making the decisions, right? You may disagree, but you do so at your own risk (just kidding).

Although I always had the deciding vote, Joey's rankings and opinions were usually not far off from mine. We knew that there would be tough decisions ahead of us and that not everyone would agree. But, sometimes you just got to say, what the fuck, and make decisions.

After the list is a capsule review of each film, usually about a paragraph, and in a few cases two or three. For more complete reviews of every film from the wiseguy point-of-view, see our website, www.

mobmovielessons.com, or get our companion movie review book, *Minestrone for the Mobster's Soul: The Movies.* The short reviews here or the longer ones in the movie book and on-line aren't some Ebert and Siskel discussion of lighting, scenery, cinema photography, and shit like that – just the stuff that the average guy (and a few broads who are into it) want to hear. There's no "Thumbs Up or Down" here either. In our line of work, thumbs are made for breaking.

At the end there's a small list of television serials like *The Sopranos* and *The Untouchables* which have provided great stay-at-home family entertainment over the years.

In our family we've always got guys imitating the actors and dishing out the quotes whether they're accurate or not. We provide a real quote for you at the start of each film review. We've had some interesting discussions with our crew on the rankings and we're sure the list can provide entertaining debates for your crew as well. A fun part was watching guys like Sammy, Tommy Numbers, and Carlo do their Godfather and Goodfellas imitations like they were heading to Hollywood – no chance of course.

This is a list you're not going to find anywhere else. There are some great films, some good ones and some rotten ones. Some were made for TV and some went direct to Blockbuster. Some you've heard of a million times and some are hard to get, but with today's internet you can find almost every one if you look hard enough. Like I said, we didn't give any thumbs, but in the end we decided to rank them—from five gats down to zero. An alphabetical list of some films that did not make the list and are "On the Bubble" for one reason or another follows the top hundred. You could probably come up with more. At the end is the list of the "Dirty Dozen: The Twelve All Time Worst Mob Movies." You might want to see some of these for laughs or with a bottle of Jack Daniels handy. On the other hand, avoid them if you're feeling depressed and have any weapons nearby.

You've already read the Lessons – now it's time to go through the list and see all the movies again. Let the actors and characters teach you the lessons you need to hear. As Hyman Roth said when they cut his birthday cake in *Godfather II:* "Enjoy."

Five Gats: Totally Mobbed Up and Great

1. The Godfather
2. The Godfather, Part II
3. Goodfellas
4. A Bronx Tale
5. Donnie Brasco
6. Casino
7. Scarface
8. The Departed
9. Al Capone
10. On the Waterfront

Four Gats: Totally Mobbed Up and Good / Partly Mobbed Up and Great

11. Gotti
12. Once Upon a Time in America
13. American Gangster
14. Eastern Promises
15. Witness to the Mob
16. Scarface ('32)
17. Boss of Bosses
18. Carlito's Way
19. Bound
20. Hoffa
21. Mean Streets
22. History of Violence
23. Little Caesar
24. The Untouchables
25. Key Largo
26. Bugsy

Three Gats: Very Good

27. The Godfather III
28. True Romance

29. The Last Don
30. State of Grace
31. King of New York
32. Mobsters
33. Things Change
34. Road to Perdition
35. Prizzi's Honor
36. Find Me Guilty
37. Dinner Rush
38. The Client
39. Hoodlum
40. The Juror
41. Ruby
42. Crazy Joe
43. St. Valentine's Day Massacre
44. The Big Heat
45. The Professional or Leon
46. Power of Attorney
47. Miller's Crossing
48. Death Collector or Family Enforcer
49. This Thing of Ours

Two Gats: Good

50. Gloria (Gena Rowlands)
51. Trial by Jury
52. The Purple Gang
53. The Rat Pack
54. Vendetta
55. Bella Mafia
56. Out for Justice
57. Knockaround Guys
58. The Last Don, Part II
59. Wisegirls
60. Murder, Inc.
61. The Brotherhood
62. Brooklyn Rules

63. The Valachi Papers
64. Gangster No. 1
65. Vendetta: Secrets of a Mafia Bride
66. Vendetta II: The New Mafia
67. 10th and Wolf
68. Suicide Kings

One Gat: Fair

69. Federal Protection
70. Hitman's Run
71. Men of Respect
72. Gangster Wars
73. Sugartime
74. Billy Bathgate
75. Wannabes
76. Mob Justice
77. Love, Honor, and Obey: The Last Mafia Marriage
78. Triggermen
79. The Pope of Greenwich Village
80. The Don is Dead
81. Witness Protection
82. The Sicilian
83. The Rise and Fall Of Legs Diamond
84. The Neon Empire
85. The Lost Capone
86. 18 Shades of Dust or Hitman's Journal or The Sicilian Code
87. Bonanno: A Godfather's Story
88. Ghost Dog: The Code of the Samurai
89. The Funeral

No Gats: Poor

90. Portrait of a Hitman
91. Protection
92. Doorway to Hell
93. Getting Gotti

94. Mafia Doctor
95. Honor Thy Father
96. The Hitman
97. Capone (1975)
98. Lansky
99. Mob War
100. The Revenge of Al Capone

25 On The Bubble

Below is an alphabetical list of 25 films that didn't crack the list of 100, either because they weren't as good or were not tied closely enough to organized crime.

American Cousins
Across 110th Street
Bullets or Ballots
Crime Boss
Dirty Deeds
El Padrino
F.I.S.T.
In the Shadows
Kiss of Death
Mister Scarface
One Eyed King
Party Girl
Payback
Perfect Witness
Point Blank
Running Scared
The Big Combo
The Killers (1946)
The Killers (1964)
The Firm
The Last Word
The Mechanic
The Outfit
The Seven Ups
Things to do in Denver When You're Dead

The Dirty Dozen: Twelve of the Worst Mob Films of all Time

1. Mafia Princess
2. Lucky Luciano
3. The Virginia Hill Story: Mistress to the Mob
4. Black Caesar
5. Hit the Dutchman
6. Killer Instinct / Mad Dog Coll
7. Boondock Saints
8. Dillinger and Capone
9. Marked Woman
10. Gloria (Sharon Stone)
11. Black Godfather
12. Chicago Syndicate

Mob Comedies

There are numerous comedy films that are "connected." This list of 30 contains some great ones, some old ones, some obscure ones, and some horrible ones.

1. *Analyze This* (1999)
Robert DeNiro, Billy Crystal, Chazz Palminteri, Joe Viterelli, and Lisa Kudrow

2. *The Freshman* (1990)
Marlon Brando and Matthew Broderick

3. *Bullets over Broadway* (1994)
Chazz Palminteri, John Cusack, Tony Sirico, and Jennifer Tilly. (Directed by Woody Allen)

4. *Midnight Run* (1988)
Bobby De Niro, Joe Pantolino, Dennis Farina, and Charles Grodin

5. *Some Like It Hot* (1959)
Marilyn Monroe, Tony Curtis, Jack Lemmon, and George Raft

6. *Wise Guys* (1986)
Danny DeVito, Joe Piscopo, and Harvey Keitel (Directed by Brian DePalma)

7. *Married to the Mob* (1988)
Alec Baldwin and Michelle Pfieffer

8. *Get Shorty* (1995)
John Travolta, Danny Devito, Gene Hackman, and James Gandolfini

9. *Mickey Blue Eyes* (1999)
Hugh Grant, James Caan, Burt Young, Vincent Pastore and Joe Viterelli

10. *Pocket Full of Miracles* (1961)
Glenn Ford, Bette Davis, Peter Falk, Ann-Margret, Hope Lange

11. *My Blue Heaven* (1990)
Steve Martin

12. *Harlem Nights* (1989)
Eddie Murphy, Richard Pryor, Danny Aiello, Redd Foxx

13. *Johnny Stecchino* (1991)
Roberto Begnini

14. *The Gang That Couldn't Shoot Straight* (1971)
Robert DeNiro, Jerry Orbach and Herve Villechaize

15. *The Crew* (2000)
Burt Reynolds, Richard Dreyfus, Dan Hedaya and Seymour Cassel

16. *The Whole Nine Yards* (2000)
Bruce Willis, Rosanna Arquette and Amanda Peet

17. Analyze That (2002)
Robert DeNiro, Billy Crystal, Chazz Palminteri, Joe Viterelli, and Lisa Kudrow

18. Brother Orchid (1940)
Edward G. Robinson, Humphrey Bogart, Ralph Bellamy and Ann Sothern

19. *Bugsy Malone* (1976)
Jodie Foster and Scott Baio

20. Eight Heads in a Duffel Bag (1997)
Joe Pesci

21. Made (2001)
Peter Falk, Jon Favreau, Vince Vaughn, Sean Combs, and Vincent Pastore

22. Crime Spree (2003)
Harvey Keitel, Abe Vigoda, Gerard Depardieu and Johnny Holliday

23. Robin and the Seven Hoods (1964)
Frank Sinatra, Dean Martin, Sammy Davis Jr., Bing Crosby, and Peter Falk

24. Hoods (1998)
Joe Mantegna, Joe Pantoliano, and Jennifer Tilly

25. *Mafia* or *Jane Austen's Mafia* (1998)
Lloyd Bridges, Olympia Dukakis, Jay Mohr, Joe Viterelli, Vincent Pastore

26. *Mad Dog Time* (1996)
Richard Dreyfuss, Ellen Barkin, and Diane Lane

27. Mob Story (1990)
Margot Kidder

28. *Oscar* (1991)
Sylvester Stallone, Kirk Douglas, and Chazz Palminteri

29. *The Godson* (1998)
Dom DeLuise and Rodney Dangerfield

30. Corky Romano (2001)
Peter Falk, Chris Kattan, Chris Penn, and Vincent Pastore

Others

Mafioso (1962) with Alberto Sordi became available on DVD in 2008.

Mafioso: The Father, The Son (2004) also became available on DVD in 2008.

Wisegal (2008) came out in March of 2008 and should be available on DVD in the future.

See mobmovielessons.com for commentary and review of these films.

Television Serials

In addition to the movies covered by this book, some of which were made for television, five classic mob television series follow. Entire books could be written about *The Sopranos* (and have been), while *The Untouchables* made both Eliot Ness and Robert Stack, American icons.

1. *The Sopranos*

2. *The Untouchables*

3. *Falcone*

4. *Crime Story*

5. *Wiseguy*

Movie Reviews Short Version

Leave the gun. Take the cannolis.
Clemenza

1. *The Godfather* (1972)

The best film ever made? *Citizen Kane*? I don't think so. *Casablanca?* You can make a case. But nothing else comes close to *The Godfather.* It's the foundation for all our lessons. Tom's *loyalty,* Don Vito's *justice,* Tessio's *betrayal,* and Luca Brasi's *respect; family, love, and religion—* everything is here. Even Fredo teaches us about *omerta.* He never rats on anybody, he just can't keep his mouth shut. *The Godfather* is our Bible (Moses might have come down from the mountain packing the DVD for all I know). Guys are quoting it today on the streets, on TV, and in mob circles as if it were playing in movie theatres right now.

The Godfather also set the standard for all Mafia films that followed. Besides its two sequels, nearly every Mafia film made for years in some way plays off *The Godfather. Once Upon a Time in America* is often called the Jewish *Godfather. Goodfellas* supposedly portrays the unromanticized *Godfather*. And *Analyze This* is the best of the many "comedy Godfathers." There's even *The Black Godfather* (see our list of worst mob movies). Not to mention Tony Soprano's crew, who mimic the movie and discuss it so much that Tony says at one point he can't stand to hear it any more.

You know the unforgettable scenes as well as I do: 1) the wedding–we all want our daughters to have a shindig like that; 2) the horse's head in the bed–that's what you call a horror scene, man; 3) Michael taking out Sollozzo and McCluskey– you could cut the tension with a stiletto; 4) Carlo getting beaten by Santino–the best ass-kicking scene on film; 5) the Baptism and murder cuts interwoven with each other at the end—I seldom go to church without thinking about that finale (of course, I seldom go to church, period). Clemenza and the cannoli, Luca Brasi's scenes, the death of Don Vito among his tomato plants, I could go on and on.

The only movie that rivals *The Godfather* is *The Godfather, Part II*. *The Godfather* was nominated for ten Oscars and won three: Best Picture, Screenplay, and of course, Best Actor (Marlon Brando). With Pacino, Caan, and Duvall splitting the vote for Best Supporting Actor, they got robbed by some guy dancing (Joel Gray in *Cabaret*). *Stronzata!* I say.

I make him an offer he don't refuse.
The Young Vito Corleone

My offer is this. Nothing.
Michael Corleone

2. *The Godfather, Part II* (1974)

Godfather II was the first sequel in movie history that was arguably better than the original. So good is DeNiro's performance as young Vito Corleone as he mimics Brando's older character in the first film; so realistic are its scenes of the vibrant immigrant-jammed streets of early New York and the island of Cuba; so fascinating and fulfilling for fans of the first movie are the depictions of the earlier Don Vito and the later Don, Michael—that for a time we had this film ranked in the number one slot.

Godfather II teaches the same lessons as the original, but it shows the darker side of "our thing." Sometimes the values clash with each other. For instance, is it really *justice* for Michael to kill Fredo, who is *family*, for his *betrayal,* when Fredo was just seeking *respect.* In the end we question ourselves and the lessons. *Part II* might be more true-to-life, but we're more comfortable with the clear cut rules set out in *GI. GII* was nominated for eleven Oscars and was awarded six. This was supposed to be Pacino's show, but DeNiro stole it as young Vito Corleone. Few of us on the Avenue, on Taylor Street, or in Cicero figured that *Godfather II* would live up to the power of *GI.* We were afraid it would spoil a perfect thing. Of course, we were blown away (in a manner of speaking) just the way you were.

I'm funny how? Funny like a clown? I amuse you? What the fuck is so funny about me?
Tommy DeVito

3. *Goodfellas* (1990)

What's it really like to be a wiseguy, one of the goodfellas? Characters such as the walking time-bomb, Tommy DeVito (Joe Pesci) and Henry Hill (Ray Liotta) give us the answers in this film based on real events in Hill's book. As much as wannabes in every tough city in America fantasize the *Godfather* characters played by Brando, DeNiro, and Pacino, they really identify more with the characters in *Goodfellas.*

Henry Hill wants to fit in, like we all do. The fear that somebody like Pesci would turn on us—"Do you think I'm funny? Funny, how?"—is almost worst than death. Tommy proves to be a total wacko wise guy, shooting the young kid, Spider (Michael Imperioli), seemingly for sport and then going to work on Billy Batts (Frank Vincent) and digging a hole for him. *Goodfellas* is not a film where people act on codes and principles. On the contrary, it proves the negative side of some of our lessons. Tommy has no *honor* and his career terminates early. Henry Hill's *ambition* and *loyalty* are to drugs rather than to the Outfit and he ends up disgraced. In the end Henry, mimics the original stool pigeon— Joe Valachi—and rats everyone out to save his ass, breaking all the Mafia codes. *Omerta* goes right out the window and it's too bad he didn't go right after it.

Now youse can't leave
Sonny

4. *A Bronx Tale* (1993)

DeNiro directs and plays a lead role (Lorenzo). Chazz Palminteri writes the screenplay based on his own life growing up and from characters and stories he heard through the mob grapevine. He names the main character, Calogero (or "C"), after himself and plays the other main character, mob boss Sonny. You can't go wrong with those credentials in this tale of an honest bus driver trying to bring up his son the right way in a neighborhood run by the mob. C is conflicted by the different life lessons taught by his real father and his "adopted" father, Sonny. After all, his old man's driving a bus, and Sonny's living the life. C learns life lessons about *trust* and *respect* from both of his dads in almost every scene. Lorenzo explains to his son that sometimes you have to compromise some of your principles in order to survive. The key scene in the film involves omerta, and even though this is a Bronx tale, it could have been an anywhere story, especially Chicago.

Fuhgeddaboudit
Lefty

5. *Donnie Brasco* (1997)

Life lessons pour out of every gun barrel and seep out of every bullet hole in this true story about the New York mob. The inner workings of our thing are exposed by undercover agent, Joe Pistone—aka, Donnie Brasco (Johnny Depp). Pistone crosses a thin line and becomes Brasco in a real sense, learning to love "the life" and all the perks that come with it. Lefty (Al Pacino) brings Brasco in as a "friend of ours" and teaches him the ways of the wiseguy. Because we know Brasco's true identity, we learn lessons that Lefty is oblivious to. Pistone plays on Lefty's *friendship* and *trust*. When some of the bosses are suspicious, Lefty shows his *loyalty,* betting his life on Brasco's reliability. He gets repaid by *betrayal*. In *Donnie Brasco*, Lefty is sent for with the implication that he is killed. In real life, Pistone saw to it that Lefty was arrested before the mob could impose *justice* on him. Lefty went down the river instead of to its bottom. Sonny was the one who was whacked for being responsible for both of them.

In a classic scene, Donnie also gives the ultimate definition of "fuhgeddaboudit" to some meddigan FBI guys.

Pistone gave up years of being with his family in order to be one of us. When he was finished so was most of his personal life. Many of the mobsters he was trying to bring down were spending a lot more time with their families than he was with his, and many were no doubt trying to put their kids on a different path. Was it worth it? If you pretend to be something, you begin to become the person or thing that you have been imagining and pretending. If you pretend long enough, you're never the same.

It's all been arranged just for us to get your money
Ace Rothstein

6. *Casino* (1995)

Ace Rothstein (Robert DeNiro) knows everything there is to know about betting lines, odds, slots, and everything else in the gambling—excuse me, I mean gaming—industry. Suckers watching this movie see exactly how their money gets taken and how they're never going to beat the house. *Casino* is based on the true story of how the mob skimmed the casino money from Vegas and how once again, a guy not keeping his mouth shut, can blow the whole operation. Joe Pesci reenacts his *Goodfellas* persona here as Nicky Santoro. Once again Pesci goes over the edge, only this time he's digging holes in the desert. Sharon Stone gives an Oscar-nominated performance as Ginger, Ace's wife.

Don Rickles get clubbed over the head with a phone, James Woods makes an appearance as a sleazy pimp. Alan King, Jerry Vale, Steve Allen, and other Vegas stars play themselves, since like most entertainers they eat this mob stuff up, real or fictional. I could tell that from my jukebox days and from the singers, musicians, and comedians who visited The Music Man and frequented St. Francis's.

If your reaction when you saw *Casino* was "Wow, Vegas probably hates this movie because it shows how easily they take everybody's money," I've got a bridge in Lake Havasu I'd like to offer you. *Casino* was great publicity for Vegas. Most people already know they're losers, that's why they play. Trust me on this—most of my net worth started here.

Lesson Number One: Don't underestimate the other guy's greed.
Lesson Number Two: Don't get high on your own supply.
Frank Lopez

7. *Scarface* (1983)

The fact that Al Pacino's *Scarface* opened during the 50-year anniversary of Paul Muni's 1932 *Scarface,* is just one reason I put this film about a Cuban drug lord on our list. Tony Montana is modeled after Tony Camonte, and Camonte was based on the real "Scarface," Al Capone. All three were obsessed with ruling their mob kingdoms and none of them was going to wait for the boss ahead of him to reach old age.

Director Brian DePalma has more techniques to work with here than they had in the early '30's. As usual, he shows a lot more of the violence, rather than letting you imagine it. The way Pacino chews up the scenery has helped make *Scarface* a classic. And this is one of Michelle Pfeiffer's first films—I wish Tony had spent more time with her. Tony teaches the lessons directly—"First you get the money (*ambition*), then you get the power (*respect*), then you get the woman (*family*)". But Tony has no *honor* and throws it (his *business*) all away. Tony teaches our lessons while famously dropping 218 f-bombs, and has some unnatural whims concerning his own sister. Like Camonte, Montana hits the top fast only to ask, "Is that all there is?" Another lesson, I guess.

My father's on his way out
Low level associate.
We're all on our way out. Act accordingly.
Frank Costello

8. *The Departed* (2006)

I hadn't realized how many years had gone by since the last great mob film until I saw *The Departed* in 2006. Look at the top ten—there isn't anything else since the mid-90's. Maybe *The Sopranos* was sucking up all the creativity and interest. It took Scorsese to break the losing streak. *The Departed* begins with one of the classic plots—two young guys grow up on the mean streets of Boston. Colin (Matt Damon) goes "bad" and joins boss Frank Costello's (Jack Nicholson) outfit. Billy (Leonardo DiCaprio) becomes a cop.

The twist that screenwriter Monahan gives the story is that the mob-connected Sullivan goes undercover in the police force to get inside information for the mob; while Costigan, the cop, becomes a mole in Costello's crime family. You've got to see the film a second time just to keep track of who is doublecrossing who. There are some well deserved shots taken at the clergy as well. Besides Nicholson, Damon, and DiCaprio, Alec Baldwin, Martin Sheen, and Mark Wahlberg show just how thin the line is between Dirty Harry and just plain dirty.

Serve the public, that's my motto.
Al Capone

Nobody who's smart goes hungry in Chicago
Johnny Torrio

9. *Al Capone* (1959)

Al Capone has ruled the streets of Chicago in films since the early 1930's. Some film critics choose *The Untouchables* as the best depiction of Capone's time, but if my vote counts (and I say it does, big time) I'd give it to this 1959 film. Rod Steiger pulls out every acting trick in his extensive repertoire to give life to Capone's brilliantly nasty character. DeNiro was great as Capone in *The Untouchables* but he didn't get nearly as much face time. Like *Gotti,* # 11 on our list, this masterpiece is a largely accurate story of the rise to power of the top boss of his time. Al was ruthless in getting to the top, but afterwards he was all *business,* a criminal genius who took advantage of the stupid Volsted Act (Prohibition) to give people what they wanted—booze, broads, and bets. His business was so well organized (and enforced) that the only thing the Feds could nail him on was a tax rap, after his accountant, Jake "Greasy Thumbs" Guzik, screws up.

Once Alphonse goes to prison, the movie ridicules him and makes him look weak so no one watching it will think well of him. He takes a beating while at "the Rock," and everybody there seems to disrespect him. While getting beaten, he keeps yelling, "I'm Al Capone, I'm Al Capone," like he's gone berserk. Let me tell you—Didn't happen. You can tell the director is playing loose with the facts because he also implies that Al met his final demise in the slammer. We all know that Scarface bought the farm in the Sunshine State years after getting out of the pen. And he didn't die catching a bullet from a rival or from the Feds, but as a result of too much careless fraternizing with the opposite sex if you get my drift.

I coulda been somebody. I coulda been a contender.
Terry Malloy

10. *On the Waterfront* (1954)

Marlon Brando, Rod Steiger, Lee J. Cobb, Karl Malden—in its time, the cast of *On the Waterfront* rivaled that of *The Godfather* made eighteen years later. As with *The Godfather*, almost everybody was nominated for an Academy Award and four of them won, including Brando of course. Judged strictly as a film, *Waterfront* is second only to *The Godfather,* and it's Marlon who makes both the masterpieces they are.

The movie's main characters, the dockworkers and union men, live and work under the influence of the Mob, rather than being involved in it themselves. Brando is Terry Malloy, a boxer who gives up a promising career when he takes a dive so the mob can clean up on some good odds. You have to wonder why his brother (Rod Steiger) didn't look out for him "just a little bit." Lee J. Cobb is the mob guy, playing a character based on Albert Anastasia of Murder, Inc.; while Karl Malden is a priest who's trying to clean things up, but who finds a lot of resistance from guys who won't rat—they all know the consequences if they do.

Betrayal at the hands of your own *family* is one theme of the film, as Terry's own brother sells him out. Otherwise Terry coulda been somebody. More positive lessons come to play when you see how strong *omerta* is in the film. The men are extremely *loyal.* You had to be to work on the docks. Any singing canaries get thrown off a roof to see if they fly. It's just *business.*

What's life about? Go through it as a man's man...suck it up, take the fall, do the time. It's about rules—parameters.
John Gotti

11. *Gotti* (1996)

Somewhere John Gotti is smiling down (or maybe smiling up) at Armand Assante's class, clothes, and demeanor that represents him in this flick that bears his name. Anthony Quinn, a made-for-mobster movie persona, is dying capo, Neil Delacroce. Unlike Gotti, his underlings show how wiseguys are already imprisoned—by their usually dull, occasionally exciting, yet always dangerous lives. Just as in *The Sopranos*, a lot of their self-image is influenced by *The Godfather.* That means that in *Gotti* you have a work of fiction (this movie) imitating a reality (wiseguys in the last quarter of the century) who are imitating a work of fiction (*The Godfather)* that is based on the book by Puzo that supposedly represents the reality of this thing of ours. No wonder these guys are fucked up.

"The Dapper Don" gets ratted out by Sammy "the Bull" Gravano (William Forsythe), who feels he has no choice. John believes his organization will greatly miss his presence, but true wiseguys never really go for all Gotti's high profile stuff. He became kind of a cult hero to the people in New York, a status that helped lead to his undoing. Almost every one of our lessons appears here as Gotti's *ambition* leads him to the top quickly. He first earns *respect* then loses it and becomes bad for *business.* The Feds have a hard time nailing him until Gravano disregards *loyalty* and *betrays* his *trust* and *friendship* and shatters the law of *omerta.* Where's the *justice* in that? Can you tell me it's better that Gotti's gone, and Sammy the Bull is still around? Where are the parameters?

I like the stink of the streets. It cleans out my lungs.
Noodles

12. *Once Upon a Time in America* (1984)

Watch this film in its uncut format, which is three hours and forty-five minutes long, to get the true feel of it. If you watch the shortened version that first played in the theatres, you will be as lost and confused as a lot of people were when it first came out. The producers thought people wouldn't sit through the longer one (and they were probably right), but fortunately with your VCR or DVD player and remote in hand, you don't have that problem. *Once Upon a Time in America* is sometimes nicknamed "The Jewish Godfather," since it traces the rise and fall of the Jewish mob and how kids develop from young street criminals to a Mafia-like organization as adults. *Friendship, loyalty,* and *ambition* lead them to some good earnings.

Here's another cast that's hard to beat. I'd point out that Robert DeNiro and James Woods provide much of the goombah action in two of the lead roles, but I don't know the yiddish for "goombah." A hot Tuesday Weld becomes Max's girlfriend, and William Forsythe is good as part of the crew, but check out the guys who had smaller parts who became fixtures in later mob movies: Joe Pesci, Burt Young, and Danny Aiello. The director was Sergio Leone—who made the great Spaghetti Westerns. Get the extra large popcorn for this one, but give it a chance. You know that "the chosen people" probably have this one on their list ahead of *The Godfather.* You just might too.

The loudest one in the room is the weakest in the room.
Frank

Quitting while you're ahead is not the same as quitting.
Chinese General

13. *American Gangster* (2007)

The mob boss with the biggest profits in New York City in the '70s was not Italian but African-American. Frank Lucas (Denzel Washington), who learned the ropes (and knives and guns) from Bumpy Johnson (see *Hoodlum*), deserved the title of this film. He's a genuine American success story, a company C.E.O. who knows how to organize; a capitalist who figures out how to buy low, cut out the middleman, and sell for huge profit; a businessman, who serves his customers by giving them a better product at a lower cost than the competition. He uses power when he has it and he's willing to share the profit when others are more powerful than he is.

Lucas writes the lesson on risk management, smart enough to know that making 20 million with no hassle is a lot better than making 40 million and being hunted down. He knows how to create and protect his brand. He's got the CIA, the U.S. military, and the New York police force on his team. When he finally meets his match, Richie Roberts (Russell Crowe) an honest cop who organizes a crew to stop him, Frank deals. Today Frank and Richie are good friends in this true story.

You play with a prince, to do business with a king.
Semyon

14. *Eastern Promises* (2007)

The so-called Russian Mafia is usually in a nasty, decrepit world of its own. This film is no exception, but it does emulate some of the traditions: family dinner scenes, oaths, ceremonies, and an unquestioned hierarchy. Nikolai (Viggo Mortensen) gets his stars (becomes a made man) in London, and joins a world of dismembered bodies, 14-year old prostitutes, kidnapping, and drugs; not exactly the world of victimless crime. Viggo went DeNiro for this role, learning Russian and buffing his body big time for a fight sequence in a Russian bathhouse. *Promises* has two scenes that challenge any film for brutality. If your squeeze is squeamish, send her for popcorn.

Look at'm, a rat in a suit
Cosa Nostra till I die
John Gotti

15. *Witness to the Mob* (1998)

This is the John Gotti story from the rat's point of view—Sammy the Bull Gravano, who came out of this thing with a slap on the wrist from the Feds after all the business he'd taken care of—nineteen bodies we know of. The producers put together an interesting lineup—Nicholas Turturro as Gravano and Tom Sizemore as Gotti. They backed them up with more than the usual suspects. Abe Vigoda is Paul Castellano, Frank Vincent (in every mob flick, it seems) is Frankie DeCicco, and Michael Imperioli and Vincent Pastore, both from *The Sopranos* have roles. They make it look as though Sammy had no choice but to squeal in order to save his own skin, but let's be straight—a rat is still a rat. The Gravano-Gotti saga is *loyalty, trust,* and *betrayal* in spades. As far as the government letting a guy off with 19 murders under his belt—that's Fed justice for you.

What are you going to do about it?
Tony Camonte

16. *Scarface* (1932)

In this old classic based on Capone's life, Tony Camonte is the name used instead of Capone. Maybe the producers didn't want to tick off the wrong people since this was being made during and right after Big Al's reign in Chicago. There's some heavy-handed movie-making in a few spots, like when Capone's, uh, I mean Camonte's, lackey almost does a comedy routine trying to use a new electronic device—the telephone, but talking pictures were only a couple of years old at the time.

Paul Muni is great, even with his phony Italian accent. He is quick to sniff out weakness in mob boss Johnny Lovo and send him to the Big House in the sky. Normally, when a guy gets whacked, I like to see the blood and damage. This film makes its point off stage in shadows, without the carnage we see in more current flicks, but, you know, I was all right with it. *Scarface* is filled with lessons and lectures against the evils of organized crime (the producers must have been under orders from the Feds), and it also hints that Tony has it on for his own sister. I guess that's supposed to add to his depravity.

Another key theme is that the government does so little to stop mob violence and control. The movie is subtitled: *Scarface: the Shame of a Nation* and instructs that "you, the public" are responsible for your government's inaction. Yeah, right. Trying to make their moral point, the producers end the film with Camonte catching a hail of bullets from the police. The real life Capone went to the pen and lived in retirement for eight years after getting out, but of course that was over a decade after the film was made.

*...as soon as these tough guys today get caught and they're facing hard
time, they sing better than Pavarotti.*
Paul Castellano

17. *Boss of Bosses* (2001)

If they ever did a movie on my life I'd want Chazz Palminteri to play
me. As Paul Castellano in *Boss of Bosses*, he has the ultimate mob boss
persona. Paul's close relationship with Carlo Gambino from the early
days to the 1980s shows you why Carlo designated him as boss of the
Gambino family on his deathbed. Paulie comes across much like Don
Vito Corleone in his personal life and his attitude toward the business.
He wants to work toward becoming more legit and white collar. He
doesn't want drugs and doesn't want to put a hit out on anyone unless
absolutely necessary. He tries to be reasonable, a don I can respect.
Paulie's methods are successful and the money flows in, but to a guy
like John Gotti, he comes across as too soft. It's Gotti who makes it
personal sacrificing *business* and *honor* for his own *ambition*.

*...emergency rooms don't save nobody. Sonuvabitches pop you at
midnight, when all they got is a Chinese intern with a dull spoon.*
Carlito

18. *Carlito's Way* (1993)

Al Pacino is Puerto Rican drug dealer, Carlito Brigante, who tries to
go straight when his sleazy attorney (sorry to be repetitious), played by
Sean Penn, gets him out of a thirty year term in the can. But the lawyer's
motivation is not just good customer service. He drags Carlito into a
battle with Latino and Italian wiseguys who you'd swear just stepped
off a future Soprano set. In fact, one of them will—Joseph Siravo,
who played Tony's father in flashbacks. Carlito wants to go straight,
but he can't let down his friends and can't resist the effect his past has
on him. *Carlito's Way* shows the difficulty of changing your entire life
and persona. That's why a lot of wiseguys give up on themselves and
concentrate instead on not having their kids follow in their footsteps.

Either pull the trigger or get that fucking thing out of my face.
Corky
I'm not apologizing for what I did. I'm apologizing for what I didn't do.
Violet

19. *Bound* (1996)

You'll wonder while you're savoring the delicious first half of *Bound* why this is even on the mob list, but after it's over, you'll see why. The lesbian romance between Corky (Gina Gershon) and Violet (Jennifer Tilly), a gang leader's goomah, gives this mob caper a twist. Corky is a handyman, uh, handygirl, who comes into Violet's Chicago apartment to fix her pipes. And man, does she. The second plot gets underway when Violet's mob boyfriend Caesar (Joe Pantoliano) comes home unexpectedly and thinks someone's keeping Violet company. He's relieved to find it's just the chick next door, thinking there's nothing to worry about.

Caesar is a mob money launderer who has two million in Benjamins sitting in a suitcase in the flat. His boss is flying in to pick up the cash and it better be there. Corky convinces Violet that she can do better in business than on her back for Caesar and they combine hot *friendship* with *ambition* to make Caesar the fall guy. There are plenty of clever twists toward the end during which you'll swear the girls can't outwit him.

I don't want the law. I want justice.
They been feedin' you dogshit! Tellin' you it's Cream of Wheat.
Hoffa

20. *Hoffa* (1992)

We can all learn from the way Jimmy Hoffa (Jack Nicholson) ran his crew and took care of his *business*, The Teamsters. He did everything to insure the success of his workers, even if that included using the mob's power against the owners when necessary. The workers, in turn, owed their *loyalty* to him and gave him his power. Of course, once the mob does you a favor, you know you'll be hearing from them again,...and again. And if your actions put the mob in danger, you just might find a final resting place at Giants Stadium in the Meadowlands. See *Ruby* for more lessons on that score.

Nicholson went all Stanislavski on the role, as DeNiro usually does. Bulking up to make sure he looked like his character, he really becomes Hoffa. Danny Devito does an excellent job as Hoffa's fictionalized loyal friend, and he directed the film as well. Armand Assante is the Mafia kingpin.

You don't make up for your sins in church. You do it in the streets. You do it at home.
Charlie

21. *Mean Streets* (1973)

Mean Streets wasn't a blockbuster hit when it first appeared, but you knew immediately that Scorsese, DeNiro, and Keitel had a *Raging Bull,* a *Goodfellas*, and other great films ahead of them. In less than a year, *Godfather II* with DeNiro began fulfilling that promise.

DeNiro plays Johnny Boy, a crazed neighborhood bullshitter and petty thief, who borrows money and never pays it back—not smart in this or any neighborhood. Charlie (Harvey Keitel) keeps taking care of this jamoke, reminding me of how we took care of Crazy Louie on our street. This *friendship* thing doesn't always make sense. Charlie has his own hang ups, though. Worrying about whether or not he's committing sins is what bothers him. It's like Johnny is his penance for all the evil he's doing. The dialogue isn't smooth or phony—the screenwriter got it right—right off the streets. The barroom brawl isn't choreographed either; it's real, reminding you of the days when you were duking it out as a kid.

He's still fuckin' crazy Joey.
Carl Fogarty

22. *A History of Violence* (2005)

Mild-mannered, unassuming Tom (Viggo Mortensen) runs a diner in a picture-perfect small town in Indiana with his two kids and wife Edie (Maria Bello). We learn that Edie doesn't know anything about Tom's past when she puts on (and then takes off) her old cheerleading outfit to show him what he's missed in one of two sex scenes in the film that rank with the best in mob moviedom. Tom seems to be living the American dream until quite by accident two stick-up men walk into his diner. When they prove violent, he is forced to blow them away.

The ensuing publicity brings in three wiseguys from Philly, led by Ed Harris, who we soon learn had his face mangled by Tom years ago and has been looking for him ever since. When Harris and friends threaten not only Tom but his family, they meet the same fate as the stick-up guys. Knowing it's just a matter of time before he is visited again by his past, Tom gets on the turnpike to Philly himself to find his brother (William Hurt), a mob kingpin, and end this conflict one way or another.

For all they that take the sword, shall perish with the sword
Matthew 16:52, according to *Little Caesar*

23. *Little Caesar* (1931)

Nobody's as good at being bad as Edward G. Robinson. As Caesar Enrico "Rico" Bandello he's at his best (or worst). Nothing else matters to him but getting to the top, kind of the Vince Lombardi (another great Italian) of mob leaders. He's tough, cruel, and power-hungry and runs his crew with an iron fist. He also lets his boys know that getting too involved with dames is "soft stuff" and he ain't about to let them screw up his operation. "Yeah, see."

His outright disregard for other human beings brings him to a fitting end. No wasting away in prison from natural causes for Rico. Like a lot of crime movies of this era, there's a lot of moralizing going on. This one starts with a quote from the Bible so you that you know retribution is going to be visited upon the evildoer by the end. (The lawmakers and staff that wrote the RICO [Racketeer Influenced and Corrupt Organizations] Act that put some of my friends away used that tortured title so they could name the law after Rico in *Little Caesar*.)

That's the Chicago way, and that's how you get Capone.
Jimmy Malone

24. *The Untouchables* (1987)

Critics went *mezzo pazzo* (half-crazy) for this Brian DePalma recreation of the Capone saga when it was released. Chicago's Union Station looks great, but the street signs, Harrison and Racine, are nowhere near where the scene is supposed to take place. And the baby carriage that goes AWOL down the steps at the train station was supposed to be a cinematic breakthrough. Okay, if they say so.

I'll take Robert Stack as Eliot Ness any time over Kevin Costner, but DeNiro plays a fantastic Capone. Trouble is, we don't see enough of him. Therefore we don't get enough direct conflict between Capone and Ness. I can't believe Bobby bulked up again like he did for *Raging Bull* just to play these few scenes. And having Frank Nitti get thrown off a roof...please. You wouldn't know David Mamet wrote the screen play if I didn't tell you. Sean Connery plays an Irish cop, one of the few who isn't on the take, and is the best reason to see this film.

You don't like the storm, Rocco? Show it your gun. If it doesn't stop, shoot it.
Frank McCloud

25. *Key Largo* (1948)

Humphrey Bogart is a war veteran and Edward G. Robinson is Milwaukee mob boss Johnny Rocco. How can you go wrong? They're hiding out in a hotel in the Keys as a hurricane passes. Afterwards, Edward G expects a big payday and a boat ride to Cuba (this is in the days boat traffic was going in that direction). Bogie helps protect Nora (Lauren Bacall) and her father James (Lionel Barrymore) who owns the hotel.

Booze, gambling, and other "forbidden enterprises" are Rocco's program and I found myself identifying a little. But good guy Bogie swung me over, especially when Rocco starts torturing his former girlfriend (Claire Trevor) who has hit the skids. There's no excuse for this. This is one of Bogie's five greatest roles.

Because we both want whatever we want, whenever we want it and we both want everything.
Virginia Hill

26. *Bugsy* (1991)

Warren Beatty is Ben, "Don't call me Bugsy" Siegel. Beatty isn't generally my idea of a wiseguy, but he might have been the perfect choice for Bugsy—someone slick enough to dream up Vegas instead of staying in his own hood. How Bugsy gets the backing of Meyer Lansky (Ben Kingsley) and Lucky Luciano, builds the Flamingo, and creates a new Vegas is well known. The key lesson in *Bugsy* is what *ambition* can accomplish if you think big. Very few people could have imagined what Vegas could become and would have had the balls to try to pull it off.

The trouble is, of course, Bugsy never lived to see Sin City's success. When the Flamingo becomes five million clams over budget (a really hefty tab in 1940s dollars), he gets bumped off for poor financial planning. I would have felt sorry for him, except that he brings himself down by his obsessive pursuit of Virginia Hill (Annette Benning). He must have felt screwing her was worth it, but he screwed himself at the same time. The boys back home thought that, besides Bugsy, a broad was ripping them off too.

Joe Mantegna is a perfect George Raft (See George in 1932's *Scarface*) and Harvey Keitel is Mickey Cohen. The Flamingo and Vegas took off soon after Bugsy's demise. *Bugsy* got ten Academy Award nominations. This is a fairly good flick, but somebody must have putting the muscle on the Oscar voters.

Just when I think I'm out, they pull me back in.
Don Michael Corleone

27. *Godfather III* (1990)

We waited sixteen years to see if Coppola could pull off another greatest sequel of all time. He couldn't. A less compelling script, George Hamilton as *consigliere* instead of Robert Duvall, and Michael allowing his sister Connie to influence his business—these elements diminish *GIII* from the start. Still, Andy Garcia as Santino's illegitimate son,

Joe Mantegna and Eli Wallach as rival mafiosi, and Sophia Coppola as Michael's daughter pull us back in. Both the Corleones and cardinals of the Church lust for power and money, sins that inevitably lead to their destruction. They also make *Godfather III* a good, if disappointing, film.

It's better to have a gun and not need it than to need a gun and not have it.
Clarence

28. *True Romance* (1993)

Pour in the personas of Dennis Hopper, Christopher Walken, and Gary Oldman. Now have James Gandolfini stir things up and get Quentin Tarantino to brew the script and direct it. You have one scary concoction. The confrontation between the customarily weird Hopper (who knows he's about to be clipped) and the usually macabre Walken, alone is worth the price of admission. Plot revolves around a young video store clerk (Christian Slater), who falls for a hooker named Alabama (Patricia Arquette), and marries her after a few days. He suddenly finds himself in possession of a shit-load of cocaine and some nasty mobsters in hot pursuit. This was Tarantino's second major film after *Reservoir Dogs*.

The most important thing in doin' business is good manners.
Borelli

Either we're dead or we ain't
Frankie

29. *State of Grace* (1990)

Ed Harris is an Irish boss who controls the action in Hell's Kitchen, while Gary Oldman is his sadistic brother who'd just as soon put a bullet in a "greaser" than give up a dime of his dough. Joe Viterelli is an Italian boss who has to impart some wisdom to these Guiness-sloshers. When an old neighborhood friend (Sean Penn) comes back after a twelve year absence, the plot thickens because he's decided to work for the law. On top of that Penn's old girlfriend (Robin Wright) is talking to a shrink about things, and all the hoods are pissed off that the Yuppies are regentrifucking their territory. The Micks look a bit crazy in this, and the Italians look like smart businessmen. I call that reality. The title *State of Grace* comes from the inner feeling Terry gets when he decides to "do what is right"—and all I got to say is I hope he was in that state when the flick ended.

This is family business and that comes first—before anything else,-- getting laid, love, your mother, God, and country.
Pippi Delana

30. *The Last Don* (1997)

Danny Aiello is a hard edged Don who doesn't want his daughter (Kirstie Alley) to marry into the wrong family, so he has her husband whacked on their wedding night. She pops a son anyway, who grows up to be a jerk-off. Joe Mantegna, the Don's chief button, grooms his own son, Cross (Jason Gedrick), to be a good earner in the business. Leave it to Aiello to show us where *family* ends and *business* begins, with the class and dignity of a true Mafia boss.

I thought people like you didn't believe in the legal process.
Jennifer, Frank's lawyer and girlfriend.
I thought people like me were the legal process
Frank

31. *King of New York* (1990)

Christopher Walken becomes king of the drug trade, proving Don Corleone was right in believing in its eventual ruination of business. He enlists Italians, Latinos, Chinese, Blacks, and just about every ethnic group in the Big Apple by blowing away anybody who resists and enlisting who's left. Once he is "king" he and his right arm (Laurence Fishburne) dole out charity to the community, want to build a new hospital, and otherwise lord over the kingdom. The public doesn't care where the financing is coming from—they love it. Cops David Caruso and Wesley Snipes realize they'll have to go outside the law to bring down this Robin Hood of controlled substances. Walken does the little dance he's become known for, and when three muggers attack him while he's screwing his chick in an empty subway car, he proves he's king of the city.

What's the secret of America? Money!...Never forget it.
Arnold Rothstein

32. *Mobsters* (1991)

Meyer Lansky, Lucky Luciano, Frank Costello, and Bugsy Siegel get their MBA (Mob Business Administration) degree like any twenty-somethings wanting to make good. Their coursework focuses on how diversity (two Jews and two Italians), *loyalty* to the corporation, and *trust* can help a *business* grow; and they show that *friendship* helps *ambition* become a reality. Numerous corpses and mutilated bodies quickly clutter their campus, though, demonstrating that their main management theory is being more violent than your average gangster. This is another telling of the Masseria – Maranzano war for control of New York in the 1920s and the creation of the five families. Anthony Quinn as Masseria heads up a mobbed up cast.

I give my word.
Gino

33. *Things Change* (1988)

Gino (Don Ameche) is an old Italian shoeshine man in Chicago who happens to be a dead ringer for a boss in the Outfit. When the mobster commits a murder, he decides to make it a perfect crime by getting Gino to take the fall. With Gino's perfect reputation, the boss figures he'll only get three years, after which the boss will set him up for the rest of his days in his native Sicily.

Gino reluctantly agrees but starts to have second and third thoughts almost immediately. When he and his handler (Joe Mantegna) take off to Vegas they're mistaken for mob big shots immediately. Gino's naive personality and honest character only add to what other mobsters and casino workers think is great cover. He says little or nothing which makes everyone fear and respect him even more. When Ameche and Mantegna are forced to meet the real boss of the West Coast, the action starts. The boss will cut them in on a big deal if they are the real thing or is sure to kill them if they're not.`

What men do after work is what made us rich. No reason to screw them at work as well.
John Rooney

34. *Road to Perdition* (2002)

Irish Godfather, John Rooney (Paul Newman) loves his lead hit man, Michael Sullivan (Tom Hanks), but follows the rule, "don't trust nobody." When Rooney becomes suspicious even of Michael, he decides he has to get rid of him. Most of this takes place in a damp, dark, dreary Midwestern city in Capone's time, but they slip in a visit to Chicago where Frank Nitti (Stanley Tucci) agrees he won't intervene in the hit on Sullivan, in other words giving Rooney the go-ahead. To get even with Capone, Michael, with his twelve year old son as his getaway driver, starts knocking off banks in Midwest towns, taking only Capone money out of the banks.

A story of fathers and sons during Capone's time, *The Road to Perdition* is paved by bloodshed, revenge, justice and ends with a summary of what we hope isn't true about the life: "This is the life we choose, the life we lead, and there is only one guarantee, none of us will ever see heaven."

If he was so fuckin' smart, why is he so fuckin' dead.
Charley

35. *Prizzi's Honor* (1985)

Prizzi's is supposed to be a "black comedy." As Pesci would say, "What's so fuckin' funny about it?" I agree with one thing—the guy playing Don Corrado Prizzi couldn't be taken seriously. But his Don Corleone imitation is so overplayed that the joke is up after his first or second sentence. There is so much mileage on this guy, I suppose that's supposed to add to the humor. Jack Nicholson is his "button man," and he hooks up with beautiful Kathleen Turner, who is also a "contractor." Talk about finding a girl with common interests. According to her, though, she "only does 3-4 hits a year." I guess Jack is supposed to be funny too, but after two minutes of watching his slack-jawed neanderthal, I was ready to go back to a cave in Sicily with my ancestors. Anjelica Huston is Jack's old girlfriend and helps to stir things up; in fact, she won the Best Supporting Actress Oscar Award for her efforts. In fact, *Prizzi's* was nominated for seven other Awards. They say if everyone at the table is laughing except you, the joke's on you. Maybe that's why I didn't get it.

I'd rather go to jail for a thousand years than to ever rat on my friends.
Jackie

36. *Find Me Guilty (*2006)

Find Me Guilty summarizes a lot of what we've been trying to present to you in this book. Federal prosecutors spent two years conducting the longest criminal trial in American history, trying to lock up twenty members of the Lucchese family. Did some of these guys deserve to be found guilty? I'll let you be the judge of that. But are the FBI and the federal prosecutors any better people? I don't think so. *Loyalty, friendship, family, omerta*—almost all our life lessons are embodied in Jackie DiNorscio (Vin Diesel), who defends himself in court for 22 months. Once he gets the jury laughing, you know how the verdict is going to come out. The FBI exposes its RICO case to be nothing but an attempt to prove that a bunch of Italians were getting together and talking. Alex Rocco is mob boss Nick Calabrese and Ron Silver is the judge who endured this seemingly non-ending debacle. Annabella Sciorra, is her usual spontaneously combustible self as Jackie's wife. The lead defense attorney, who slowly realizes Jackie's shtick is working in the courtroom, is played by Peter Dinklage, a midget who easily has the highest stature of any of the lawyers. But it's Vin Diesel who represents our thing in *Find Me Guilty* as well as anybody has, for better or worse.

We're not leavin' here till we're partners in the business.
Black and Blue

37. *Dinner Rush* (2000)

Restaurateur/book-maker Louis (Danny Aiello) sends his son Udo to chef school, and he returns making all these fancy new dishes that people in Tribeca just eat up. "No sausage and peppers on my menu," says Udo. Locals mob the place not just because of the *nuovo menu* but also because they think the place is mobbed up. The plot thickens faster than Louis' *salsa putanesca* when he brings in another chef, Duncan, who cooks old school, southern Italian. Trouble is Duncan is an addicted gambler (one of my favorite type of people). When Duncan gets deeply into debt, two goons, known as "Black" and "Blue," come to collect. They like the restaurant so much, though, that they tell Louis he's going to have to franchise out to Goombah, Inc. or his favorite chef will be trying to cook from underneath a stone slab. Louis is forced to come up with his own option to protect his interests. Fast-talking waitresses, a detective who is a regular customer, and patrons you'd either like to punch out or take out fill the restaurant and you get a behind the scenes look at how the dishes are prepared. Louis teaches plenty of lessons on taking care of *business* and keeping your *respect* while you do. A violent beginning and a violent ending are perfect bookends for the plot.

Thanks...you've been a real pain in the ass.
Mark, to the D.A.

38. *The Client* (1994)

When a little kid witnesses the suicide of a Mafia lawyer, he becomes the object of a mob search led by Barry "The Blade" Moldano (Anthony LaPaglia) to shut him up. He wanders around the courthouse until he finds Love; that is, lawyer Reggie Love (Susan Saradon) to protect him. The D.A. (Tommy Lee Jones) is not much better than "The Blade" because he's only interested in the kid testifying, rather than protecting him. The mob guys come off stupid, the Feds even stupider, and the kid and his protectress have to fight both of them.

Maybe the three grand's worth it, huh? I remember the days when you could get a guy here (for a hit) for what, forty bucks?
Dutch Schultz
We live in inflationary times.
Sulky

39. *Hoodlum* (1997)

Equal rights means black people get a chance at the rackets too. "Bumpy" Johnson (Laurence Fishburne) helps the Queen of Policy wrest control of the numbers game in Harlem from Lucky Luciano (Andy Garcia) and Dutch Schultz (Tim Roth). Tie this in with *American Gangster*, in which Frank Lucas picks up where Bumpy left off.

All you need to say is two words. Two specific words..... "Not guilty."
Teacher

40. *The Juror* (1996)

"You've been selected for jury duty," is that letter we all hate to receive. Annie (Demi Moore) seems almost happy to get it and have the chance to put some Mafia guys away. Right there I figured she deserves to "get it." Teacher (Alec Baldwin) does everything he can to see she utters those two sweet little words, "not guilty," or no other words ever again. This is worth seeing if only for James Gandolfini, who brings psycho Teacher into the family. He's ready for his Soprano role after this. *The Juror* ends with a chase scene in Guatemala. I didn't even know the Mafia had a crew down there.

When election time comes around these guys better remember who put 'em there.
Tony Ana

We deliver the votes for Kennedy in Chicago, knowing he bites the hand that feeds him.
Sam Giancanna

The government of the United States has a secret policy with organized crime. They plan hits.
Jack Ruby

41. *Ruby* (1992)

If you see *The Rat Pack* (#53 on our list), you can then continue that story here. When JFK got hit and two days later Ruby (Danny Aiello), a hood from Chicago, took out Oswald, it didn't take a genius to figure out who was involved. The mob got him elected, got him fixed up with high class hookers (like Candy Cane in this movie), and then got stepped on. The Warren Commission whitewashed everything with a report that had more holes in it than Santino at the tollbooth. Here's a version of what really happened.

Isn't it funny how things you get on the sly always seem better?
Joe

42. *Crazy Joe* (1974)

Crazy Joey Gallo (Peter Boyle) was a greedy Brooklyn wild man who was willing to stand up to anyone in the five families until he was killed in a clam bar in Little Italy in 1972. *Ambition* leads Gallo to take on the mob because he feels he's not getting *justice*; i.e., his part of the action. He and his crew battle a gang boss played by Eli Wallach, who gives a performance he later re-enacts in *Godfather III*. Joe winds up in the slammer when he gets set up by the Don. While in the joint he hooks up with Willy (Fred "The Hammer" Williamson) and "the brothers" really take to him. When he gets out of jail after eight years, the only way to have the muscle to take back what is his is to align with "the Blacks." Cement mixers and chicken grinders are used to interesting effect, and there are some lessons about this thing of ours thrown in along the way.

I like a guy who uses his head for something besides a hatrack.
Capone

43. *St. Valentine's Massacre* (1967)

If they had offered this kind of history class in high school, maybe I wouldn't have gotten thrown out. Besides chronicling organized crime in Chicago under Capone and Bugs Moran (North Side), *Massacre* offers complete stats on almost every member of each crew, complete with birth dates, origins of birth, aliases, and number of hits to their credit. Jason Robards is no Steiger, DeNiro, or Muni in portraying Big Al, but he does a decent job. Bugs sets himself up by referring to us as *greaseballs* and *wops.* He could at least have been more original. The February 14, 1929 slaughter of the Bugs Moran mob (minus Bugs) is accurate down to how the bodies fell after the machine gun fire.

The lesson in *Massacre*, of course, focuses on *business.* If you want to say I'm partial to Capone because he was a Chicagoan, go ahead. Why not? His crew guns down a whole slew of mobsters, something the cops wish they could have done. Otherwise he is just protecting his *businesses*, which were mainly gambling, liquor, and prostitution, all illegal at the time and all okay today in certain areas. What's not to like?

The main thing is to have money. I've been rich and I've been poor. Believe me, rich is better.
Debbie Marsh

44. *The Big Heat* (1953)

Officer Bannion (Glenn Ford) is on a one-man mission to put some *big heat* on a mob crew headed by a sadistic Lee Marvin, who decorates Gloria Grahame's face with a pot of hot coffee at one point, and uses another broad's hand as an ashtray to put out his cigarette. Bannion gets little support from his fellow cops, who are either on the mob's payroll or keeping their heads down. Ford, who usually played the cowboy in the white hat in Westerns, gets that hat a little blood-spattered here, plowing ahead with a mob crusade without any regard for the people, usually

women, he puts in harm's way. One lady who gives him information
winds up dead along the highway after being tortured. Then his own
wife gets blown up in a car. He's the good guy, sure, but he puts his
thing, his *business*, ahead of *family*. It's no accident the movie ends with
Bannion leaving the precinct telling one of the boys to "keep the coffee
hot."

*Hey, it's your money, I mean I'm just holding it for you, you know, like
a bank, except, you know, better than a bank because banks get knocked
off, you know, no one knocks off old Tony.*
Tony

45. *The Professional* (1994) or *Leon*

Leon (Jean Reno) is a kindly hit-man brought to the States by mob
boss, Tony (Danny Aiello), as a "cleaner." He'll clean up any mess
Tony has gotten into by eliminating the opposition. He accidentally gets
12-year old Natalie Portman as an apprentice when her entire family
is wiped out by corrupt DEA agents, led by a viciously crazed Gary
Oldman. Being a professional, he makes sure no child gets left behind
while teaching his craft, and she learns by doing. This is a curriculum
usually glossed over in middle school.

I don't respect the law. It's justice I respect.
Joseph Scassi

46. *Power of Attorney* (1995)

Power of Attorney's bad script is saved by Danny Aiello's fine
acting, as "reformed" mob capo Joseph Scassi. Under indictment for
murder, Scassi pretends he's a changed man. He makes donations to
the community just like our own boss used to do. He embodies our
life lessons—"I don't respect the law; it's justice I respect," he says to
explain his actions. And he claims to be persecuted because his name
ends in a vowel (which would put a lot of us in trouble). In reality,
he's just done a stint in the slammer and doesn't want to go back. The
plot really revolves more around lawyer Paul Delacrocce (Elias Koteas)

and whether he should stay a public prosecutor or go for the dough by helping out Scassi whose innocence he's not really sure about.

Now if you can't trust a fix, what can you trust? For a good return, you'd have to go back to bettin' on chance—and then you're back with anarchy, right back in the jungle.
Johnny Caspar

47. *Miller's Crossing* (1990)

Miller's Crossing is a clash between Irish and Italian mobsters over a Jewish bookie. Is this a great country or what? Johnny Caspar (Jon Polito) wants a bookie (John Turturro) clipped because it seems he's tipping off other gamblers about how Johnny is betting. Gamblers figure that if Johnny is betting big, the fight must be fixed, because Johnny "don't bet on no chance things." Johnny is losing dough and, after all, it's un-American for him to be doing all the work to fix the fights and somebody else is getting in on the rewards. Leo (Albert Finney), head of the Irish mob, tries to save Bernie, not in the interests of business, but because he is in love with Bernie's sister. All this could have been avoided just by taking care of *business*. Leo is fortunate to have his right hand man (Gabriel Byrne) show him what *loyalty* is all about. If you're Irish, the scene where Leo sprays bullets from his "Tommy Gun" to the background music of "Danny Boy" is sure to bring tears.

Don't you know that it's cheaper to kill you than to pay you?
Anthony, local capo

48. *Death Collector* (1975) or *Family Enforcer*

Joe Pesci's first film didn't make much of a splash in 1975, five years before *Raging Bull*. He plays a local kid who makes good as a debt collector, mob-style. By showing *respect* for those in the *family,* character actor Joe Cortese ensures success of the *business*. Frank Vincent also shows up in this one and takes his obligatory beating. This film sometimes appears on a tape titled "Great Mob Movies." Though it's rated low by critics and the public alike, it's a must-see for Pesci fans—and, hey, that means just about all of us, right?

Twenty-first Century Criminals, Twenty-first Century Payoffs
Tag line

49. *This Thing of Ours* (2003)

This Thing of Ours is the real thing. As authentic as Puzo, Scorsese, and DeNiro are in writing, directing, and acting in mob movies, they can't be any more authentic than Danny Provenzano, who did all three here and was then indicted in Jersey soon after the film was completed on almost exactly the same charges as his character—extortion and breaking the thumb of a guy who renigs on an $182,000 loan. I've heard of method acting but does this guy get into his character or what? Danny is the nephew of Anthony Provenzano, late of the Genovese family, and distributors decided to open *This Thing of Ours* in New York, Jersey, and Florida at the time of Danny's trial. Danny copped a plea to extortion and got sent up for ten years (anything for publicity, I guess) Frank Vincent, Vincent Pastore, James Caan, and others add more realism if that was needed. Plenty of great goombah action takes place as the boys meet and greet over pasta and poker to plan a twenty-first century heist using computers to skim off a few cents off millions of bank accounts, amounts so small that people won't notice. Sounds like mainstream Wall Street to me, a perfect scam until everyone gets greedy.

--"they will always strike at what you love."—*It's nothing for me to blow someone's brains out, believe me. I just hope it's someone I know.*

50. *Gloria* (1980)

A hundred years from now people can get a look at what New York and New Yorkers looked like in1980 by pulling *Gloria* out of the film can, out of its tape box, out of its DVD sleeve, or dial it up on the chip implanted in their head or whatever the fuck they have going for them then. They'll see the most authentic collection of crummy streets and signs, decrepit bartenders and hotel clerks and waitresses, graffitied subway cars, native New York cab drivers (there's a whole species onto itself in this film), and, yes, a bunch of pretty legit mob guys who are not only bad, but stupid enough to let Gloria plug a large number of them. John Cassavetes wrote and directed this story which features Gena Rowlands playing one tough mob moll who runs through the New York streets evading and killing mobsters, while caring for a six year old whose entire family has been whacked.

There was peace when people like me ran things…in your world people go bankrupt, in mine they go to sleep.
Rusty Pirone

51. *Trial By Jury* (1994)

Similar to *The Juror,* #40 on our list, this came out two years earlier. Armand Assante's character is looking at a permanent trip up the river on RICO and murder charges. Both he and the prosecutor want a beautiful woman with a kid on the jury so they can "influence" her. They get their wish. This time it's William Hurt doing the juror-stalking, though Assante joins him in the end.

I've got a few words to say gents. Let the word get around, we're all Mafia.
Mr. Licovetti, from Chicago

Being locked in the closets and beat up and burned and sexual stuff—and to come out from under it—I mean, it's lovely. I mean, most people like me end up on death row, or in the graveyards, or prison.
Robert Blake, commenting on his childhood (from IMDB, Internet Movie Data Base, www.imdb.com)

52. *The Purple Gang* (1959)

The reputation of Detroit's Purple Gang rivaled Chicago's when I was a kid. The usual war for control of the rackets in Mo-Town is told here, with Robert Blake providing the main muscle. Barry Sullivan plays the Eliot Ness-type who tries to bring him to justice. The casting of Blake, the previous "Our Gang" series kid was prophetic, as he went on to star as TV's Baretta, was one of the killers in *In Cold Blood*, and then came close to winding up on Death Row himself.

I figure if power doesn't mean you have the opportunity to work with people you love, then you really haven't got any.
Sinatra

53. *The Rat Pack* (1998)

After fondly reminiscing about Frank, Dino, Sammy, songs, booze, broads, movies, television, and Vegas shows this film gradually fades into what it's really about: extortion, fraud, betrayal, and murder. How Ol' Blue Eyes helped JFK get elected, how he got stiffed by the new President because of his ties to organized crime, and how the mob reacted to all of this comprise the plot, while Mantegna and Liotta play the leaders of the Pack.

Why do they hate us?
Gaspare Marchesi
Look at what we've achieved.
Macheca

54. *Vendetta* (1999)

A generation before my Sicilian ancestors were crowding into New York City in the early 1900s, the Mafia was getting its first start in America in New Orleans. Rich Southerners figured they could replace the slaves they had lost twenty years before with "dagos" and "wops" and treat them the same way. When "them uppity immigrants" showed they were going to control their own lives and jobs, the Southern fat cats treated them like they were used to treating former slaves, resulting in the largest vigilante lynching in the country's history. This true story features Christopher Walken as the ruthless, aristocratic tyrant who runs the city behind the scenes. He whips the locals into a frenzied orgy of killing while remaining behind his gentile facade.

The Mafia are bound by their own laws.
Sophia

55. *Bella Mafia* (1997)

A "female Godfather" film had to be made sooner or later. When Mafia leader Don Luchiano (Dennis Farina) and his top capos are bumped off, the women in the family feel the need to take over. Vanessa Redgrave, Jennifer Tilly and Nastassja Kinski begin by revenging the assassinations of their men, but that's only the start. Nastassja ultimately becomes the hottest, if least realistic, head of a crime family you'd ever want to see. And really, what do we call her, The Godmother?

While to the stranger's eye one street was no different from another, we all knew where our "neighborhood" somehow ended. Beyond that, a person was...a stranger. Arthur Miller (raised in Brooklyn) quoted at the beginning of *Out For Justice.*

56. *Out For Justice* (1991)

You can't criticize the mob for every violent thing some self-styled wannabe wise guy does, either in real life or in the movies. We don't like being stereotyped any more than anybody else. In *Out for Justice* Richy (William Forsythe) is a berserk crack addict who the news media make out to be a wiseguy. When Richy clips a cop, he brings down the wrath of the cop's partner, Gino (Steven Seagal). *Justice* becomes a battle between Richy, a brutalizing killer, and Gino who single-handedly kicks the hell out of about fifty guys as he searches for this *pezzo di merda* who's hiding out in Brooklyn. Action and authentic dialogue from Brooklyn, this film must have reduced the neighborhood unemployment rate by 50%. Salvatore Bonanno, Salvatore "Sonnie" Mignano, Beneditto Bongiorno, Julius Nasso, Jr., Vincent Nasso, David Basulto, and Sonny Zito are just a fraction of those in the cast who got billing in this film but were hardly ever seen again.

It used to be there was a way of doing things and things got done. Now everybody's feelings are involved.
Teddy

57. *Knockaround Guys* (2001)

Old World mob bosses (Dennis Hopper and John Malkovich) have standards and work hard to get things done. Newer generation wannabes like Hopper's son (Barry Pepper) and his friend (Vin Diesel) just knock around, thinking they were born with a platinum pasta fork in their mouths. They don't have what it takes to be wiseguys, yet they can't get a job because new age employers think they're connected. When they screw up a simple money pick-up in a small town in Montana, the old guard has to take over. *Mob Slackers* might have been a better title.

An eye for an eye.
Cross

58. *The Last Don, Part II* (1998)

Part Deux of *The Last Don* is not worthy of Mario Puzo, who must have worked on this film just before he passed away (at least, his name is on the writing credits). The Don (Danny Aiello) dies soon after the film begins, starting a string of senseless violence by his protege Cross (Jason Gedrick) to get control of the mob. Though Joe Mantegna's character died in the first movie, the director wisely resurrects him in Part Two as a *"ghost consigliere."*

We're a family here. I don't train you so you can quit next weekend.
Frankie Santalino

59. *Wisegirls* (2002)

Mira Sorvino and Melora Walters both have secrets, but it's Staten Island wisegirl Mariah Carey who eventually finds them both out. They are waitresses at Il Santalino, a joint so connected even the busboy is packing. The wiseguys in the flick have lost all parameters, dealing in drugs, plugging each other, and treating the girls like what they get from the Italian butcher. It's fun to see the girls be wise in more ways than one.

Let me tell you somethin' about women. I never met one that didn't need a rap in the head, and pretty often.
Reles

60. *Murder, Inc.* (1960)

Peter Falk shows that at one time he could out-Cagney the best of them. He takes, takes, takes, whatever the hell he wants, including May Britt, a hottie in the late 50s. The title refers to the name given to Anastasia's murderous crew at the time, but the film's facts are questionable and a moralizing voiceover at the end is laughable.

I'm in! I've always been in, haven't I?
Vince Ginetta

61. *The Brotherhood* (1968)

Kirk Douglas plays a mob boss from the old school pitted against his younger brother who wants to take the family business in new directions in this pre-*Godfather* tale which includes a grand Italian wedding, the traditional kiss of death, battles for power, and members hiding out in Sicily till things settle.

There's a big difference between fear and respect.
Michael (Freddy Prinze, Jr.)
All roads lead to Rome, Mikey
Carmine (Scott Caan)

I knew stealin' was supposed to be a sin, but I learned to live by a different set of rules.
Michael (Freddie Prinze Jr.)

62. *Brooklyn Rules* (2007)

Like *Mean Streets, Rules* is a realistic portrayal of the relationships between made guys, connected guys, and guys who were straight but were loyal to where they came from. Scott Caan (James' son) and Freddie Prinze Jr. are two of the three who come of age in the neighborhood. One starts running with the mob, one starts college, and the third is an average kid who wants to belong and who makes the sign of the cross or prays every time he passes a church or a statue of the Virgin

Mary. The streets of Brooklyn clash with the corridors of college and religious upbringing. For instance, neighborhood mob captain (Alec Baldwin) uses the meat slicer in a butcher shop to give a Van Gogh to a Nam vet who keeps Gook ears around his own neck to prove to himself that he's tough, but who was absent the day the neighborhood business rules were passed out. The college guy won't take shit from badasses in the hood, even if they're connected, especially in front of his college girlfriend, Ellen (Mena Suvari). The big boss is always hovering in the background here, like he did on Chicago's West Side. When Caesar is rubbed out in the battles that ensue after Paul Castellano is killed, the three heroes wind up in Gotti-land, where all previous deals are off. These guys could have been me and DB forty years ago in Chicago instead of Brooklyn.

(Not everything in *Brooklyn Rules* was realistic. Writer Terence Winter, who wrote many *Soprano* episodes, had one of the kid's mothers make a lasagne so bad nobody ever wanted to eat it. No Italian mother makes a lasagne that bad; she'd be put straight by the other ladies. Hell, I'd give her my recipe).

He'll be all right. He's as strong as a bull.
A doctor

63. *The Valachi Papers* (1973)

Joe Valachi (Charles Bronson)—the original rat, the guy who first gave up the words, *cosa nostra*—this is his story. All the family tree analysis in New York goes back to him. He takes the oath complete with ceremony, including the burning of the paper in his hands, and in the end gives it all up. *Papers* makes it appear that Vito Genovese gives Valachi no choice but to go to the cops to save his skin, but it doesn't fully explain why. Besides Bronson, the bulk of the actors are native Italian since this had to be filmed in Italy because of the protests of fellow *paesans* in the U.S. The worst part of this rat-fink mess for Valachi was that he had to spend the rest of his life in the slam anyway. Didn't Joe know how to plea-bargain? Without him the movie industry wouldn't have known about Cosa Nostra, the ceremonies, and other details about "the life." He opened the door to a treasure of great films that followed. We know, though, that a rat is still a rat.

It's... the... good life
To be free, and explore the unknown
Tony Bennett (opening soundtrack)

64. *Gangster No. 1* (2000)

Gangster No. 1 shows that wiseguys in England can have just as tough a life as in America. Malcolm Macdowell is a godfather in his 60's, looking back to his younger days, when the cold-blooded Limey eliminated his opposition in any way possible, especially by de-roofing them. Sound track and party scene are pure pre-Beatle.

People want guns, people need guns. I can get them. We can get them.
McLeary
Somebody's got to perform this service.
Latella

65. *Vendetta: Secrets of a Mafia Bride* (1991)

"'Vengeance is mine,' sayith the Lord," is one Biblical verse not often featured in Sicilian Sunday sermons. When a little girl sees her mother raped by her uncle, sees her shot seven years later, and sees her father clipped by a hitman, she's programmed thinking vengeance just might be what she wants to major in. Nancy Alt plays the grown woman who gets involved with the mob led by Eli Wallach and his *consigliere* Burt Young. While seeking her vendetta, she unknowingly falls for her father's killer (Eric Roberts), marries him, and then finds out the truth a minute later. It makes for one helluva wedding reception.

You don't understand. I loved Sean. Even when I shot him, I loved him.
It was vendetta. I am family.
Nancy (Carol Alt)

66. *Vendetta II: The New Mafia* (1993)

In this sequel to *Vendetta I*, Nancy (Carol Alt) whacks bridegroom Eric Roberts in front of three hundred guests before she can even get cake all over her face or throw the bouquet (of course "none of them knows nuttin'" once the cops arrive). But she's already pregnant with the killer's kid. Boss Eli Wallach convinces her to give the kid up and hide out in Sicily. The only place a single woman this hot can hide in the Old Country is in a convent, which she does, until a newspaperman comes snooping, notices what's under the nun's duds, and falls for her, habit and all.

The Mafia in this city's gone. You know what omerta means? It means how much time do I get off my sentence.
Joey

67. *10th and Wolf* (2006)

As the war to kick Iraq out of Kuwait is winding down in 1991, Tommy Santoro (James Marsden) is pissed off the U.S. didn't complete the job and get Saddam. (You know the one, that's where Bush 41 kicked all kinds of butt with a half million of our best, as opposed to his kid who Ramboed into Iraq with his dick in his hand.)

Tommy wants to get rid of Saddam single-handedly, and when he gets drunk enough to try one night, he fails and gets court-martialed. Federal agents (including Brian Dennehy), however, give him a chance to keep his ass out of prison by infiltrating the Philly mob of his old neighborhood near 10th and Wolf. He wants no part of it at first, but when he finds his brother and cousin also are in trouble and can be saved, he chooses *blood* over *omerta*. A rat is always a rat, but sometimes lessons clash.

If I ever find out that you laid your hands on that little girl again, me and Mr. Mantle are gonna pay you a visit, my friend.
Lono

68. *Suicide Kings* (1997)

Mafia kingpin Carlo Bartolucci (Christopher Walken) is retired for years until four college-age kids pull him back in by kidnapping him in order to trade him for a sister who they think has been kidnapped by the mob. They tie him to a chair and cut off a finger. Still, who do you think will win this confrontation?

I was just a big earner.
Frankie

69. *Federal Protection* (2001)

Armand Assante plays Frankie, a Chicago chop-shop operator. He looks, though, more like Nick Nolte after the cops picked him up on that drunk-driving beef than the slick boss he resembles in most of his films. This is another version of who's gonna rat on who (or whom). After the big boys make Swiss cheese out of him but fail to finish the job, he offers to go into witness protection to survive. When the Feds do their job with their usual level of competency, a housewife in Salt Lake City makes him. Armand is forced to take matters (and the housewife) into his own hands.

Killing's never the right thing.
Tony

70. *Hitman's Run* (1999)

Tony (Eric Roberts) is a Catania family hit man who dishes out more lead to more people than a Chinese toy factory. Nevertheless, the Feds put him into witness protection. It happens. This time both the FBI and the CIA are involved so it's no surprise that their computer gets hacked and his identity is compromised. After offing what seems like a hundred guys, at the end Tony has the balls to say, "Killing's never the right thing."

A tale told by an idiot.
Macbeth

71. *Men Of Respect* (1991)

If your kid has to read *Macbeth* in school, have him see this play instead of buying the Cliff Notes. John Turturro plays wiseguy Mike

Battaglia who takes over the mob after hearing some gypsy fortunes that say he should. Boss Rod Steiger is wiped out while Dennis Farina, Stanley Tucci, Peter Boyle, and Vinny Pastore play some of Shakespeare's other roles, and there's a big gangland war at the end.

....there's three kinds of people in this world: those who never gamble, those who enjoy gambling and those who own the tables.
Arnold Rothstein to Lucky Luciano

72. *Gangster Wars* (1981)

This is another tale of the Masseria – Maranzano war in the 1920's and how it produced the rise of Rothstein, Luciano, Lansky, and Seigel. All the authentic names are used except for the curious fact that Lansky is called Lasker. A chance to see Richard Castellano (Clemenza) play Masseria. Other films tell the family founding legend better though.

Sugar in the morning, Sugar in the evening....
The McGuire Sisters

73. *Sugartime* (1995)

Sammy "Momo" or "Mooney" Giancana (John Turturro), who falls for Phyllis McGuire (Mary Louise Parker), was not the pussy-whipped fool he's shown to be here, even though he was gaga for Phyllis McGuire of the McGuire Sisters. Sure he built Villa Venice nightclub (where most West Side schools had their proms) for her, But being one of Capone's and Nitti's right hand men, he had plenty else going for him, including sharing a mistress with JFK in the 60s. *Sugartime* shows this was more than a coincidence and that the Kennedy brothers' crackdown on the mob might have led to JFK's assassination. Still, for us, the theme warns against "soft stuff" as much as Edward G. Robinson does in *Little Caesar.*

I'm not his girl, he's my gangster.
Drew

74. *Billy Bathgate* (1991)

Dustin Hoffman's takes his turn at making his mob movie bones, playing Dutch Schultz, taking a dorky kid under his wing, and helping him rise in the organization. Billy makes Henry Hill look like Don Corleone. Why Nicole Kidman (who is Dutch's moll) gives it up for him I don't know. Dutch doesn't do well with the Upstate N.Y. jury either.

Angelo: *Some fuckin' yuppie called me a Guido and told me to go home and catch "The Sopranos."*
Santo: *Then why didn't you cut off his balls so he could sing like a soprano.*

75. *Wannabes* (2000)

A couple of young neighborhood guys starting up the ladder to becoming made guys try to take the spotlight away from the screw-up son (Joseph D'Onofrio) of mob boss Santo Maneri (Joe Viterelli). Viterelli plays it like a wannabe Brando-Gandolfini in this Soprano-influenced rehash of every mob-cliche in the book. Sounds like just my cup of espresso.

Vinny, you rat me, I'll know before I get there. You'll never hear the hammer click.
Gus Farace

76. *Mob Justice* or *Dead and Alive: The Race for Gus Farace* (1991)

Neither *honor* nor *omerta* is on display in this true tale of connected guy, Gus Farace (Tony Danza), who kills a cop and spends the next ninety minutes of the film on the lamb. Danza's not my idea of a menacing mobster, but the rest of the cast balances him out. He's protected by mob chief (Frank Vincent), but his cousin (Nicholas Tuturro) rats on him. Samuel L. Jackson shows up on the side of law enforcement this time, but is eliminated less than a third of the way through.

A Sicilian woman is like a dog. Sometimes you get a good master, sometimes you don't.
Advice from Sicilian mother to her daughter

77. *Love, Honor, and Obey—The Last Mafia Marriage* (1993)

Rosalie Profaci Bonanno tries to show it's tough to be the wife of a wiseguy in this version of the *family* legend featuring Ben Gazzara as Joseph Bonanno. Based on Rosalie's rat-out best seller.

Hear this music? It's all about greed and all the trouble it can get you into.
Ben Cutler (Pete Postlethwaite)

78. *Triggermen* (2002)

Small time Limey hoods hit Chi-town for a holiday but get involved in a mob hit when they pick up a satchel of cash waiting for the real killers. They decide to follow through rather than give up the money in this third black comedy on our list.

These WASPS, they outgrow people. Italians outgrow clothes.
Paulie
Little Italy got their own law and order. You wanna know something. It's the only neighborhood in the whole city where little kids and old ladies can still walk the streets at night.
Police Officer

79. *The Pope of Greenwich Village (1984)*

Sinatra sings "Summer Wind" while two-bit hood Eric Roberts gets himself and his cousin Mickey Rourke into scrapes with the mob and its boss Bed Bug Eddie (Burt Young) that only the Pope could escape from. At the end they're still walking and talking (or pontificating, if you will) which is surprising since you'll want to whack Roberts' character Paulie yourself halfway through the flick. Mercifully, the mobsters only remove one of his thumbs, duly amputated by mob quasi-surgeon, Frank Vincent.

Pope is an early flick in both Roberts' and Rourke's careers, proving that a lot of artists do their best work when they're young. Rourke's long time honey, Daryl Hannah finally walks out on him. Her lack of screen wardrobe would have made the real Pope cop a plea on that celibacy statute, but she can't convince Rourke to forsake his whacked out, drugged up, (okay, fucked up) cousin for her. No soft stuff for him. That's blood loyalty a Madura or DiBruno can appreciate.

Your wife should be one of us. I mean, our women, they understand, they don't ask questions.
Angelo

80. *The Don is Dead* (1973)

Don Paul takes a dirt nap at the start of this film and the *ambitions* of three Vegas families outstrip their common sense. Mob war chops the three families down to two, headed by Anthony Quinn and Abe Vigoda, as they continue double-crosses and scams that would never have fooled a Corleone.

Everybody's connected. I can't even go to my own crew. If they talk...to me, they're dead.
Bobby "Bats"

81. *Witness Protection* (1999)

There's no free lunch when the Feds are paying, especially if it means going into witness protection. When Bostonian Bobby "Bats" Batten (Tom Sizemore) is found skimming off the mob, a contract goes out on him. After an attempted hit that fails, he decides that turning state's evidence is better than winding up six feet under prematurely. After a few years, though, he thinks differently. Being stuck with the old lady (even if it is Mary Elizabeth Mastrantonio) twenty-four hours a day in some mid-sized town in Kansas or Montana, and working his ass off in a dorky job while in witness protection, are worse for a big city wiseguy than going to jail or getting whacked.

I love you, blood and all.
Giuliano

82. *The Sicilian* (1987)

"So die, all who betray Giuliano" is the calling card of this Sicilian Robin Hood played by Christopher Lambert and created by Mario Puzo. Along with a wing man (John Turturro) he thinks is *loyal*, he earns *respect* and *honor* among the people. This conflicts with the business plan of the chief of his clan, Don Masino Crocce, who never learned to share. In the end, he learns as most of us do, "you can't trust nobody."

The bullet hasn't been made that can kill me.
Legs Diamond

83. *The Rise and Fall of Legs Diamond* (1960)

Legs Diamond (Ray Danton) shows the guts and ambition to muscle into Arnold Rothstein's turf, get him clipped, and take over. Legs also uses any good looking dame he can to help his rise in Arnold's organization. Dyan Cannon's Dixie feeds him inside info on the mob, while Alice (Karen Steele), Legs' girlfriend, doesn't give herself enough credit as a looker and lets Legs walk all over her (in a manner of speaking). Trouble is, even though he goes Gotti on the flashy front, he doesn't follow the rules of staying available and taking care of business.

Can an old man give you advice on his birthday? Don't get involved—go to college.
Max

84. *The Neon Empire* (1989)

I guess Manhattan or Times Square might come to your mind when you hear the title of this film, but if you're like I am, you thought one thing—Vegas, baby. Pseudonyms are used for Bugsy Siegel (Ray Sharkey) and Meyer Lansky (Martin Landau) to give the writers even more freedom than usual to dick around with the facts in this legend of the founding of the city of bright lights, gambling, drinking, and whoring. Sounds like a little social club I used to have. Sure, whatever plays there, stays there—that mostly means your money.

People still drink, they cheat, they steal, and they kill. That's the way it always was and that's the way it always will be and nobody is ever gonna change that.
Capone

85. *The Lost Capone* (1990)

Al's brother, Jimmy Capone, clubs a guy with a Louisville Slugger, runs off to Nebraska, becomes a marshall, and changes his name. Who knew? Al's devotion to family values leads him to try to get Jimmy to come home and help in the family business. Eric Roberts is not high on my list of Capones, but both Dominic Chianese and Ally Sheedy kept me interested.

In this life we got here, nothin's what it seems to be.
Vincent

86. *18 Shades of Dust* or *Hitman's Journal* or *The Sicilian Code* (1999)

You'll get excited just reading the cast: Danny Aiello, Vincent Pastore, William Forsythe, and Aida Turturro; and smaller parts played Frank Pellegrino, a Soprano FBI agent, and Raymond Serra, who's been around the crime movie block. You'd expect big things, wouldn't you? Instead, Aiello's aging mob enforcer Vincent Dianni spends a lot of time talking to himself, doubting a lot of things he's done, and wondering what the future holds. I'm talking about the real future, as in heaven or hell. *Dust* flies in the face of a reality in which wiseguys don't spend a lot of time psychologizing, introspectionizing, and second guessing "the life."

It wasn't the first time politicians reached out to us for help and then betrayed us. America has a very distorted view of our world. Mafia is a process, not a thing.
Joseph Bonanno

87. *Bonanno: A Godfather's Story* (1999)

Joseph "Bananas" Bonanno was 96 when this film (based on his own book of the same name) opened, so maybe he was losing his marbles. Three different actors play Joe at three stages in his life in this search for *respect* that is embarrassing to him and to our thing. Tony Nardi plays him as middle-aged for most of the movie. Martin Landau is the oldest of the Joes, and Edward James Olmos makes an appearance as Salvatore Maranzano—here are two actors who could have done a lot more in the Mafia genre.

Old Bonanno tells the story as if he's reading to us, but I guess that's to emphasize that it's from his own book. He gives kind of a disclaimer saying,

Omerta, however, does not mean that a man cannot say what he feels.

What does that mean? That he has the go ahead to write a book about it?

If he leaves here alive, he will eventually return to kill, because he'll be driven by the fear that one day we'll change our minds. There's one shell in the chamber. Kill him. I'm not doing it. Either you do it or we'll set him free, and you can wait for him to return.

A family elder to Ray

After young Ray shoots the man, he is handed the shell and told:
Carry this with you. Nothing will cost you more.

88. *The Funeral* (1996)

Talk about your dysfunctional families! Christopher Walken is at his psycho best and his brother Chris Penn, rest his soul, is in a different world. They react the only way they can to their third brother, Vincent Gallo, being whacked by a rival gang. He appears in flashbacks and makes sure their fate is sealed because they must avenge his untimely demise no matter what. Penn's character is such a candidate for anger management that he attacks the guy bringing flowers for the funeral. Their wives, Anabella Sciorra and Isabella Rosellini, don't exactly help cool things down.

I mean, I can't just call him up. Instead, he contacts me every day through a bird.
Louie

89. *Ghost Dog: The Code of the Samurai* (1999)

Mafia rules vie against Samurai rules when *Ghost Dog (*Forest Whitaker) becomes a hit man for the mob because he considers himself a servant to his master, a wiseguy who saved his life. When the mobsters decide to come after him anyway, he must defend himself, while still being true to his Samurai code (kind of like a Japanese Machiavelli thing). This is not easy with lessons like, *if a warrior's head is suddenly cut off, he should still be able to perform one more action.*

Personal. What the fuck does "personal" mean? Personal in this business don't mean a goddamn thing.
Max

90. *Portrait of a Hitman* (1977)

When a contractor gets an order, he should carry it out. Nothing should stand in the way of his assignment. He's a professional. Not Jack Palance, who plays the softest hitter of all time, an artist who whacks guys as a side job.

I want you to look at me before I kill you.
Sal

91. *Protection* (2001)

More bad press for the WP program. Stephen Baldwin goes Valachi when he realizes the mob wants him dead anyway, but the Fed protection plan is about as bogus and poorly run as its Iraqi war plan.

I wouldn't plead guilty to havin' an appetite.
Mileaway

92. *Doorway to Hell* (1930)

"Every time I think I'm out, they pull me back in." In 1930 it was called the doorway to hell—it only swung one way and you couldn't walk back out. Mileaway (James Cagney) shows his partner Louie that even "soft stuff" (a dame) can't help him walk back through that door.

The system versus the street...the street won and the people lost.
Diane Giacalone, the Prosecutor

93. *Getting Gotti* (1994)

Lorraine Bracco plays the prosecutor who went after Gotti for years, helping him earn his "Teflon Don" moniker. She rants, raves, screams, and yells in front of a judge who makes Lance Ito look like Solomon. This is a docudrama, which must mean based on truth with a lot of bullshit thrown in.

...just a few more jobs, then (I'll) get out....
Danny

94. *Mafia Doctor* (2003)

The Mafia is ahead of its time here in setting up a Public Service Corps. Nicky (Paul Sorvino), a Mafia strongman, sends young Frank Siena (Danny Nucci) to medical school in Italy, all expenses paid. The catch is that when he returns, his public service is to the Mafia. This way any sudden trauma incurred by wiseguys can be handled without having to go to a regular hospital monitored by authorities. No filling out all those complicated forms. House calls? You better believe he'll be making them. Extra prescriptions? No problem. And forget about that Hypocratic oath thing, they got their own oath.

I can't stand it any more
Rosalie Bonanno

95. *Honor Thy Father* (1973)

Salvatore Bonanno, Joe's son, told his story years before Rosalie
and Joe himself told theirs. For a family whose patriarch revered
omerta, these people have had more biographical material published
about them than Abe Lincoln. This adaptation of Gay Talese's book
features Raf Vallone as the old man (Joe Bonanno) and Joseph Bologna
as Sal. There's a rare opportunity to see Richard "Clemenza, Take the
cannolis," Castellano here. He portrays a Sartre-reading minor capo,
Frank Labruzzo, but his deathbed hospital scene will make you gag.
Bill's wife (Brenda Vaccaro) screams out near the end of the film, "I
can't stand it anymore." I've got to admit I couldn't either.

....we don't eat no snails.
Marco

96. *The Hitman* (1991)

Lessons on *respect* and *trust* are violated here in a movie that just
plain doesn't make a lot of sense. The fact that it features Chuck Norris
avenging himself against that bad-assed crew—the Seattle mob—tells
you something. What are they, some kind of a coffee-crew? Or a grunge-
gang? Then you notice this mess also has French-Canadian and Middle
East mobsters involved as well. To make matters worse, the boss, Marco
(Al Waxman), issues one of the all time ugly Mafia warnings—
  We'll teach these French fiends how expensive it is to move into a
neighborhood where we don't eat no snails.
  When the French guy meets Grogan (who's representing Marco),
he's also surprised that Grogan isn't Italian and says,
  I don't catch the odor of oregano we expected.
  He then decides he wants a message sent back to that "garlic breathing
pig." Norris tries to pit the Italians against the French-Canadians and
also against an Iranian crew. Iranians? In keeping with the rest of his
creative ethnic slurs, he calls them "camel jockeys."

Chicago is a beer-drinkin' town—no law can change that.
Johnny Torrio

97. *Capone* (1975)

Ben Gazzara's Capone blows people away at breakneck speed in this version of his rise to the top; at the same time the film pays little attention to his business smarts. John Cassavettes plays Frankie Yale, Capone's Brooklyn boss, who gets wiped but after the first five minutes of the movie. A pre-*Rocky* Sylvester Stallone is Capone's right hand man, Frank "The Enforcer" Nitti. This film fucks big time with the facts, making Nitti into a rat who turns in evidence of tax evasion on Capone so that he can take over the mob. Never happened.

...you'll have to watch because I won't be there—the government will be running not only gambling, but prostitution and drugs. Why? Because that's where the money is.
Lansky

98. *Lansky* (1999)

Richard Dreyfuss takes his turn as a Mafia big shot, depicting an elderly Meyer Lansky (the brains behind a lot of the mob's early success) in a series of flashbacks after trying to fight extradition from Israel.

Godfather, he's interfering with my business, my legitimate business, which is sanctioned by you. This is a direct insult to me, Godfather. He wants my territory and I cannot sit idly by, Godfather, I ask you permission to do what I must do.

99. *Mob War* (1989)

Jake LaMotta, the real "Raging Bull," is so bad playing a mob boss that the director is forced to refer to him as "Godfather" over and over, hoping you get the picture.

When the final tally is told, I have done more good than bad.
Capone

We will have no honor until the man who gave the order is dead. I want Cermak. Our blood demands it.
Capone

100. *The Revenge of Al Capone* (1989)

Capone is raked over the coals one more time, as he supposedly runs his operation from jail after the income tax conviction. Ray Sharkey's Capone is at the bottom of my list of actors who've portrayed Al. This version also tries to smash the Eliot Ness legend.

A Note from the Authors

Although Bobby Madura and Joey DiBruno are fictionalized characters, most of the events that take place in *Minstrone for the Mobster's Soul: Life Lessons from the Movie Mafia* occurred in the lives of the guys we grew up with, and in a couple of cases, we were inadvertently part of the action. We've changed the names of most of the places and people to protect the innocent and, yeah, sometimes the guilty too.

Both our mothers worked in the offices of one company controlled by the Outfit in Chicago. When the "loan officer" for the company, someone they saw every day, was found in the trunk of a car, they brought the story home, though none of the details. Our friends ran a social club very similar to St. Francis. Neighborhood buddies did get killed and jailed; they did rob stores and "borrow" cars, and we sometimes were along for the ride. As kids, we did some minor pilfering ourselves, vandalizing schools and shopping at the five finger discount stores. We knew kids who got out of the Our Lady of Angels fire, though we went to other schools.

We grew up seeing how the city and the neighborhood worked. Somehow, no doubt through the hard-working examples of our parents and their insistence on our education, we made it out. One of us became a basketball coach and the other became a teacher. We kept in touch with a few of the guys who made it out too.

Minestrone is not meant to justify anything negative our characters, our friends, or we did growing up. Rather, it's meant as a peek into the positive. Why is *The Godfather* the most popular movie ever made and why is *The Sopranos* the top dramatic television series ever made. Is it because the movies and television "romanticize" the mob or the Mafia? That answer is up to you. Our focus is on the positive values these and dozens of other mob films portray, values that are deeply ingrained in our society, and ones that we think make these movies speak to today's audiences.

We also don't mean any disrespect to the members of any ethnic groups mentioned either. We had to quote the way guys really talked when necessary; as a matter fact, many of you will note that far worse is heard on the street. Some do-gooders who don't live in the real world may get upset with the philosophy Bobby and Joey espouse. It isn't necessarily ours, although we agree with a lot of what they say. For the rest of you—can you handle the truth? We think so.

Bob Ociepka
Bruno Ociepka
(July 2008)

FILMOGRAPHY OF QUOTED WORKS

1. *The Godfather.* Puzo, Mario (writer), Coppola, Francis Ford (director). (1972). Paramount Pictures.

2. *The Godfather, Part II.* Puzo, Mario (writer), Coppola, Francis Ford (director). (1974). Paramount Pictures, The Coppola Company.

3. *Goodfellas.* Pileggi, Nicholas, Scorsese, Martin (writers), Scorsese, Martin (director). (1990). Warner Bros. Pictures.

4. *A Bronx Tale.* Palminteri, Chazz (writer), DeNiro, Robert (director). (1993). B.T. Films, Inc., Penta Entertainment Limited, Price Entertainment, Tribeca Productions.

5. *Donnie Brasco.* Pistone, Joseph D., Woodley, Richard, Attanasio, Paul (writers), Newell, Mike (director). (1997). Tri Star Pictures, Mandalay Entertainment, Baltimore Pictures, Mark Johnson Productions.

6. *Casino.* Pileggi, Nicholas, Scorsese, Martin (writers), Scorsese, Martin (director). (1995). Universal Pictures, Syalis DA, Legende Enterprises, DeFina- Cappa.

7. *Scarface.* Stone, Oliver, Trail, Armitage, Hecht, Ben, Hawks, Howard (writers), DePalma, Brian (director). (1983). Universal Pictures.

8. *The Departed.* Monohan, William, Mak, Siu Fai, Chong, Felix (writers), Scorsese, Martin (director). (2006) Warner Bros. Pictures, Vertigo Entertainment, Initial Entertainment Group (IEG), Plan B Entertainment.

9. *Al Capone.* Ward, Malvin, Greenberg, Henry F. (writers), Wilson, Richard (director). (1959). Allied Artists Pictures.

10. *On the Waterfront.* Johnson, Malcolm, Schulberg (writers), Kazan, Elia (director). (1954).   Horizon Pictures, Columbia Pictures Corporation.

11. Gotti. Capeci, Jerry, Mustain Gene, Shagan, Steve (writers), Harmon, Robert (director). (1996) (TV) Home Box Office (HBO).

12. *Once Upon a Time in America.* Grey, Harry, Benvenuti, Leonardo, Medioli, Enrico, Arcalli, Franco, Leone, Sergio, Kaminsky, Gastaldi, Ernesto (writers), Leone, Sergio (director).   (1984). Embassy International Pictures, PSO International, Rafran Cinematografica, Warner Bros. Pictures, Wishbone.

13. American Gangster. Zaillian, Steven, Jacobson, Mark (writers), Scott, Ridley (director). (2007). Universal Pictures, Imagine Entertainment, Relativity Media, Scott Free Productions.

14. *Eastern Promises.* Knight, Steven (writer), Cronenberg, David (director). (2007). Astral Media, BBC Films, Corus Entertainment, Focus Features, Kudus Film and Televsion, Scion Films Limited, Telefilm Canada.

15. *Witness to the Mob.* Weiser, Stanley (writer), O'Sullivan, Thaddeus (director). (1998). (TV) NBC Studios, Tribeca Productions.

16. Scarface. Trail, Armitage, Hecht, Ben, Pasley, Fred, Miller, Seton I., Mahin, John Lee, Burnett, W.R. (writers), Hawks, Howard, Rosson, Richard (co-directors). (1932).   The Caddo Company.

17. *Boss of Bosses.* O'Brien, Joseph, Kurins, Andris, Shames, Laurence, Cunningham, Jere (writers), Little, Dwight H. (director). (2001). (TV) Bleecker Street Films.

18. Carlito's Way. Torres, Edwin, Koepp, David (writers), DePalma, Brian (director). (1993).   Bregman/Baer Productions, Epic Productions, Universal Pictures.

19. *Bound.* Wachowski, Andy, Wachowski, Larry (writers and co-directors). (1996). Dino DeLaurentis Company, Spelling Films.

20. *Hoffa.* Mamet, David (writer), DeVito, Danny (director). (1992). Canal & Jersey Films, Twentieth Century-Fox Film Corporation.

21. *Mean Streets.* Scorsese, Martin, Mardik, Martin (writers), Scorsese, Martin (director). (1973). Taplin-Perry-Scorsese Productions.

22. *A History of Violence.* Wagner, John, Locke, Vince, Olson, Josh (writers), Cronenberg, David (director). (2005). New Line Productions, Bender Spink, Media Film Producktion, Munchen & Company.

23. *Little Ceasar.* Burnett, W.R., Lee, Robert N., Faragoh, Francis Edward, Lord, Robert, Zanuck, Darryl F. (writers), LeRoy, Mervyn (director). (1931). First National Pictures.

24. *The Untouchables.* Fraley, Oscar, Ness, Eliot, Mamet, David (writers), DePalma, Brian (director). (1987). Paramount Pictures.

25. *Key Largo.* Anderson, Maxwell, Brooks, Richard, Huston, John (writers), Houston, John (director). (1948). Warner Bros. Pictures.

26. *Bugsy.* Jennings, Dean, Toback (writers), Levinson, Barry (director). (1991). Baltimore Pictures, Desert Vision, Mulholland Productions, Tri Star Pictures.

27. *The Godfather Part III.* Puzo, Mario, Coppola, Francis Ford (writers), Coppola, Francis Ford (director). (1990). Paramount Pictures, Zoetrope Studios.

28. *True Romance.* Tarantino, Quentin, Avary, Roger (writers). Scott, Tony (director). (1993) Morgan Creek Productions, Davis – Films, August Entertainment.

29. *State of Grace.* McIntyre, Dennis (writer), Joanou, Phil (director). (1990).   Cinehaus, Orion Pictures Corporation, Rank Organisation. The.

30. *The Last Don.* Puzo, Mario, Eliason, Joyce (writers), Clifford, Graeme (director). (1997)   (TV Mini). Konigsberg/Sanitsky Company.

31. *King of New York.* St. John, Nicholas (writer), Ferrara, Abel (director). (1990).   Caminto, Rank Organisation, The, Reteitalia Scena International.

32. *Mobsters.* Mahern, Michael, Kazan, Nicholas (writers), Karbelnikoff, Michael (director). (1991). Universal Pictures.

33. *Things Change.* Mamet, David, Silverstein, Shel (writers), Mamet, David (director). (1988).   Columbia Pictures Corporation, Filmhaus.

34. *Road to Perdition.* Collins, Max Allan, Rayner, Richard Piers, Self, David (writers), Mendes, Sam (director). (2002). Dreamworks SKG, Twentieth Century-Fox Film Corporation, Zanuck Company, The.

35. *Prizzi's Honor.* Condon, Richard, Roach, Janet (writers), Huston, John (director). (1985). ABC Motion Pictures.

36. *Find Me Guilty.* Lumet, Sidney, Mancini, T.J., McCrea, Robert J. (writers), Lumet, Sidney (director). (2006). Crossroads Entertainment, Bob Yari Productions, MHF Zweite
Academy Film, One Race Productions, Three Wolves Productions, Yari Film Group (YFG).

37. *Dinner Rush.* Shaughnessy, Rick, Kalata, Brian S. (writers), Giraldi, Bob (director). (2000).   Access Motion Picture Group, Giraldi – Suarez – DiGiaimo Productions.

38. *The Client.* Grisham, John, Goldsman, Akiva, Getchell, Robert (writers), Schumacher, Joel (director). (1994). Alcor Films, Regency Enterprises, Warner Bros. Pictures.

39. Hoodlum. Brancato, Chris (writer), Duke, Bill (director). (1997). United Artists Pictures.

40. *The Juror.* Green, George Dawes, Tally, Ted (writers), Gibson, Brian (director). (1996). Columbia Pictures Corporation.

41. *Ruby.* Davis, Stephen (writer), MacKenzie, John (director). (1992). Kuzui Enterprises, Polygram Filmed Entertainment, Propaganda Films, Rank Organisation, The.

42. *Crazy Joe.* Gage, Nicholas, Carlino, Lewis John (writers), Lizzani, Carlo (director). (1974). Columbia Pictures Corporation. Dino deLaurentis Cinematografica, Persky-Bright Productions, Produzione Cinematografiche Inter. Ma. Co.

43. St. Valentine's Day Massacre. Browne, Howard (writer), Corman, Roger (director). (1967). Los Altos Productions.

44. *The Big Heat.* Boehm, Sydney, McGivern, William P. (writers), Lang, Fritz (director). (1953). Columbia Pictures Corporation.

45. *The Professional (Leon).* Beeson, Luc (writer and director). (1994). Gaumont Les Films du Dauphin.

46. Power of Attorney. Barmash, Jeffrey, Erschbamer, George, Himelstein, Howard, Wilson, Roger (writers), Himelstein, Howard (director). (1995). Cinevu Films, Small World Entertainment.

47. *Miller's Crossing.* Cohen, Joel, Cohen, Ethan, Hammett, Dashiell (writers), Coen, Joel (director). (1990). Circle Films, Twentieth Century-Fox Film Corporation.

48. *Death Collector (Family Enforcer).* DeVito, Ralph (writer and director). (1975). EPOH Productions.

49. *This Thing of Ours.* Bohus, Ted A., Provenzano, Danny (writers), Provenzano, Danny (director). (2003). Austin Film Group, Dylan's & Skyler's Releasing, Metal Shop Productions.

50, Gloria. Cassavettes, John (writer and director). (1980).   Columbia Pictures Corporation.

51. *Trial By Jury.* Katz, Jordan, Gould, Heywood (writers), Gould, Heywood (director). (1994).   Morgan Creek Productions.

52.. *The Purple Gang.* DeWitt, Jack (writer), McDonald, Frank (director). (1959).   Allied Artists Pictures.

53. *The Rat Pack.* Salem, Kario (writer), Cohen, Rob (director). (1998). (TV) Home Box Office (HBO), Original Film.

54. *Vendetta.* Gambino, Richard, Prager, Timothy (writers), Meyer, Nicholas (director). (1999) (TV). Home Box Office (HBO).

55. *Bella Mafia.* LaPlante, Lynda (writer), Greene, David (director). (1997).   The Konigsberg Company.

56. *Out for Justice.* Henry, David Lee (writer), Flynn, John (director). (1991).   Warner Bros. Pictures.

57. *Knockaround Guys.* Koppelman, Brian, Levien, David (writers and co-directors). (2001).   New Line Cinema, Lawrence Bender Productions.

58. *The Last Don Part II.* Puzo, Mario, Eliason, Joyce (writers), Clifford, Graeme (director). (1998).   (TV Mini). Konigsberg/Sanitsky Company.

59. *Wisegirls.* Meadows, John (writer), Anspaugh, David (director). (2002).   Lions Gate Films, Leading Pictures, Intermedia Films, Anthony Esposito Champion Entertainment, IMX Communications, Inc., Lions Gate Entertainment, Essential Films, RGH/Lions Share Pictures.

60. *Murder, Inc.* Barr, Mel, Feder, Sid, Turnik, Irve, Turkus, Burton (writers), Balaban, Burt (director). (1960).   Twentieth Century-Fox Corporation, American Broadcasting Company (ABC).

61. *The Brotherhood.* Carlino, Lewis John (writer), Ritt, Martin (director). (1969). Paramount Pictures.

62. *Brooklyn Rules.* Winter, Terrence (writer), Corrente, Michael (director). (2007). Cataland Films, Eagle Beach Productions, Hannover House, Southpaw Entertainment, Straight Up Films.

63. *The Valachi Papers.* DeRita, Massimo, Geller, Stephen, Maas, Peter, Maiuri, Ardvino (writers), Young, Terrence (director). (1973). DeLaurentis Intermarco S.P.A., Euro-France Films.

64. *Gangster No. 1.* Ferguson, Johnny (writer), McGuigan, Paul (director). (2000). British Screen Productions, British Sky Broadcasting (B Sky B), Film Four, Filmboard Berlin-Brandenburg (FBB), Little Bird, NFH Productions, Pagoda Film, Road Movies Film Produktion.

65. *Vendetta: Secrets of a Mafia Bride.* DeConcini, Ennio, DiFiore, Alan, Margolin, Stuart, Modignani, Sveva Casati (writers), Thomas, Margolin, Stuart (director). (1991). (TV). Reteitalia, Titanus, Tribune Entertainment.

66. *Vendetta II: The New Mafia.* Mondignani, Sveva Casati, Ross, Brian, Thomas, Ralph L. (writers), Thomas, Ralph L. (director). (1993). Filmline International, Inc., Titanus.

67. *10th and Wolf.* Steele, Allan, Moresco, Robert (writers), Moresco, Robert (director). (2006). Suzanne DeLaurentis Productions.

68. *Suicide Kings.* Stanford, Don, McKinney, Josh, Goldman, Gina, Rice, Wayne Allan (writers), O'Fallon, Peter (director). (1997). Dinamo Entertainment, Eyes 'n Rice Live Film, Mediaworks, Inc.

70. *Federal Protection.* Smith, Craig (writer), Hickox, Anthony (director). (2001) Federal Protection. Chariot Communications, Inc.

70. *Hitman's Run.* Barker, Eric, Olson, Josh (writers), Lester, Mark L. (director). (1999). Hitman's Run Productions.

71. *Men Of Respect.* Reilly, William, Shakespeare, William (writers), Reilly, William (director). (1991). Arthur Goldblatt Productions, Central City Films, Grandview Avenue Pictures.

72. *Gangster Wars.* DeKoker, Richard (writer), Sarafian, Richard C. (director). (1981). Universal TV.

73. *Sugartime.* Burke, Martyn, Roemer Jr., William F. (writers), Smith, John M. (director). (1995). (TV) Home Box Office (HBO), Pacific Western.

74. *Billy Bathgate.* Doctorow, E.L., Stoppard, Tom (writers), Benton, Robert (director). (1991). Touchstone Pictures, Touchwood Pacific Partners.

75. *Wannabes.* DeMeo, William (writer and director), Addessi, Charles A. (director) (2000). Artisan.

76. *Mob Justice (Dead and Alive: The Race for Gus Farace).* Markle, Eric, Beebe, Dick (writers), Markle, Peter (director). (1991). (TV). Concorde – New Horizons, Patchett Kaufman Entertainment.

77. *Love, Honor, and Obey – The Last Mafia Marriage.* Bonanno, Rosalie, Christopher Canaan (writers), Patterson, John (director). (1993). (TV). CBS Entertainment.

78. *Triggermen.* Johnston, Tony (writer), Bradshaw, John (director). (2002). First Look International, Gemini Film Productions, International West Pictures (IWP), Now Entertainment Group, T-Men Productions, Trimuse Entertainment, Inc.

79. *The Pope of Greenwich Village,* Patrick, Vincent (writer), Rosenberg, Stuart (director). (1984). United Artists.

80. The Don is Dead. Albert, Marvin H., Trumbo, Christopher, Butler, Michael Phillip (writers), Fleischer, Richard (director). (1973). Universal Pictures.

81. Witness Protection. Sabbag, Robert, Theriault, Daniel (writers), Pearce, Richard (director). (1999). (TV). HBO NYC Productions, Turtleback Productions.

82. *The Sicilian.* Puzo, Mario, Shagan, Steve, Vidal, Gore (writers), Cimino, Michael (director). (1987). Gladden Entertainment.

83. *The Rise and Fall of Legs Diamond.* Landon, Joseph (writer), Boetticher, Budd (director). (1960). United States Pictures.

84. *The Neon Empire.* Anhalt, Edward, Hamill, Pete (writers), Pierce, Larry (director). (1989). (TV). Fries Entertainment, Richard Maynard Productions.

85. *The Lost Capone.* Bacon, James, Gray, John (writers), Gray, John (director). (1990). (TV). Patchett Kaufman Entertainment.

86. *18 Shades of Dust (Hitman's Journal).* Centetiempo, John, Hogan, Michael (writers), Aiello III, Danny (director). (1999). Shades Productions, Inc., Westside Pictures, Inc.

87. *Bonanno: A Godfather's Story.* Bonanno, Bill, Bonanno, Joseph, Lalli, Sergio, Donnelly, Thomas Michael (writers), Poulette, Michael (director). (1999). Armeda Ltd., Daniel L. Paulson Productions, Les Productions La Fete, Inc.

88. Ghost Dog: The Code of the Samurai. Jarmusch, Jim (writer and director). (1999) Pandora Filmproduktion in association with Arbeitsgemeinschaft der offentlich-rechtlichen Rundfunkanstalten der Bundesrepublik Deutschland (ARD) in association with Degeto Film in assoication with Plywood Productions. Bac Films. Canal+. JVC Entertainment.

89. The Funeral. St. John, Nicholas (writer), Ferrara, Abel (director). (1996). C & P Productions, MDP Worldwide, October Films.

90. *Portrait of a Hitman.* Yablonsky, Yabo (writer), Buckhantz, Allan A. (director). (1997). Program Hunters, Inc., Wildfire Productions.

91. *Protection.* Kelly, Jack (writer), Flynn, John (director). (2001). Alliance Atlantis Communications, Faulkner – Bibo Productions, Inc., LeMonde Entertainment.

92. Doorway to Hell. Brown, Rowland, Rosener, George (writers), Mayo, Archie (director). (1930). Warner Bros. Pictures.

93. *Getting Gotti.* Henderson, James S. (writer), Young, Roger (director). (1994). (TV). CBS Television, Aquarius TV, Artisan Entertainment, New Films International.

94. *Mafia Doctor.* Palmisano, Louis C., Lerman, Rhoda, Leekley, John, Bradford, Rebekah, Fox, Ray Errol (writers), Chapple, Alex (director). (2003). (TV). Carlton America, Michele Brustin Productions.

95. *Honor Thy Father.* Carlino, Lewis John, Talese, Gay (writers), Wendkos, Paul (director). (1973). (TV). Halycon Productions, Metrodmedia Productions.

96. *The Hitman.* Carmody, Don, Geoffrion, Robert, Thompson, Galen (writers), Norris, Aaron (director). (1991) Twighlight Motion Picture Seven Ltd. Partnership.

97. *Capone.* Browne, Howard (writer), Carver, Steve (director). (1975). Santa Fe.

98. *Lansky.* Dan, Uri, Eisenberg, Dennis, Landau, Eli, Mamet, David (writers), McNaughton, John (director). (1999). (TV). Frederick Zollo Productions, HBO Films, Home Box Office (HBO).

99. *Mob War.* Ingvordsen, J. Christian, Weiner, John (writers), Ingvordsen, J. Christian (director). (1989) GMUS Ltd., Reel Media International, Starlight.

100. *The Revenge of Al Capone.* Wynn, Tracy Keenan (writers), Pressman, Michael (director). (1989). (TV). River City Productions, Inc., Unity Productions, Inc.

The Krays. Ridley, Phillip (writer), Medak, Peter (director). (1990). Fugitive Features, Parkfield Entertainment.

Johnny Stecchino. Cerami, Vincenzo (writer) Begnini, Roberto (writer and director). (1991) Cecchi Gori Group Tiger Cinematografica, Penta Films, Silvio Berlusconi Communications.

The Freshman, Bergman. Andrew (writer and director). (1990). TriStar Pictures.

BIBLIOGRAPHY OF QUOTED BOOKS

Born to the Mob. Saggio, Frankie and Rosen, Fred (writers). (2004). Thunder Mouth Press, an imprint of Avalon Publishing Group, Inc.

Covert: My Years Infiltrating the Mob. Delaney, Bob and Scheiber, Dave (writers). (2008). Sterling Publishing Co., Inc.

Donnie Brasco. Pistone, Joseph D. (1987).

Five Families: The Rise, Decline, and Resurgence of America's Most Powerful Mafia Empires. Raab, Selwyn (writer). (2005). Thomas Dunne Books, St. Martin's Press.

Omerta. Puzo, Mario. (2000). Random House.

Underboss, Maas, Peter. (1997). Harper Collins.

Bob Ociepka lived near Chicago and Ashland avenues until he was eight, and near Grand and Pulaski until he left for college. A legend among Chicago high school basketball coaches, he was inducted into the Chicago Catholic League Hall of Fame in 2000, and has spent the last twenty years as an assistant coach in the NBA. Bob is the author of two previously published books–*NBA Offenses I* and *NBA Offenses II*.

Bruno Ociepka grew up near Division and Ashland and lived for many years in the same two-flat with his cousin, Bob, near Grand and Pulaski. He taught in high school and business college for 25 years and is the author of seven training texts in the travel and tourism industry.

Printed in the United States
152086LV00001B/26/P

9 781593 305054